This is a wide-ranging exploration of the similarities and differences between ancient Greek and ancient Chinese science and philosophy, concentrating on the period down to AD 300. Professor Lloyd studies such questions as the attitudes towards authority, the practice of confrontational debate, the role of methodological inquiries, the development of techniques of persuasion, the assumptions made about causal explanation, and the focus of interest in the study of the heavens and in that of the human body. In each case the Greek and Chinese ways of posing the problems are carefully distinguished, to avoid applying either Greek categories to Chinese thought or vice versa. Throughout, the characteristics of the science produced are related to the values of the societies concerned and to the institutional framework within which the scientists worked. Professor Lloyd shows that the science produced in each ancient civilisation differs in important respects, and relates those differences to the values and social institutions in question.

ADVERSARIES AND AUTHORITIES

IDEAS IN CONTEXT

Edited by Quentin Skinner (General Editor), Lorraine Daston,
Wolf Lepenies, Richard Rorty and J. B. Schneewind

The books in this series will discuss the emergence of intellectual traditions and of related new disciplines. The procedures, aims and vocabu-
laries that were generated will be set in the context of the alternatives
available within the contemporary frameworks of ideas and institutions.
Through detailed studies of the evolution of such traditions, and their
modification by different audiences, it is hoped that a new picture will
form of the development of ideas in their concrete contexts. By this
means, artificial distinctions between the history of philosophy, of the
various sciences, of society and politics, and of literature may be seen
to dissolve.

The series is published with the support of the Exxon Foundation

A list of books in the series will be found at the end of the volume.

ADVERSARIES AND AUTHORITIES

Investigations into ancient Greek and Chinese science

G. E. R. LLOYD

*Professor of Ancient Philosophy and Science,
University of Cambridge, and
Master of Darwin College*

CAMBRIDGE
UNIVERSITY PRESS

Published by the Press Syndicate of the University of Cambridge
The Pitt Building, Trumpington Street, Cambridge CB2 1RP
40 West 20th Street, New York, NY 10011–4211, USA
10 Stamford Road, Oakleigh, Melbourne 3166, Australia

First published 1996

Printed in Great Britain at the University Press, Cambridge

A catalogue record for this book is available from the British Library

Library of Congress cataloguing in publication data

Lloyd, G. E. R. (Geoffrey Ernest Richard), 1933–
Adversaries and authorities: investigations into ancient Greek
and Chinese science / G. E. R. Lloyd.
p. cm. – (Ideas in context)
Includes bibliographical references and index.
ISBN 0 521 55331 8 (hardback) ISBN 0 521 55695 3 (paperback)
1. Science – Greece – Methodology – History. 2. Science – China –
– Methodologt – History. 3. Science, Ancient. I. Title.
II. Series.
Q127.G7L55 1996
509′.31– dc20 95–38071 CIP

ISBN 0 521 55331 8 hardback
ISBN 0 521 55695 3 paperback

Contents

For Nathan Sivin

Preface

The year 1987 marked a turning point in my studies in ancient
science. I owe it to my seminar audiences in Beijing in that year
that they brought home to me the desirability, or rather I should
now say the necessity, of studying neither ancient Greek science
nor its Chinese counterpart in isolation. This is not with the
object of assessing the strengths and weaknesses, the superiority or inferiority, of either tradition, let alone in order to engage
in the pointless exercise of establishing chronological priorities.
Rather, the features of either tradition that scholars working in
just one of them tend to take for granted turn out to be anything
but unproblematic: in many cases they relate to key issues for
our understanding of what 'science' itself meant for the society concerned.

There is nothing automatic about the ways in which different
inquiries – say what we call medicine, or astronomy, or mathematics – were developed and practised in the ancient world. On
the contrary, the particular ways in which they were raise deep
and difficult questions, to answer which we have to engage in a
sustained analysis of the conditions under which the inquirers
worked and of the societies in which they operated. Why were
the problems defined in the ways they were? What expectations
were entertained for adequate solutions? Whom were the investigators trying to convince and how did they hope to do so? What
was the institutional framework within which they worked? How
were they recruited and organised (if they were organised)? What
were their motivations and aspirations, what, indeed, their sources
of livelihood?

Since 1989 I have been engaged in a wide-ranging study of
these questions in collaboration with Nathan Sivin, where we
have been exploring anew the whole field of Chinese and Greek

science from circa −300 to circa +200, that is, roughly, down to the time when Buddhist and Christian influences came to be major factors in China and in Greece respectively. Our aim in this project is, precisely, first to relate Chinese and Greek science far more closely than is ordinarily done to their respective social, cultural, political and institutional backgrounds; and secondly to examine *both* those backgrounds *and* the intellectual products – the science done – in each case in the light of the other, that is, keeping the *comparison* between China and Greece constantly in mind.

The present collection of essays is not the envisaged prime outcome of that collaboration, although it is undertaken very much in the spirit that animates it and what I owe to Professor Sivin will be evident throughout. Rather, what is presented here is in the nature of a set of sighting shots, the record of some preliminary forays that I have made in the past five years, in lectures, seminars or contributions to conferences or workshops, in Europe, North America and the Far East. If I write, obviously, as primarily a Hellenist, it will also be evident that I do so as one who is far from content with remaining within the conventional boundaries of a Hellenist's agenda.

Most of these papers have appeared in earlier versions in journals or in conference proceedings, but all have been revised and in some cases substantially modified in response to criticism and in the light of further reflection. The tentativeness of many of the arguments advanced will be apparent, as also will their speculative nature. But they are designed to suggest new lines of inquiry and are offered in the hope of stimulating further discussion.[1]

The major methodological difficulties stemming from the lacunae and bias of our sources will be aired in Chapter 1. Brief observations on the structure and authenticity of the chief Chinese texts used will be made, as necessary, when they are first introduced,[2] and so also similarly, though more rarely, with the

---

1. Readers may be referred to Sivin's two volumes of selected essays 1995d, 1995e for a number of detailed new analyses of aspects of the materials to be discussed in our joint book.
2. The volume edited by Loewe (1993) now makes easily accessible authoritative and up-to-date views on the provenance and dating of all the major Chinese texts of the period with which I am concerned.

primary Greek texts. While the chief periods under investigation are, as noted, the Greek world before Christianity became a dominant influence, and the Chinese world before Buddhism did there, I have not here stuck rigidly to authors writing before the end of the +2nd century, but have allowed myself the occasional reference to later texts, especially on the Greek side when these appear to work, in the main, within pagan traditions.

Acknowledgements

My foremost debt has already been mentioned. This is to Nathan Sivin, who has guided and inspired all my work on topics related to Chinese science – and not just on the questions investigated here – and who has also given me the benefit of constant critical advice on issues both specific and strategic. This has saved me from many inaccuracies and errors, while those that remain are, of course, entirely my own responsibility.

I have learnt much on questions to do with Chinese mathematics from Karine Chemla, Catherine Jami and Donald Wagner, with the last of whom I have engaged in extensive correspondence relating to the interpretation of particularly problematic texts in Liu Hui, and with the first of whom I have exchanged views on many other topics as well, not least in connection with the issues raised in recent numbers of *Extrême-Orient Extrême-Occident*. Karine Chemla has also been kind enough to give me detailed comments on many aspects of the arguments in this book.

I have benefited from detailed discussions of the similarities and differences between Chinese and Greek medical case-histories with Elisabeth Hsü, who has been engaged in a detailed study of the *Canggongzhuan* and related texts.

Then more generally I owe much to all those who have allowed me to consult them on a wide variety of problems related to the subject-matter of these essays and their background, to Myles Burnyeat, Christopher Cullen, Mark Lewis, Michael Loewe, David McMullen, David Sedley, Robert Wardy.

Not least I wish to record my thanks to Bridie Andrews, who was – with Professor Zhen Li – the first to encourage me to read classical Chinese texts in the original, and to all those who have participated in the groups undertaking such readings in Cambridge over the past five years.

As noted in the Preface, these studies stem from talks given on various occasions in different places across the world in recent years, and my thanks go both to my hosts, for their hospitality, and to my audiences, for their constructive comments. Thus an earlier version of Chapter 1 was presented to the Greek-China workshop in Cambridge in 1991, at Tohoku University, Sendai, later that year (the volume entitled *Is it Possible to Compare East and West?*, edited by H. Numata and S. Kawada, Tokyo 1994, contains the papers given to the Sendai conference), at the Taiwan National University, Taibei, in 1992, and at the Scuola Normale at Pisa in 1993.

Chapter 2 derives from a presentation to the Cambridge Philological Society in 1993, the original version of which was published in the *Proceedings* XL, 27–48.

Chapter 3 amalgamates the arguments of a submission to a McGill conference on medical traditions and their epistemologies in 1992 (which I was, however, unable to attend in person: the proceedings, edited by Don Bates, have been published by Cambridge University Press, 1995, under the title *Knowledge and the Scholarly Medical Traditions*), and those of a paper given to a conference on method organised by Jyl Gentzler at Amherst in 1993 (the proceedings of which are forthcoming from Oxford University Press).

Chapter 4 is a much expanded version of a contribution to the number of *Extrême-Orient Extrême-Occident* devoted to 'Regards obliques sur l'argumentation en Chine', published as volume 14, 1992.

Chapter 5 stems from a contribution to a conference on causation, held at Saint-Germain-en-Laye, under the auspices of the Fyssen foundation, in 1993, the proceedings of which have been published under the title *Causal Cognition*, edited by D. Sperber, D. Premack and A. J. Premack, Oxford 1995.

Chapter 6 develops themes from an article I published in *Dialogos* 2, 4–23, in 1995.

Chapter 7 stems from a contribution to the numbers of *Chinese Science* devoted to a Festschrift for Nathan Sivin, and earlier versions were given as lectures at Pittsburgh in 1992 and at Yale in 1993.

The original ideas developed in Chapter 8 stem from a further contribution to an *Extrême-Orient Extrême-Occident* set of papers on number (16, 1994) and from seminar papers presented in Cambridge in 1993–4.

An earlier version of Chapter 9 was given as a University lecture at Cornell in 1992. Finally material in Chapter 10 was presented at Toronto (as a Stubbs lecture) in 1993, at Seoul National University later that year, at Zurich in 1994, and at McGill and Harvard in 1995. The Stubbs lecture will be included in a volume entitled *Modes of Thought*, edited by David Olson and Nancy Torrance, to be published in 1996 by Cambridge University Press.

Notes on editions

Chinese

Ancient Chinese texts are cited as follows:

春秋繁露 (*Chunqiu fanlu*), of 董仲舒, Dong Zhongshu, in the edition of 賴炎元 (Lai Yanyuan), Taibei, 1984, cited by *juan* and page number.

韓非子 (*Hanfeizi*) in the edition of 陳奇猷 (Chen Qiyou), Shanghai, 1958, cited by *pian* and page number.

漢書 (*Hanshu*) in the edition with commentary by 顏師古 (Yan Shigu), Zhonghua shuju, Beijing, 1962, cited by *juan* and page number.

淮南子 (*Huainanzi*) in the edition of 劉文典 (Liu Wendian), Shanghai, 1923, cited by *juan* and page number.

黃帝內經 (*Huangdi neijing*: 'Inner Canon of the Yellow Emperor'). The 靈樞 (*lingshu*: 'Divine pivot') and 素問 (*suwen*: 'Basic questions') recensions are cited according to the edition of 任應秋 (Ren Yingqiu), Beijing, 1986, cited by *pian, zhang* and where necessary page number. The 太素 (*taisu*: 'Grand basis') recension is cited according to the edition of Kosoto Biroshi, Osaka, 1981.

晉書 (*Jinshu*) in the Zhonghua shuju edition, Beijing, 1974, cited by *juan* and page number.

九章算術 (*Jiuzhang suanshu*: 'Nine Chapters of the Mathematical Art') in the edition of 錢寶琮 (Qian Baocong), *Suanjing shishu*, Beijing, 1963, cited by page number.

呂氏春秋 (*Lüshi Chunqiu*) in the edition of 陳奇猷 (Chen Qiyou), Shanghai, 1984, cited by *juan* and *pian* number.

論衡 (*Lunheng*) of 王充 (Wang Chong) in the edition of 劉盼遂 (Liu Pansui), Beijing, 1957, cited by *pian* and page number.

馬王堆 (*Mawangdui*) medical texts, according to Vol IV of *Mawangdui Hanmu boshu*, Beijing, 1985, and the 五星占 (*wuxingzhan*) from *Zhongguo tianwenxue shi wenji*, Beijing, 1978.

孟子 (*Mengzi*: 'Mencius') in the Harvard-Yenching Institute Sinological Index Series, Supplement 17, Beijing, 1941, cited by the sections of that edition.

墨子 (*Mozi*), in general, in the edition of 張純一 (Zhang Chunyi), but for chapters 40–45 I rely on the edition of A. C. Graham, London and Hong Kong, 1978, cited by the sections and pages of that work.

史記 (*Shiji*) of 司馬遷 (Sima Qian) in the Zhonghua shuju edition, Beijing, 1959, cited by *juan* ('chapter'), page and where necessary column number.

太平御覽 (*Taiping yulan*) in the facsimile of the Sung edition produced by Shangwu yinshu guan, Shanghai, 1960, cited by *juan* and the original page number.

荀子 (*Xunzi*) in the Harvard-Yenching Institute Sinological Index Series, Supplement 22, Beijing, 1950, cited by *pian* and line number.

戰國策 (*Zhanguoce*) in *A Concordance to the Zhanguoce*, Institute of Chinese Studies, Ancient Chinese Text Concordance Series, Hong Kong, 1992, according to the State and chapter number, page and line of that edition.

周髀算經 (*Zhoubi suanjing*: 'Arithmetic Classic of the Zhou Gnomon') in the edition of 錢寶琮 (Qian Baocong), *Suanjing shishu*, Beijing, 1963, cited by page number.

莊子 (*Zhuangzi*) in the Harvard-Yenching Institute Sinological Index Series, Supplement 20, Beijing, 1947, cited by *pian* and line number.

Greek and Latin

I cite the major Greek and Latin authors by standard editions, for example the fragments of the Presocratic philosophers according to the edition of H. Diels, revised by W. Kranz, *Die Fragmente der Vorsokratiker*, 6th ed. (Berlin, 1952) (referred to as DK), the works of Plato according to Burnet's Oxford text, the treatises of Aristotle according to Bekker's Berlin edition. The works of Euclid are cited by the edition of J. L. Heiberg *et al.*, revised by E. S. Stamatis, those of Archimedes by Heiberg's edition, revised by Stamatis (referred to as HS with the volume number), Ptolemy's *Syntaxis* by the edition of J. L. Heiberg (volumes 1 and 2 being referred to as H I and H II respectively), his *Tetrabiblos* by the edition of F. Boll and E. Boer (Leipzig, 1940) and his *Harmonics* by the edition of I. Düring (Göteborg, 1930).

Greek and Latin medical texts are cited, for preference, according to the *Corpus Medicorum Graecorum* and *Corpus Medicorum Latinorum* editions (referred to as *CMG* and *CML* respectively), together with the *Corpus Medicorum Graecorum Supplementum Orientale*. Thus for the Hippocratic treatise *On Ancient Medicine*, I use *CMG* I 1, for *On the Nature of Man CMG* I 1, 3, for *On Regimen CMG* I 2, 4, while for Galen's

On Sustaining Causes (*De Causis Contentivis*) I use *CMG Suppl. Or.* II, and so on. But for Hippocratic treatises not included in *CMG*, I use E. Littré, *Oeuvres complètes d'Hippocrate*, 10 vols, Paris, 1839–61, cited as L followed by the volume number and page. For Galen's works not included in *CMG*, I use the edition of C. G. Kühn, Leipzig, 1821–33, cited as K followed by the volume number and page.

Abbreviations for Greek works are those used in the *Greek-English Lexicon* of H. G. Liddell and R. Scott, revised by H. S. Jones, with Supplement (1968). Thus Simplicius, *In Ph.*, refers to Simplicius' work *In Aristotelis Physica Commentaria*, ed. H. Diels (*Commentaria in Aristotelem Graeca*, Vols IX and X), Berlin, 1882–95.

Modern

All modern works are cited by author's name and year of publication. Full details are to be found in the bibliography on pp. 232ff.

Throughout this book the practice of writing dates as BC and AD is avoided by the use of − and + respectively.

With the exception of 'Confucius' and 'Mencius', all Chinese names and words are transliterated according to the Pinyin, not the Wade-Giles or other, convention. This is done throughout including in the quotations from authors who use other systems.

CHAPTER 1

Comparative studies and their problems: methodological preliminaries

The aim of this introductory chapter is to review some of the methodological issues involved in the comparison between ancient Greek and Chinese science. First, what does it mean to use the term 'science' at all in this context? Secondly, what, given the limitations and the bias in our sources, can we realistically hope to achieve in such a study? Thirdly, what are the primary questions we should be addressing, and how should we address them, that is, within the framework of what assumptions?

Some preliminary points need to be made on each of these three topics. First, it is obvious that in antiquity we are not dealing with science as we know it today, that is, with the highly institutionalised practice that is carried on in modern universities and research laboratories. On the strictest interpretation of science, we have to concede that the term is not applicable to anything before the present century. But that is, no doubt, to be unduly restrictive, and I shall use the term conventionally as a place-holder for a variety of specific inquiries we can identify in both Greece and China. Three of the most prominent, which will occupy much of our attention throughout, are astronomy, mathematics and medicine: a fourth is cosmology and whatever passes as natural philosophy or physics: others that could be added are geography, optics, harmonics, mechanics and so on.

All of these terms for specific domains are, to be sure, themselves problematic – and not just because two of them, mathematics and medicine, stretch beyond the bounds of what some would count as science. In each case we have to rid ourselves of the prejudices generated by modern expectations of how each of these subjects is to be pursued – the teleological assumption that bedevilled so much of the early history of science. Rather,

1

the primary task is to analyse what the ancient investigators themselves thought they were trying to do, their conceptions of their
subject-matter, their aims and goals.

This is not to say, of course, that we can ever put ourselves in
their shoes. All history has, to be sure, to be evaluative: none can
be neutral. That in turn means that it is not merely a matter of
reporting what the ancients *said* they were doing, as if we have
to take their word for it: for we clearly can and must inspect what
they actually did and reflect (as the ancients themselves sometimes did) on the matches and mismatches between what some
claimed to do and what they did, between theory and practice.
But how *they* saw the subjects they were engaged in must be our
starting-point.

So I take 'astronomy' to encompass what *they* included in the
study of the heavens. That comprised not just calendar studies,
and the description of the constellations and investigation of the
movements of the sun, moon and planets, but also – in both
Greece and China, though in different ways – the study of celestial omens or other attempts to predict events on earth, in other
words what we call astrology. Again by 'medicine' I mean whatever theories and practices of healing we find. And similarly 'mathematics' must be held to comprise the study of numbers and
figures, however that was pursued and with whatever ambitions,
including, for instance, the ambition to master the universe by
cracking its numerological codes.

My second initial question related to how much we can hope
to achieve. We are faced with formidable difficulties stemming
from the nature and limitations of our sources. All of our evidence, for Greek and for Chinese antiquity, has been mediated
through distinctive and long-drawn-out processes of transmission,
and both the information we have, and the gaps in it, reflect the
judgements of those who have participated in those processes.
Every act of recording or commenting on the ideas or practices
of earlier periods incorporates such judgements. We have to ask
ourselves why the texts that have been preserved, were preserved,
and conversely why those that have not been, were not. Similarly,
the interpretations of commentators have to be read against the
background of their interests and motivations. We are particularly disadvantaged because of the shortcomings and the bias in
our sources, on the Chinese side for the Mohists, for example,

and on the Greek, for the –5th-century atomists and for many of the early Hellenistic medical writers and astronomers.

Those of us who study ancient periods should not delude ourselves that our subject-matter is simple, just because the evidence is often rather impoverished. It is salutary to remind ourselves of the complexity of the problems of interpretation that some of our colleagues who deal with later periods face, for example in the West those who have wrestled with the problems surrounding the circumstances of the industrial revolution, or those relating to any of the major modern political revolutions East or West. They are all recognised to be extremely difficult to characterise reasonably, let alone to explain or understand. *We* should not expect to do *better*: we can hardly expect to do a fraction as well, with the far less detailed documentation available for the types of interpretative problems we face.

My third question concerned how we should go about our task of comparing. This may best be approached, in the first instance, indirectly, with two negative points about how *not* to do so. These relate to the dangers of generalisation even *within* a single culture, and to some of the converse problems attending the attempt to make direct comparisons between individual theories and concepts *across* cultures *as if* they were addressed to the *same* issue. I shall call these the anti-generalisation point and the anti-piecemeal point.

The anti-generalisation point covers a variety of negative recommendations. One particular tactic that I have recently attacked elsewhere (Lloyd 1990) represents generalisation carried to extraordinary lengths. This is the appeal to a distinct mentality as what is in play in China or in ancient Greece. My first objection to that is that, whatever credibility such talk may have, it provides not even the beginnings of an explanation, but at most a statement of what has to be explained. Moreover, secondly, as such a statement, it obscures rather than clarifies the issues, since it locates the problems in the scarcely directly investigable domain of the *mental*. The whole argument then often turns out to be circular, since the evidence for the mentality hypostasised *is* the evidence that that mentality is supposed to explain.

However there is a further difficulty, not just with talk of mentalities, but with *any* grandiose generalisation about Greek, or Chinese, ways of thought, and that is that they make the unjustified assumption of a *uniformity* in the relevant characteristics across different domains and at different periods. Take first periods: we must surely be very cautious about most of the generalisations that purport to hold true of the *whole* of Chinese thought before the Qin unification (in −221), let alone of the four centuries after that unification *as well.* On the Greek side, Hellenists are well used to working with rough and ready periodisations, archaic (down to the end of the −6th century), classical (to the death of Alexander in −323), Hellenistic (to the fall of Alexandria to Rome in the late −1st century), and so on. Yet there too all the diversity tends to get set aside all too readily when the grand generalisation about *Greek* thought is attempted.

A similar point holds also for the differences between *domains.* We must surely be prepared to recognise that what may be true of mathematics (either in China or in Greece) may not be the case also of medicine, or again of natural philosophy, or again of technology. The circumstances in which each of these was practised and developed vary very considerably in both ancient civilisations, and we had better not ignore that in striving for grand syntheses.

As far as Greece goes, we should go further. It is no good attempting generalisations about 'Greek medicine' that relate to, and are based on, a study of just Hippocratic medicine and its successors. Indeed Hippocratic medicine itself is far from homogeneous. It was all the product of *literate* individuals at least, but that does not take us very far. Nor will it do to take whatever we happen to believe to be genuinely Hippocratic in Hippocratic medicine as the basis for generalisations about Greek medicine as a whole. Any attempt at a general overview of ancient Greek medicine has to take into account four or five distinct other traditions as well, difficult as it is to reconstruct some of these, thanks (again) to the bias in our sources.[1] There is, for example, temple medicine, and the medicine of the itinerant purifiers, and again that of the root-cutters and the drug-sellers, and again that of female healers ('midwives'), the last especially poorly represented in our extant evidence. No more, on the Chinese side, should we underestimate the diversity of the ancient – and indeed living – traditions of healers there.[2]

1. Some of the complexities of the relations between these rival traditions of medicine in ancient Greece are analysed in Lloyd 1983.
2. See, for example, Sivin 1987, pp. 20ff.

But it is not just medicine that offers a good illustration of the anti-generalisation point. The same is true, if to a lesser degree, of Greek mathematics, for besides the Euclidean axiomatic-deductive tradition, there are others, such as that represented by the metrical geometry of Hero of Alexandria, and again the algebraic tradition that culminates in Diophantus. The same is true, too, of philosophy in Greece. There too I would resist any sweeping generalisation to the effect that there is just the *one* notion of *what philosophy is* at work in *all* the individuals we lump together under that rubric.

The diversity *within* philosophy, or mathematics, or medicine, or technology, *may* be greater in ancient Greece than in ancient China. That is possible, though it is also possible that the diversity in ancient Greece is just better documented. We shall address questions to do with the dialectical presentation of Greek thought in Chapter 2. However, in the case of medicine, the pluralism of literate and non-literate traditions is sufficiently well attested in both China and Greece to make the point, even while we may recognise that the ways in which different individuals responded to that pluralism vary in the two cultures: for instance, some reacted to others' views by accommodating them as far as possible, but others by attacking or rejecting them, or using them as a basis of a claim for the superiority of their own solutions to the problems. Yet as a general methodological warning, the dangers of generalising *across* the principal domains we are dealing with should be obvious enough.

My other preliminary negative point, the rejection of a 'piece-meal' approach, is, in a way, the converse of the first. It is clearly not possible, without courting disaster, to proceed to a comparison and contrast between individual theories or concepts seriatim in China and Greece *as if* they were addressing the same questions. Worse still would be the assumption that the questions they were addressing were the ones we consider important in twentieth-century science.

Thus we cannot start from the Greek side, let us say, by identifying some particularly prominent theory or concept and then asking what the Chinese equivalent is – as if it is a foregone conclusion that there will *be* any such equivalent. We cannot assume, in the periods we are dealing with, that there *is* a single set of theories or concepts fundamental to early science that will turn out to play analogous roles in both China and Greece. Indeed the very diversity in the forms that mathematics, astronomy, medicine and natural philosophy took in ancient times, and the implications of that diversity for our understanding of the origins of science, will be two of the central themes of these studies.

Some examples will bring out the importance of the anti-piecemeal point. Take what seems a fundamental Greek notion, *phusis*, 'nature', where we have to be particularly careful since we often unguardedly take *our* idea of 'natural science' to be more or less continuous with theirs. Now on the Greek side, the concept of *phusis* is extremely complex and in many respects it does not at all behave in the way we might expect.

First it is as much normative as descriptive. Of course, our own notion of 'nature' is too. Even so the normative use of *phusis* is particularly strongly marked, and it encompasses some surprising items, as when humans are said by Aristotle (*On the Parts of Animals* 656a10ff) to be the only creatures where the natural parts are in their natural positions. Secondly, *phusis* covers much that we might think has to belong to culture, not to nature – as when Aristotle defines humans as by *nature* political animals, or more strictly as animals that live in city-states (e.g. *Politics* 1253a2f), or when he treats slavery as a *natural* institution (*Politics* 1253b14ff, 1254a17ff).

The Greek concept of *phusis* is problematic, controversial and disputed. The argument I have developed elsewhere (Lloyd 1991a, ch. 18) is that those ancient disputes are not just contingent or accidental. Rather, the concept was forged in controversy. Many of those who used it in the early classical period did so as a means of legitimating their way of doing what they held to be proper science and philosophy. They used it to put down rivals, not just from among traditional claimants to wisdom, but also from among their own immediate competitors who also claimed to be philosophers, sophists or whatever.

But what is essential for our purposes here is that there is no straight equivalent to *phusis* in classical Chinese. Of course, a variety of terms, 天 (*tian*, heaven), 物 (*wu*, things), 性 (*xing*, character), 理 (*li*, pattern), 道 (*dao*, the way), 自然 (*zi ran*, spontaneity, literally 'self so'), do service perfectly adequately, in different contexts, to express ideas where the English translation would be in terms of nature, the Greek in terms of *phusis*, or their cognates. Yet that is still not to say that there is a concept of nature in classical Chinese, just the one, nor that it was a major preoccupation. Rather, the evidence from ancient China shows how well they got along *without* any such central preoccupation.

So what we must at all costs avoid is the assumption that there is a single concept of nature towards which both Greeks and Chinese were somehow struggling, let alone that it was *our* concept of nature as in 'natural science'. It would introduce massive distortions in the interpretation of both Greek and Chinese science if we took it that the work of ancient investigators was targeted at that goal: I stress once again that we must resist any such teleological assumption.

The ancients were not to know the future. They could not anticipate the eventual development of natural science, however much some of those responsible for some of the later developments in European science were to claim, for their part, that they were following and elaborating ancient traditions. Of course, in the history of those later developments, we can trace the use, and transformation, of ancient ideas, and also the rhetoric of both the appeal to, and the rejection of, antiquity. But if we are to understand how *phusis* was used in –5th-century Greece, we have to locate that term in –5th-century argument and debate, to identify the aims and ambitions of those who used it then, to see how they used the inquiry they dubbed the 'investigation concerning *phusis*'.

We cannot assume that the ancient Chinese, for their part, had our concept of 'natural science' as their goal either, let alone that they were fumbling towards some ancient Greek notion of *phusis*. The point can, of course, be tested. One of the more promising texts in which to do so is the 自然 (*zi ran*) chapter, of the 論衡 (*Lun Heng*) of 王充 (Wang Chong) in the +1st century, even though he is, from several points of view, an exceptional and idiosyncratic writer. His chief articulating contrast is that between 有為 (*you wei*) and 無為 (*wu wei*) (very roughly, 'ado' and 'no ado'), and he has some subtle points to make about spontaneity and intentionality, as we might put it. There are, to be sure, points of similarity to ancient Greek discussions that focus on *phusis* and other concepts such as *proairesis* (choice). But evidently to see Wang Chong's programme as working towards *those* ideas is drastically to distort *his* polemic with *his* rivals and opponents. His chief concern is to pour cold water on the attribution of intentionality to a variety of things, particularly some that had often been taken as signs or omens.

That is an example where I began from the Greek side, with *phusis*. But there is no shortage of similar examples where the same holds true if we start from Chinese concepts. One has only to think of the splendidly rich materials relating to the classical notion of the *dao*. Almost anything can be said to have a *dao*, whether objects or skills. Thus a plant may, though this is not a matter of its eternal essence conceived statically, but rather of the way it grows, and there can be a *dao* of any number of human activities, from butchery to calligraphy. Then again the *dao* is the proper path of life, the one the sage follows spontaneously, and as such the goal, though not an item of theoretical knowledge that secures understanding, but rather an internalised mode of being and doing.

What was the Greek equivalent? Parmenides, to be sure, speaks of philosophy in terms of ways, using the word *hodos*. Yet he has both a Way of Truth *and* a Way of Seeming. It would have seemed paradoxical in the extreme, to Chinese of the classical period – by which I here mean down to the end of Han times in +220 – to admit that there could be a *Way* of *Seeming*. Again some favour *logos* as closer to Chinese concerns. But clearly that juxtaposition, too, reveals more differences than it does similarities, not least because of the presuppositions of expressibility that Greek *logos* generally entails.

The harder the point is pressed, the clearer it should become that any such pursuit of an equivalent takes the *wrong question* as its starting-point. Of course, *dao* is a very special term, and so might be thought exceptional. But the point can be made with plenty of others, 氣 (*qi*, breath, 'pneuma'), 陰陽 (*yin yang*, the negative and positive principles), 天 (*tian*, 'heaven'), concepts to which we shall be returning in the studies that follow – and that is before we appeal to more domain-specific concepts, such as, for example, 邪 (*xie*, 'heteropathy'), used in medicine.[3]

So far my principal points have been negative ones and serve to underline the complexities of the task that faces any comparativist history of ancient science. Yet it may be possible to

----

3. See Sivin 1987, pp. 49, 102ff.

glean some positive recommendations from the negative ones I have so far made. I do not just mean the necessary, but not very helpful, stipulation to be as scrupulous as possible about recontextualising the materials we are dealing with, making sure that we do full justice to the *original* debates and concerns in *each* of the separate areas in *each* period in *both* great ancient civilisations. No doubt it would be better to *begin* any attempt at comparison and contrast only *after* deeply immersing ourselves in *everything*. To that, I would just say that the whole point about methodology is to try to develop appropriate procedures not to cut corners, but to give focus to our inquiry. Besides, methodology, whether conscious or not, is inevitable, in that however unselfconscious a scholar's methods and assumptions may be, they will be pervasive. So they had better be as explicit as we can make them.

One suggestion that may be thought to emerge from my anti-piecemeal reflections is that we should not begin with a comparison between the *answers* or *results*: we should ask first what the *questions* were to which the answers were thought to be the right answers. I have insisted that we cannot assume that the theories or concepts were addressed to the same questions. So it follows that we must problematise the questions.

What were the questions or problems that the Chinese were concerned with that led to the answers they gave being the answers they were? And what, similarly, were the key questions or problems on the Greek side? Thus instead of trying a direct comparison between Chinese and Greek physical speculation, as if both were answers to the *same* questions, we should explore first, for example, what the Chinese considered to be the important issues to which talk of the five phases, 五行 (*wu xing*), provided the basis of an answer.[4] Again, what did the Greeks think to be the key questions they were answering with their talk of elements, *stoicheia*?

Let me come back to elaborate both the general point, and the particular example of phases and elements, a little later. But let me first mention three obvious objections my proposed question-oriented approach might be thought to run into. First

---

4. The most recent authoritative study of the development, and range of application, of this concept is Sivin 1995c: cf. also Graham 1989, pp. 340ff, and see further below, pp. 122ff.

it looks as if my way of putting it (asking what the questions are, to which the answers were thought to be the right answers) involves or presupposes a certain type of determinism – as if the answers were *determined* by the questions. But no: because it is not as if the answers were entirely *uniform* in either China or Greece. While the language of the five phases was common to many writers from Han times (–2nd century) onwards, and the five were generally agreed (namely 木, *mu*, 火, *huo*, 地, *di*, 金, *jin*, 水, *shui*, that is, roughly, 'wood', 'fire', 'earth', 'metal' and 'water'), there was still plenty of variety in the way they were used and even about how far they are to be used. Thus their introduction into medicine marks an important turning-point in the development of medical speculation. Much more obviously, in the example I took before, while just about everyone agreed on the importance of the *dao*, knowing what the *dao* was, or rather how to follow it, or more strictly actually following it, was what sagehood was all about. This was not for the ordinary person.

So too, on the Greek side, even among those who, from the –4th century onwards, agreed that for physical theory you needed elements, the variety of answers is almost as great as the number of philosophers who put them forward. Atomic theories competed with continuum ones, monistic theories with pluralist ones, and there were plenty of different kinds of pluralism in the field. Aristotle's privileging of earth, water, air and fire was just one of several such, and although it came to be the most influential ancient Greek theory, the impression of its dominance over its rivals strengthens the further from antiquity one goes.

But then the second objection, and the third, to my approach are that, if we work at a different *level*, in our comparisons, turning to questions or problems, rather than to theories or concepts, we shall never have anything significant to say about the *contents* of theories, only about their forms, and worse still, we shall often be going well beyond anything for which we have direct evidence in the ancient Greek or Chinese texts themselves, since in many cases they do not address my second-order questions, of the questions their theories are directed at, explicitly. So one objection would insist that the substance of the Greek and Chinese theories in question is going to slip through the net of our inquiry, and the other is that that inquiry is, in any case, going to have to be all too speculative.

A concession has to be made to the first of these two objections immediately. Of course, the question-oriented investigation will have nothing concrete to say about why this, that, or the other, Greek element theorist had the particular theory he had at the moment he proposed it (as opposed to having something to say, we may hope, about why Greek theorists in general focussed on *elements*). We are not, that is to say, ever going to be in a position to say why, exactly, Diogenes of Apollonia revived a monistic theory based on the element air in the late −5th century.[5]

Whether we shall ever be in any position to give any kind of *explanation* of the phenomena at that level is doubtful, though the internal dialectic of the argument between Greek element theorists provides *some* kind of story of how they saw the strengths and weaknesses of differing concrete responses to the problems at different historical conjunctures. But it is surely over-optimistic to a degree to think we could ever arrive at a hard-edged explanation of the contents of the particular contributions made by specific individuals at different stages in any of the main domains of inquiry we are concerned with. We cannot recapture the thought-processes of Archimedes in his bath. If that is accepted, it can hardly be thought a fundamental objection to bring against the question-oriented investigation I propose.

The objection of rank speculativeness – when we have to go well beyond what our authors themselves talk about – is obviously more problematic. The only response is to rest one's case on the results obtained. It is a question of how *well* the job can be done, how speculative, how far removed from the direct textual evidence, one has to be, how suggestive or fruitful the results appear to be, for example in relating together previously unconnected areas or aspects of ancient investigations. Critical evaluation must always involve an element of judgement, and so of subjectivity. But that does not mean *unconstrained* subjectivity, not if the evaluation makes the best use of criticism. Not that any results can be claimed to be anything like definitive, and most, in our state of knowledge, must be acknowledged to be decidedly tentative.

Let me now come back to the particular case of elements and

5. For a first orientation on the work of Diogenes of Apollonia, see Kirk, Raven, Schofield 1983, Laks 1983.

phases to try out some ideas primarily on the Greek side. Why, the issue is, did the Greeks so often focus on the question of the underlying elements – to which they gave so many divergent answers? Why this preoccupation with the simplest units to which everything else can be reduced, with what is in itself unchanging but is itself the ground of change, with foundations? I stress that the elements are in themselves unchanging, for even when they interact, as the elements they are they have determinate characteristics.

No doubt the answer has to be complex. No doubt some might favour an approach to the question via an analysis of the very structure of the Greek language.[6] But while some have suggested a connection between the subject-predicate structure of Greek and other Indo-European languages, and a focussing on *substances*, we have to remark that, even if we accepted that, that would still be well short of providing even the beginning of an answer to why those substances, the physical ones at least, should be themselves analysed in terms of their *elements*.[7]

A more promising approach may be suggested if we focus on the very divergence of Greek element theories which is such a striking feature of them, especially when contrasted with the relatively stable consensus, in China, at least from Han times on, both on the identity of the five phases and on the relationship between phases and *qi*. Why were so many different answers given in ancient Greece to the – different – question of the constituent elements of things? Why do we find so many different solutions proposed, by Presocratic philosophers, by Plato and Aristotle, by the Stoics and Epicureans, not to mention also by dozens of medical writers who also propounded physical theories? That divergence relates, obviously, to the intense competitiveness of Greek intellectual life, to the rivalry between groups as well as within them. The point would be that, to outdo the competition,

6. The parallel attempt to explain aspects of Chinese philosophy through an analysis of features of classical Chinese was tried by Bloom 1981 and Hall and Ames 1987, whose theses have, however, been extensively criticised by Graham 1989, pp. 389ff, cf. Harbsmeier 1981 and forthcoming, and most recently subjected to blistering attack by Wardy 1992 and forthcoming (a).
7. Hypotheses of linguistic determinism in the manner of Sapir and Whorf are dubious, to put it mildly, at the best of times: but they are also manifestly futile wherever, as repeatedly happens with Greek, there is massive diversity within the concepts developed within the same natural language.

you needed a theory you could call your own. Even when you took over other people's ideas, you often modified them, and the end-product was often stridently proclaimed to be brand new, the author's personal discovery, the solution, indeed, to problems that had defeated everyone else.[8]

The first stage in my argument would be that that competitiveness stimulated the very diversity we noticed in the answers to the question of the underlying elements, though reservations about the nature of Greek adversariality will be necessary in due course (Chapter 2). But if it is presumably uncontroversial that competitiveness can contribute to our understanding of the *diversity* of element theories, can it do anything to help explain why *element* theories? I hope a little, with a further argument that goes like this.

Ideally, to win the competition, you needed not just a theory you could claim as your own, but one you could present as true, better still as certain. Of course, you could proceed – the Greeks often did proceed – by *eliminating* rival theories, deploying destructive arguments to undermine the claims of the opposition. The hope was that that left only your own preferred theory standing. But *constructively* the hope was to *demonstrate* that theory, indeed many claimed that they had done so, and had, indeed, shown its *necessity*. There were, to be sure, many different modes of demonstration developed in ancient Greece (see Chapter 4), but certainly one powerful tradition, from the –4th century onwards at least, took proof *more geometrico* – in the geometrical manner – as its ideal. The essence of that was valid deduction from axiomatic starting-points (or from intermediate starting-points that themselves could be deduced from the axioms). We shall be returning to this theme several times in the studies that follow.

It is not fortuitous, I would say, that from the –4th century the standard name to cover whatever different starting-points you needed – definitions, axioms or common opinions, postulates or hypotheses – is, precisely, elements, *stoicheia*.[9] That may seem an

8. This point is fully documented in Lloyd 1987a, ch. 2, 'Tradition and innovation', where I grant, of course, that the balance between those two trends changes appreciably after the classical period in Greece.
9. The history of the development of this term has been traced especially by Burkert 1959.

outrageous suggestion to traditional Greek scholars who might protest on two scores especially. Elements may or may not have been the original title of whatever work Hippocrates of Chios wrote in the late −5th century that led to the late commentators, such as Proclus, suggesting that he started the development that culminated in Euclid's extant treatise of that name.[10] But (the first objection would be) is it not clear that the definition of the indemonstrables, and the clear recognition that there must be such, are comparatively late developments, certainly later than Hippocrates, and maybe not before Aristotle himself? Moreover, secondly and more fundamentally, although the same term 'elements' may crop up in both physics and mathematics, the differences in application in those two fields rule out any such connection as I have suggested.

I would concede something to both objections, but not retreat entirely. Obviously the terminology of elements took time to develop in both natural philosophy and mathematics. In philosophy it first appears in a technical sense in Plato, even though some of the basic ideas can be expressed *via* other concepts, such as *archē*, beginning, starting-point, principle. To be sure, in mathematics the elements are propositions, in physics the basic constituents of substances. However my sticking-point is that in physics, as in mathematics, the concern with *element* theory is a concern for secure foundations. In mathematics these are the foundations from which the rest of mathematics can, in principle, be deduced: and in physics they are the foundations of all physical explanation, the − in themselves unchanging − constituents that underlie all physical change.

What I suggest, then, is that theorising about physical elements corresponds, at least in part, to a perceived need to take over the high ground in physical theory, to have a secure vantage point from which to defeat the opposition. If you could persuade people of the correctness of your view of the elements, then much of the rest of your physical theory could be held to be secure.

Indeed if you did *not* have a reasonably plausible element theory, it would be difficult to make a beginning in physics, in

10. Proclus, *In Euc.* 66.7ff. At 66.14–68.6 Proclus refers to a sequence of mathematicians between Hippocrates and Euclid who continued and extended work on the elements.

the Greek sense of the study of nature, at all. Even those theorists who do not claim that their element theories are necessary,
nevertheless are often clear as to the *type* of elements they insist
on. Plato would illustrate the point. He is undogmatic about the
specifics of his geometrical atomism. In the *Timaeus* (54ab) he
draws back from an account of why the half-equilateral is the
fairest of triangles, saying that 'if anyone could refute us and
discover that it is not so, we do not grudge him the prize' – for
his would be the victory of a friend, not an enemy. At the same
time, he is absolutely clear about the type of account to be given
both of the elements and of the physical world as a whole, namely
a teleological one, revealing their order.

However, the trouble was, of course, that obtaining agreement
to *your own* view of the physical elements was appreciably more
difficult than doing so in mathematics. The paradox was that
the more that Greek physical theorists strove for certainty, the
further that goal receded. The demand, in its strongest form,
was for the incontrovertible. But every time some Greek physicist
claimed that it had been achieved, the claim was challenged: no
sooner had some such claim been made by one Greek theorist
than it was implicitly or explicitly rejected by another.

But that did not mean that they abandoned the pursuit –
not even when the viability of the whole endeavour was subject
to withering attack from the radical sceptics of the Hellenistic
period. *Their* version of scepticism itself, indeed, may be held to
reflect the very view I am talking about, for their whole argument
was that *no* foundational claim as to the nature of underlying reality is justified, and they saw very clearly that competing foundation claims undermined one another. There was as much to be
said against, as for, any and every dogmatic position, so the proper
response was to withhold judgement. Yet that did not stop their
contemporaries from continuing in the vein of classical Greek
physical speculation, trying out one theory after another in a bid
to secure the foundations for the study of nature.

Let me now take stock of where my argument has reached and
of the proposals I should recommend on the general methodological issues that are my main theme here. Most of what I had
to say initially is negative and admonitory, rather than positive
and constructive in character, namely the anti-generalisation and

the anti-piecemeal points. But on the more positive and construct-ive side, the gist of my argument is that we should consider, in the first instance, why certain *questions* come to be the focus of attention. We must examine, that is, what the Greeks or the Chi-nese took to be the leading problems, and why, and what criteria they adopted for an adequate account.

Our problematising of the questions must extend all the way to how the subject-matter of each inquiry was understood, and what each was meant to cover. We cannot take 'medicine' or 'astronomy' as givens, for there is nothing automatic about how health and disease were construed, or the body itself, or the heavens, and the same applies even more forcefully when we are dealing with such overarching concepts as 'order' or 'harmony'. We cannot take it for granted that a focus on causal explana-tion (for instance) will be uniform, nor indeed that concepts of 'cause' will be (cf. Chapter 5). Nor indeed can we assume that, in general, methodology, when explicitly invoked, always plays the same role in the economy of the presentation of arguments (cf. Chapter 3). Even in a concrete case like the use of dissection, what looks like the very same practical technique is deployed in very different ways and used for quite different purposes in China and in Greece (Chapter 9).

All of this means that the agenda that we set ourselves must – as we said – include (even if it is not limited by) the inquiry into the conditions under which knowledge, or what passed for it, was produced, and the conditions under which those who claimed to do the producing worked.

To begin to understand the principal products of Greek philo-sophy and science we certainly have to explore, among other things, such questions as how you became a wise man, *sophos*, what the available roles for different types of wise man were (whether philosophers, sophists, mathematicians, statesmen or even healers),[11] how you won a reputation in your field, how you related to your teachers (if you admitted to having teachers) and how you won followers, supporters, pupils, and what you expected of them. We have to go into the perceived or assumed *values* of philosophy and science, what they were thought to be *for*, and

11. I have explored aspects of the rival claims made to the title of wise man (*sophos*) and to wisdom (*sophia*) in Lloyd 1987a, ch. 1, pp. 83ff especially.

that takes us inexorably into the values of the society in which the philosophers and scientists operated. So what may start out as internalist questions about the underlying problems as the ancients saw them are indissociable from externalist issues to do with values, ideologies, the statuses of different claimants to prestige, the interactions of power and knowledge.

Similarly on the Chinese side, where similar questions yield, as we shall see, *very* different answers – not that a single set of answers will do for *every* domain, let alone *every* period, on *either* side – the anti-generalisation point.

To be sure, the invocation of externalist factors is not an end to the matter. From another point of view, the values of the societies in question, and the fundamental institutions that underpin them, themselves stand in need of explanation. We can and should pursue questions to do with their origins and developments and with the variety of modes of expression of ideologies. That variety itself stems in part from the work of philosophers and scientists themselves: so the *interaction* of internalist and externalist considerations, and the feed-back effect between them, must be allowed for.

But the goal is not, and cannot be, some *ultimate* explanation, in terms of *explanantia* that are not in turn themselves *explananda*. As for the relevance of the externalist factors that can be invoked to afford insight into Greek or Chinese science, one way of assessing that is, precisely, to exploit the comparisons and contrasts between the two. The key test will be to evaluate the strengths of the *correlations* that can be suggested between, on the one hand, social and institutional factors, and, on the other, the nature of the scientific inquiries produced, in either society.

Investigations into the sociology of knowledge may look as if they just relate to the *form* of theories, or concepts, or debates, or the ways in which wise men, whether Chinese or Greek, chose to present themselves or their activities. They may look as if they leave the *contents* of speculations, in either society, as hard to comprehend as ever. To be sure, there are plenty of tricky problems to do with specific contents that this part of my question-oriented and sociological approach is not going to help with. Indeed some problems, at the point where we ask why this or that theorist produced, at a particular juncture, precisely the proposed solutions they did, may not be soluble at all. I mentioned

Diogenes of Apollonia, where we may distinguish the question of
why he based his revival of monism on air, from the study of why
he started his work (as we are told) by insisting that the starting-
point (*archē*) should be indisputable (*anamphisbē´tēton*).[12] The latter, procedural, remark speaks volumes about how *he* perceived
what he had to do in order to persuade.

But I would hold that one need not be too defensive in the
face of the invocation of the form–contents dichotomy, at least
insofar as that very dichotomy can be called into question. We
can make the point particularly well with regard to mathematics,
for that is the domain that would appear to present the most
difficulty, for it is there that assumptions that we *can* drive a
wedge between form and content may be most deeply rooted.
Yet as Karine Chemla especially has shown,[13] it is precisely by seeing that what we might think of merely as the *style* of mathematical reasoning has fundamental consequences for the reasoning
itself, that we can hope not just to gain a greater understanding
of Chinese mathematics on the one hand, Greek mathematics
on the other – each, we must recall, in its considerable variety –
but also of the best way ahead in the comparisons and contrasts
between them.

Similarly the contents of philosophical, and medical, debates
cannot, or rather should not, be divorced from the *modes of conduct* of the debates themselves (written or oral, real or imaginary), including the styles of adversariality, or consensuality,
adopted, the appropriation or rejection of others', or of traditional, views, the whole gamut of the variety of the tactics of
persuasion. This will be the subject-matter of our next study and
of Chapter 4.

But if no one should underestimate the difficulty of the work
of comparing and contrasting, the value of the endeavour lies in
the hope of deparochialising the history of ancient science. As a
Hellenist, I know how difficult it is for us to get away from the
assumptions that the Greek way of doing things was the natural
or inevitable way of doing them, that the Greeks' view of the

12. Diogenes of Apollonia, Fr. 1. In an analogous fashion, but in a very different context,
    the author of the Hippocratic treatise *On the Art*, ch. 4, *CMG* I 1, 11.5ff, suggests that
    the starting-point of an account should be what will be agreed by everyone.
13. See Chemla 1990a, 1990b, 1991, 1992a, 1992b and cf. further below, p. 61 at
    n. 18, pp. 152ff at nn. 21ff.

questions to be asked focussed on the right ones to pose, the only ones that count, that the Greeks' preoccupations with *their* ideals, models, goals, are the preoccupations that provide the necessary, if not the sufficient, conditions for the eventual development of modern science.

The best way of disabusing ourselves of those assumptions is by using all the considerable resources available for the investigation of *other* ways of doing things, other perceptions of key questions, ideals, goals, preoccupations – difficult as the work is. Do Greek philosophy and science reflect fundamental features of Greek society, Greek politics, the Greek language, Greek literacy, or again Greek economic circumstances or technology or even geography? And if so, how? And so, mutatis mutandis, also for China. The only way we have of even beginning to test the strengths and weaknesses of any of these or other explanatory schemata, or of seeing which aspects correlate with which, is by resolutely looking across the borders at our colleagues on the other side – that is, across the institutionalised walls that our universities have created as barriers between our specialisations. This is the guiding spirit that drives the studies that follow.

CHAPTER 2

Adversaries and authorities

This chapter undertakes a first exploration into the institutional background of ancient Greek and Chinese science by way of a critical examination of a number of common assumptions concerning the styles and modes of intellectual exchange favoured in each. I shall focus especially first on issues to do with adversariality, that is, with the cultivation – or the avoidance – of polemical confrontation, and secondly, on authority, and the use of the appeal to such in a bid to resolve problematic questions. By authority figures I mean those who are invoked as support or justification for a particular idea, theory or practice: it is not that such figures are necessarily held to be infallible or immune to criticism, though it is obvious that the more they are criticised, the less weight they carry for constructive purposes.

These two are not symmetrical subjects. Appeals to authority, for instance, are often overtly or covertly polemical. However, the two rubrics together will allow discussion of a fair number of the salient features of the styles of intellectual exchange cultivated in Greek and Chinese science.

My argument will proceed in three stages. My starting-point is what I take to be a common view of a fundamental contrast. On the one hand, as has been a recurrent topos at least since Burckhardt, the Greeks exhibited highly developed agonistic traits in every part of their culture, from gymnastic competitions to theatrical ones, across the board in their legal and political experience, and in many aspects of their intellectual life, philosophy and science included. On the other, it has often been claimed that the Chinese were irenic rather than polemical and rejected aggressive adversariality of any kind.[1]

---

1. Such a view influences the analyses offered by Nakamura (1960), e.g. part III, chh. 7 and 12. The idea of a radical contrast, on this score, between the West and China goes back at least as far as Voltaire, whose *Au Roi de la Chine* dates from 1771.

The first stage of my discussion will be to see what can be said *for* such a view and also whether analogous contrasts appear *prima facie* plausible with regard to attitudes towards authority. The second stage will then be to submit those suggestions to a severe critique, to point out some of the major qualifications and reservations that have to be entered for any such thesis to be acceptable.

This in turn will lead me, in the third and most substantial part of this study, to revise the central questions we need to focus on, to move from a descriptive to the – admittedly far more difficult – explanatory mode, to consider not just what is the case, but why. Whatever we make of purported contrasts (stage 1) or similarities (stage 2), the key issue throughout is why the diverse styles of attitudes or of exchange should have been cultivated in the forms they were.

For the purposes of this chapter, I shall concentrate on just two topics especially. The first is the role of what are conventionally, but in certain respects misleadingly, called 'schools' of philosophy or science in Greece or in China – where in Greece one of the chief terms is *hairesis*, 'sect', literally 'choice', while in China the main term is 家, *Jia*, one of whose primary meanings is simply 'family'. The second relates to the typical audience or addressee of scientific and philosophical works: at whom were they targeted, whom were they trying to persuade?

It goes without saying that, on issues as complex as these, any ambition to offer a decent general analysis, let alone one that could claim to have explanatory power, has to be tempered by a due recognition of the diversity of the material under consideration and of the difficulties of interpretation it poses. The positive theses I have to offer must accordingly be understood as no more than tentative suggestions and themselves subject to qualifications and reservations.

I

For our first stage we may begin with the famously agonistic Greeks and the less famously irenic Chinese of our chosen period. Any acquaintance with early Greek natural philosophy immediately brings to light a very large number of instances of philosophers criticising other thinkers – whether perceived as fellow philosophers or not.[2] Thus Xenophanes attacks Homer and Hesiod by name (Fr. 11, cf. Frr. 12, 14–16), and Heraclitus not just Homer, Hesiod and Archilochus, but also Xenophanes, Pythagoras and Hecataeus (Frr. 40, 42, 56, 57, 106). Possible implicit criticisms are even commoner and may even go back to points at which Anaximander diverges from Thales.[3] Xenophanes satirises Pythagoras' belief in metempsychosis in Fr. 7, Heraclitus may have Anaximander in mind in Fr. 80,[4] Empedocles implies disagreement with Parmenides,[5] and so on.

This is not just a feature of *early* Greek philosophy. Plato is generous, sometimes, to some of his predecessors, notably Parmenides, but criticises most of the Presocratics, including him, as well as the poets and the sophists, both as collectivities and as individuals. Homer, in particular, though much used, is subjected to blistering attack. Those who engaged in the inquiry into nature in the mechanistic, anti-teleological mode are labelled atheists in *Laws* 10, 885cd, 888e–890a, where the Athenian Stranger recommends dire sanctions for any who do not mend their ways, imprisonment first, followed by death if they do not recant, 907d–909d.

Aristotle, too, one of our major sources for his predecessors, of course, criticises them all more or less severely, not least Plato himself. Although in that case it is sometimes difficult to distinguish criticisms of Plato himself from those of views held by Platonists,[6] he attacks Plato by name often enough for the point to be made. From the list of occasions when philosophers are

2. Those conventionally categorised as 'philosophers' before Plato are, in any event, unlikely to have considered themselves as all engaged in the same one inquiry. *Sophos* (wise man) and *sophistēs* ('sophist') are, and remain, terms with fluctuating and indeterminate reference: cf. Lloyd 1987a, pp. 91ff.

3. Two such points relate to the choice of the Boundless, rather than any determinate substance such as Thales' water, as principle (see Aristotle, *Physics* 204b24ff) and to the answer to the question of why the earth is at rest (Aristotle, *On the Heavens* 294a28ff, 295b10ff).

4. Where Anaximander had described the relations between certain cosmic factors as governed by order (they pay the penalty, *dikē*, to one another for their injustice, *adikia*, Fr. 1), Heraclitus Fr. 80 insisted that 'justice', *dikē*, is 'strife', *eris*.

5. With Empedocles Fr. 17.26, for instance, compare Parmenides Fr. 8.50ff. But Empedocles agrees with Parmenides, as does Anaxagoras, that nothing comes to be from not-being. With Parmenides Fr. 8.6ff, compare Empedocles Fr. 8 and Anaxagoras Fr. 17.

6. As Jaeger 1948 made much of, Aristotle sometimes includes himself among those holding the Platonist views he criticises, as for instance in the first book of the *Metaphysics*, 990b8f, 22ff.

attacked by name in the Hellenistic period, by Epicureans, Stoics, Sceptics and the rest, one could pretty well reconstruct the main lines of the development of Hellenistic philosophy itself. Indeed in several cases that is, precisely, how we have to proceed, to reconstruct the contributions of individual Hellenistic philosophers, when we do not have their own writings.

Nor is this just a matter of 'philosophy', howsoever understood. Hippocratic texts join in the criticism of named Presocratics, Melissus in *On the Nature of Man* ch. 1, Empedocles in *On Ancient Medicine* ch. 20. They attack fellow doctors and their writings, naturally, even more commonly, beginning with the criticism of the authors and revisers of the lost work called *Cnidian Sentences* in *On Regimen in Acute Diseases*, and including attacks that imply that *every* other doctor is wrong.[7] Much later, Hippocrates, idolised by some, was criticised extensively by, among others, Celsus and Soranus, while Galen uses his interpretation of Hippocrates as a stick to beat his rivals and opponents, not just Lycus – the 'bastard of the Hippocratic sect' – and such other favourite enemies of Galen's, such as Julian, but also Sabinus, Quintus, Numesianus, Stratonicus, Aephicianus, and even his own teachers, Satyrus and Pelops.[8]

One might think, perhaps, that Greek mathematics at least might be an exception. Since we have almost no extant texts from before Euclid, that can hardly be confirmed or refuted there. Euclid himself, to be sure, adopts a studiedly impersonal style in the *Elements* and his other works. But for evidence for hard-hitting polemic in Greek mathematics, one need go no further than Pappus, who in the *Collection* not only offers criticisms of Archimedes and Apollonius, no less, but, as Serafina Cuomo (1995) has now shown in detail, engages in a sustained debate with contemporary and near-contemporary mathematicians, both the admittedly unnamed mathematician whose study of the problem of the mean proportionals is criticised at length in book 3, and also named individuals such as Carpus and Sporus.

---

7. Thus *On Regimen in Acute Diseases* sets out to describe matters of great importance that are not understood by doctors (ch. 3, L II 238.8ff) and *On Regimen* refers repeatedly to the discoveries the author has made, which, he says, 'none of my predecessors attempted to understand' (III ch. 69, *CMG* I 2, 4, 200.28ff, cf. further below, p. 195). Other examples of the sweeping criticisms that some Hippocratic writers make of other doctors are documented in Lloyd 1987a, ch. 2, pp. 57–70.
8. The evidence is set out and discussed in Lloyd 1991a, ch. 17, pp. 400–2.

As for my companion topic of authority, it is certainly true that the use of authority figures grows very considerably in the Hellenistic period, Euclid, Archimedes in mathematics, Hippocrates in medicine, Socrates and Plato in philosophy, and so on.[9] Yet two points have to be borne in mind. First, it is well known that what is attributed to those and other worthies is often very much the construct of the Hellenistic writer doing the attributing. I showed that in some detail where Galen and Hippocrates are concerned – claiming that if Hippocrates had not existed, Galen would certainly have had to invent him, but then also that in a sense he did (Lloyd 1991a, ch. 17, at p. 416). But the treatment of Plato by 'Platonists' of one type or another would also exemplify the point.

Moreover, secondly, the *lack* of great authority figures for the writers of the classical period is striking. Homer was so treated in certain quarters, but is attacked more often than revered by Xenophanes, Heraclitus, Plato, as we have noted. Of course the Greeks had their Seven Wise Men, though there was never complete agreement about who the Seven were. But with the exception of Thales, it is not as if their teaching cut much ice in natural philosophy or science. Parmenides, as remarked, was much respected, but it is not as if the invocation of his name was warranty enough for the positions with which he was associated.

But what about the less famously irenic Chinese? Two of the earliest extant texts that mention the differences between different philosophical groups and individuals both make the point. These are the 'syncretist' *Tian Xia pian*/'chapter' ('Below in the Empire' in Graham's translation) in the 莊子, *Zhuangzi* compilation,[10] and the account of the philosophical groups in the final 'chapter' of the 史記, *Shiji*, compiled by 司馬遷, Sima Qian, where Sima Qian records the views of his father Sima Tan. The *Tian Xia* chapter dates, perhaps, from the –2nd century, and Sima Tan died in –110, while the *Shiji* was written not much later, around –90.

---

9. This is discussed in Lloyd 1987a, ch. 2, pp. 101–8. As Manuli 1983 stressed, it is important not to underestimate the extent to which, in Greece, the commentary is used as a vehicle for the expression of original ideas. In China, a similar point holds also, for example, of the mathematical commentaries of Liu Hui on the *Nine Chapters of the Mathematical Art*.
10. On the various strata, their composition and dates, in the *Zhuangzi* compilation, see Graham 1981 and 1989, pp. 172ff, 306ff.

The *Tian Xia* chapter refers sweepingly to '100 *Jia*' but also to named individuals, the legendary Lao Dan (putative author of the *Dao De Jing*), but also several historically more reliably attested persons, 墨翟, *Mo Di* (founder of the Mohists), Sung, Xing, Yin Wen and indeed Zhuang Zhou (Zhuangzi) himself. Each of these is criticised at points, but each is said to have grasped some part of the ancient tradition of the Way, and to have 'got wind of' and to have delighted in this. Precisely the same expression is used no less than five times throughout the chapter in order to make the point (*Zhuangzi* 33: 16–17, 34–5, 42–3, 55 and 63–4).

In a similar fashion, in Sima Qian's *Shiji* 130, Sima Tan first goes through the ideas of the groups he calls by the titles (1) *Yin Yang*, (2) Confucians, (3) Mohists, (4) the law *Jia* (法家, *Fa Jia*: the conventional translation is 'Legalists'), and then (5) the *Jia* labelled as that of 'names' (名家, *Ming Jia*: the common rendering 'Sophists' is a typically disastrous attempt to assimilate Chinese thinkers to Greek models).[11] Then he turns to the 道, *Dao*, as he recommends it. All five of the groups first mentioned come in for criticism, but again all five are said to have taught things that are 'not to be neglected', 'not to be changed', 'not to be dispensed with', 'not to be altered' or 'to which one cannot not pay attention' (*Shiji* 130: 3289, 2–5). Moreover one of the great strengths of the *Dao* Sima Tan himself recommends is that, according to him, it encompasses the best in all the other groups' teachings (*Shiji* 130: 3289, 6).

There are, to be sure, serious problems about the extent to which either of these two accounts of early Chinese philosophical groupings can be accepted as historically reliable: we shall come back to some of these later. But that does not affect the point we are concerned with at the moment, and at this stage in our argument, namely the way in which the interactions of the groups are *represented*. Certainly in both *Zhuangzi* and the *Shiji* the emphasis is not on points at which the groups they refer to disagreed, proposed ideas that are incompatible with one another, or were otherwise competing with one another, but rather on what each of them had positively to contribute, how each succeeded, at least in part, in grasping some part of the *Dao*.

11. The differences between *Ming Jia* and Greek sophists are well brought out by Reding 1985, though he continues to write of Chinese sophists.

As for the topic of the authority of the past, that might be thought to be equally easy to show, at this first stage in our discussion. Chinese thinkers of many different philosophical persuasions were repeatedly harking back to the teachings of the Sage Kings. Sometimes, to be sure, that is just for form's sake, and sometimes it masks covert criticisms of contemporary figures, shown up as inferior by contrast to the great models of the past. Nevertheless the idea that there is past wisdom, that there were, once, Sage Kings, is a commonplace.

Thus Confucius already presents himself not as an innovator, but as a transmitter – later he was to be represented as the recoverer – of earlier wisdom, a wisdom associated with the pre-dynastic reigns of Yao and Shun, and the three dynasties of Xia, Shang and Zhou. The Mohists, too, often invoke the Sage Kings, and even otherwise idiosyncratic characters such as Zhuangzi and the +1st-century sceptic Wang Chong also cite ancient authorities with apparent respect. In the *Tian Xia* chapter I have already cited, what each of the philosophers mentioned is *praised* for is getting some part (even if not the whole) of the *ancient* tradition of the Way.

II

So at the first stage in the argument, it may seem that a major contrast can be suggested between ancient Greek and ancient Chinese intellectuals, the former constantly criticising one another, the latter seeking the common ground, often under the banner of the revival of past wisdom. However, it is easy to see that the thesis suffers from serious limitations and weaknesses.

Take first the Chinese and authority. Just as there are some texts that praise the Sage Kings, so there are others that problematise that move. In the *Hanfeizi*, named after 韓非, Han Fei (c. −280 to c. −233), who composed at least some of the work though other parts were put together under the Han, we find an argument based on the time that has elapsed since the founding of the Zhou – seven hundred years – so people are unable to fix which is the genuine wisdom of that time. Nor can they be sure of the genuine Confucianism or Mohism. As for inquiring into the Way of Yao and Shun, three thousand years ago, 'may I suggest that one can hardly be certain of it? To be certain of it without evidence is foolishness, to appeal to it though unable to be certain of it is fraud.'[12]

Again the 呂氏春秋 (*Lüshi Chunqiu,* also composed around the middle of the −3rd century), has a section (15, 8) entitled 察今, *cha jin* 'scrutinising the present', that suggests that the standards or principles (法, *fa*) laid down by former kings were important for their times: but the times did not come down with the standards. So the only thing to do is to ask *why they set the standards they did. The answer is man, but 'I myself am a man. Therefore if I scrutinise myself, I may know other men, if I scrutinise the present, I may know the past.'* This is not a rejection of the values of ancient wisdom, but a warning that one should not follow the 'fixed' standards and ignore the times they were for, even though in a sense past and present are one. Besides, the canons (books) of the principles of the former kings have come down through earlier generations, and 'some people have added to them, others have subtracted from them'. So there are problems of authenticity, and textual criticism should not be neglected.'[13]

Even more importantly, the relations between different Chinese intellectuals were sometimes very far from being irenic. The *Zhuangzi* compilation contains plenty of lampoons of Confucius, as in the famous confrontation with 'Robber Zhi' (*Zhuangzi* 29). According to the *Tian Xia* chapter, the Mohists were divided among themselves, with different groups interpreting the Mohist canon differently, but each claiming that they were right, and according to *Hanfeizi* (50: 1080), sectionalism or factionalism characterise contemporary Confucians[14] as well as the Mohists. The chief representatives of the *Ming Jia,* namely 惠施 Hui Shi (−3rd century), and 公孫龍 Gongsun Long (−2nd century), are not only renowned for their disputatiousness but are treated with near contempt by many of the writers who refer to them.[15]

There are, too, specific issues on which different thinkers took up diametrically opposed positions in explicit opposition to one another. One of the best known is the conflict on whether human

12. *Hanfeizi* 50: 1080, trans. Graham 1989, p. 273.
13. *Lüshi Chunqiu* 15, 8, trans. Graham 1989, pp. 214f, modified.
14. However, as will be noted shortly, p. 31, the term for 'Confucian', namely 儒 (*ru*), is often used loosely.
15. As Hui Shi is in *Zhuangzi* 33: 69–87, cf. Graham 1989, pp. 75ff, 82ff.

nature is inherently good, bad, or indifferent. 告子, Gaozi, had argued that human nature is indifferent, but 孟子, Mencius, held that it is good, while his view was later contradicted, in turn, by 荀子, Xunzi, who thought that human nature is bad. Mencius in the late –4th century quotes Gaozi (and is our main evidence for him) and Xunzi in the next century is explicit in citing and disagreeing with Mencius.[16]

This is not just a feature of ethical disagreements. In cosmology, one view, 蓋天, *Gai Tian* (literally canopy heaven), held that the heavens are a circular canopy set over a central, square, earth, but another, 渾天, *Hun Tian* (enveloping heaven), held that the heavens are a sphere. These views are related to observational procedures and instruments, and they were sometimes combined. However, they did not always just live in amicable harmony, since, as Christopher Cullen has shown,[17] there were distinct attempts to settle the issue between them. As for calendar studies and the establishment of cycles of eclipses, overt disputes over the competing claims of one system over another punctuate the close on two thousand year history of the official Astronomical Service from Han times down to the last imperial dynastry, the Qing.[18]

In mathematics, too, Chinese mathematicians frequently criticise the work of their predecessors. 劉徽, Liu Hui, in the +3rd century, points out the inaccuracies in the 九章算術 (*Jiuzhang suanshu*: 'Nine Chapters of the Mathematical Art'), the text from the +1st century on which he is commenting, and then two centuries later, 祖晅, Zu Geng, in turn congratulates himself on being able to solve problems that had defeated everyone else, Liu Hui included (see Wagner 1978a and 1978b).

In medicine, finally, we have some detailed evidence of disagreements not just on points of theory, but also at the level of clinical practice. The 倉公傳 (*Canggongzhuan*) containing the biography of 筸于意, Chunyu Yi, as presented in Sima Qian's *Shiji* 105, in particular, contains the records of twenty-five case-histories. On no fewer than nine occasions, Chunyu Yi distinguishes his own prognoses and treatments from those of other practitioners, sometimes just certain unnamed doctors, but twice

---

16. Mencius 6A/6, and the chapter in *Xunzi* entitled 性惡 (*Xing E*) 'Our Nature is Bad' (23) discussed by Graham 1989, pp. 117 and 244ff.
17. See Cullen forthcoming, and cf. further below, pp. 162f and p. 170.
18. See especially Sivin 1969, and cf. further below, pp. 167f.

other doctors whom he names. In one case (20, in Bridgman's numeration), his own account is greeted with derision by a doctor called Xin, though Chunyu Yi's predictions turn out to be correct.

Another case (22) is even more revealing. There Chunyu Yi treats a patient who is himself a doctor, called Sui, who had already begun treating himself. Called in by Sui to examine him, Chunyu Yi comments that the treatment begun is quite inappropriate: but then Sui justifies it by citing the authority of a semilegendary figure from the past, 扁鵲, Bian Que. That in turn elicits from Chunyu Yi the response: 'How far your account is [from the truth].' Although Bian Que spoke as he did, there is a whole range of diagnostic questions that have to be evaluated before trying to apply his ideas. There are certainly rules for examination, but when the practitioners who apply them are ignorant, they are no use at all. Here a dispute about a particular case leads Chunyu Yi to draw a more general methodological moral: knowledge of the learned texts is evidently far from enough on its own to make someone a successful practitioner.[19]

So much by way of just some of the qualifications to the picture of the purportedly irenic and authority-oriented Chinese that I sketched at the outset. But the account I originally gave on the Greek side, too, could be criticised for downplaying important factors, not just the increasing role of appeals to authority in the Hellenistic period, but also the syncretist tendencies that are prominent at least in certain writers and traditions.

Thus in medicine, it is well known that, when it suits him, Galen represents Hippocrates, Plato, Aristotle and even sometimes the Stoics, as being broadly in agreement with one another, especially when the point on which they are taken to agree is one that Galen himself endorses. Such a move also enables him, on such occasions, to claim priority for Hippocrates and at the same time to rebut any charge that he, Galen, suffers from the *philotimia* – ambition – that afflicts his rivals, in their zeal to introduce new theories.[20]

19. Sima Qian, *Shiji* 105: 2810–11. On the relations between book learning and practical experience in Chunyu Yi's account of his own training, see Sivin 1995. The *Canggongzhuan* has been analysed by Bridgman 1955 and is the subject of a forthcoming study by Elisabeth Hsü.
20. I have discussed Galen's opportunism in citing previous authorities in favour of his own theories in Lloyd 1988, and his eagerness to rebut the charge of *philotimia* in Lloyd 1991a, ch. 17, p. 400 and n. 8.

But in Greek philosophy, the most notable example of attempts
to reconcile past authorities is the bid, in many neo-Platonic commentators, to have Plato and Aristotle agree. They do this sometimes, it is true, by way of an argument that distinguishes levels
of comprehension, for which certain Platonic precedents could
be cited. In that view, the Aristotelian theory can be said to be
correct, but at a lower level of understanding than Plato's highest
insights.[21] But however justified, the synthesis produces some, to
us quite strange, amalgams of Aristotelian physics and Platonic
metaphysics.

III

But if we find, as we do, that many of the generalisations initially
suggested about Greek and Chinese attitudes stand in need of
substantial qualification, that is bound to make more complex
our next task of trying to understand the underlying factors at
work. What kind of explanatory schemata should we be looking
for here in the first place?

Evidently, first, no account in the purely psychologising mode
will do – as if it were a matter of the Greeks as a whole, or groups
of them, or even particular individuals, just being more disputatious than the Chinese, all of them or some of them. That would,
in any event, merely redescribe – or rather misdescribe – the
explananda, and all that does is to push the problem one stage
further back. For *why* the Greeks, or some of them, should have
been (if they were) so particularly disputatious, why the Chinese,
or some of them, not, still remains totally unclear.

I am not, to be sure, claiming that anything like a full-scale
causal explanation is going to be possible with regard to the subjects we are dealing with – not even with the most thorough
exploration of the whole gamut of social, political, technological and economic factors influencing those two ancient societies through their complex and varied histories – factors which,
as noted (p. 17), themselves pose further problems for understanding. What I offer here is limited to two possible lines of

21. See further p. 54 at n. 7 on Proclus' use of the distinction between mathematics and
    dialectic, for example *In Euc.* 3.1ff, 4.18ff. Similarly he draws a further sharp contrast,
    in the Proem to *Hyp.* 2.1ff, 4.13ff, between Platonic philosophy and conventional
    astronomy, but engages in an extensive examination of the latter.

argument that relate to the institutions of science and philosophy. These are first, the role of more or less well-defined groups – 'schools' or sects – of scientists and philosophers, and secondly, the question of different types of targeted audiences for scientific or philosophical work.

As I noted at the beginning, it is customary to speak of 'schools' in both China and Greece, but in both cases we have to proceed with the utmost caution. First, China. It is obvious that the reference to one hundred *Jia* in the passage from *Zhuangzi* that I cited (p. 25) is mere hand-waving.[22] Even the six groups mentioned in Sima Tan's account, in Sima Qian, are a very mixed bunch. The idea that there is a *Jia* of 'Daoists' is, as Sivin (1978) has shown, quite chimerical, not least because just about every philosopher, and not just philosophers, claimed to follow the Dao. In some writers (though not, to be sure, in *Shiji* 130 itself), the term 'Daoist' tends to become a residual category, applied to those who appear to show no other affiliation. Again, the word for 'Confucian' (儒, *ru*) sometimes seems to imply no more than membership of the learned elite, and as for 'neo-Confucian', that modern term has been applied to quite different periods and to revivals of very diverse types (Nylan and Sivin 1987).

Obviously those who were charged with the responsibility for cataloguing the works of earlier writers found it convenient (they still do) to have labels to attach to them. Some such factor is at work already in the Han dynasty bibliographical compilations, such as that in ch. 30 of the 漢書 (*Hanshu*) compiled by Ban Gu (+32 to +92) (see, for example, Graham 1989, pp. 379ff). But there is sometimes little real justification for the labels thus applied.

But in the cases where we can talk of more coherent groups, we must ask two fundamental questions. First, did you have to belong to a *Jia*? Secondly, what did it mean to do so?

Evidently some individualists, both in the Warring States period (c. –480 to –221) and later, fit very uneasily into any of the main conventional categories, even when we can accept these as meaningful for more than merely bibliographical purposes. I mentioned Wang Chong in the +1st century, and even Zhuangzi

22. There are similar references to '100 *Jia*' in Sima Qian, *Shiji* 130: 3291, 2 and 3320, 1, for example.

himself (who lived much earlier, in the −4th century) might be considered a further example, although he and the writings named after him are usually labelled 'Daoist'. But the contrast is with the Mohists, where the *Tian Xia* chapter informs us that the same canon of texts was adopted by various later-generation Mohists even when they are there represented as diverging in their interpretations (above, p. 27).

Outside philosophy, the circumstances are rather different. In medicine, the important groupings are less prominently labelled. Research on the various recensions of the 黃帝內經 (*Huangdi neijing*: 'Inner canon of the Yellow Emperor') and their relations to even earlier medicine, as documented, for instance, also in the 馬王堆, Mawangdui, medical texts of the −2nd century, is now beginning to bring to light something of the work of synthesis, and the appropriation of earlier ideas and practices, in the versions of the *Huangdi neijing* that have come down to us (see especially Yamada Keiji 1979, Keegan 1988).

Again, in astronomy, from some points of view the most important dividing line comes not between one *Jia* and another, but between those who were, and those who were not, holders of official posts, for example eventually in the imperial Astronomical Bureau. The running was made very much by those who were. When an outsider suggested an innovation, a revision of an eclipse cycle, for instance, then if it won acceptance, he often found himself converted into an insider with a post within the Bureau.[23]

But what did it mean to belong to a *Jia*? The essential points come out of a recent study by Sivin 1995a. The chief role of the *Jia* was, undoubtedly, to preserve and transmit the teachings of a master, generally in the form of a canon, 經, *Jing* (literally 'warp'). For that reason, Sivin's preferred rendering of *Jia*, in some contexts though certainly not in all, is 'lineage', taking lineage to refer to 'a relationship between masters and disciples over several generations that is ritually centred on the transmission of a charismatic written text. It is no coincidence that the word *Jia* designates this relationship, since it was used from the

---

23. A number of instances, including that of the great eleventh-century astronomer and polymath, 沈括, Shen Gua, are discussed in Sivin 1969, and Huang Yi-Long 1991 discusses the continuation of this tactic right down to the debates with the Jesuits in the seventeenth century.

Zhou on for many fictive kinship relations, i.e. those patterned on the ties between fathers and sons that involve passing on some patrimony (業, *ye*). It *implies* that the transmission will continue, but there is no literal expectation that it must do so' (Sivin, personal communication).

Each successive generation of scholars had first to memorise the *Jing*. Being able to recite it came before being able to understand it, for explanation of the meaning of the text would only come after the student had shown a mastery of the words of the text itself. In some cases, moreover, access to learning the text is obtained only after a process of initiation. We have an instance of this in the 靈樞 (*Lingshu*) recension of the *Huangdi neijing*. There the Thunder Duke purifies himself for three days, and seals his oath by cutting this arm and smearing blood, before having the text of the book put into his hands by the Yellow Emperor.[24]

Now certain features of the relations both between and within the different *Jia* have already been noted. As we saw in stage 2, there are plenty of cases of Chinese philosophers disagreeing with others and criticising them, including others with a broad allegiance to the same authority figures. We mentioned the divergent views on human nature expressed by Gaozi, Mencius and Xunzi. The last two are separated by sixty years or so, but both represent themselves as in some sense followers of Confucius.[25] Factionalism is a charge brought against both 'Confucians' and Mohists: as we saw (pp. 26f), Han Fei could develop that point to claim that it was not at all clear what the founding figures were supposed to stand for.

At the same time it should be emphasised that as a general rule allegiance to your own immediate teachers in your *Jia* is unquestioned. This was part of your duty as the transmitter of the *Jing*. Your *Jia* was in a real sense your family, and as such owed filial respect: so you would no more think of turning against your teacher and criticising him than doing so against your own father.

The case of the doctor Chunyu Yi, who tells us a good deal

24. Sivin 1995a at n. 25, on *Lingshu* 48.1, 396ff. Cf. also Keegan 1988, pp. 233–8.
25. That does not inhibit Xunzi when it comes to criticising many *ru* as worthless. See Graham 1989, p. 236, who further points out that Xunzi's position is in part a reaction to the challenge of those who were later categorised as 'Legalists'.

about his early training and apprenticeship, illustrates that it was perfectly possible, in medicine, to have a succession of teachers, for he mentions that he learnt first from Gongsun Guang and then from Gongsheng Yangqing (*Shiji* 105: 2794–6, 2815–16). Yet we must also remark, first, that Chunyu Yi passes on to his second teacher on the recommendation, and with the approval, of his first, and secondly, that there is no question of Chunyu Yi criticising either.

In these circumstances, the role of debates in and between different groups in China is rather different from the expectations generated by the title of Graham's book, *Disputers of the Tao* (Graham 1989, cf. also Kroll 1985–7). Dispute, 辯, *bian*, is in any case often a highly pejorative term, at least in certain contexts when used intransitively, where its meaning is not 'discriminate between' (as its homophone, 辨, *bian*), but 'to be argumentative' or 'disputatious'.[26] That use is found not just in Warring States writers, such as Mencius, but also in Han dynasty ones, such as the later 'syncretist' strata of *Zhuangzi*.[27] Discussion, 論, *lun*, is acceptable, though that may be more a matter of explaining a point of view than of arguing. Certainly 'eristic' and other terms are available in Greek to express disapproval of contentious argument: but in one respect, at least, Greek dialectic leaves more room for acceptable face-to-face argument with partners and opponents than is usually the case in China. This was in that the Greeks eventually came to formalise rules of procedure – for example concerning the roles of questioner and answerer – that allowed dialectic, as a joint endeavour, to be clearly distinguished, in principle at least, from eristic.[28] A thesis under examination could then formally be dissociated from its proposer – and its attacker – allowing a certain distancing of the ideas under discussion from those doing the discussing.

This is not to deny that argument has an important role in China too, not least as a means of maintaining and defending

---

26. I am grateful to Professor David McMullen for clarification on this point.
27. See, for example, Mencius 3B/9, *Zhuangzi* 33: 30, 74, 79, 86. Graham 1989, pp. 167ff, has, however, argued for a positive role for *bian* (辯) as argumentation, among the Mohists, but this in a sense related to the cognate *bian* (辨), discriminate, applied to distinguishing right from wrong. In the Mohist Canon (A 74) 'argumentation' is defined as 'disputing over the converse. To win in argumentation is to fit the fact'.
28. Aristotle, *Topics* book VIII, systematises these rules of procedure: see, for example, Moraux 1968.

the position of the *Jia*, even sometimes a position within one. But it is certainly not *fundamental* to the activity of the *Jia*, whose primary role, as I noted, was the preservation and transmission of a body of learning. That role places the principal emphasis on the authority of the text. The suggestion would be that it is the *Jia* structure that leads as a general rule to an emphasis on the irenic and on authority – not that there are not many exceptions to that rule.

Now many more of the features of Chinese *Jia* apply also to Greek philosophical and medical groups than a stage-one analysis might anticipate. Actually that is true about warnings to the effect that many so-called sects, *haireseis*, are the construct of scholars, ancient or modern. There is no need to elaborate on that here, except just to recall how *imaginary* such institutions as the medical 'schools' of Cos and Cnidos, or even the Hellenistic sect of 'dogmatists', are.[29] Again, in Greece as in China, many individuals fall outside any group, particularly in the –5th and –4th centuries.[30]

At the same time, some features of the operation of most Greek schools or sects diverge sharply from what we know of China. First, it is clear that Greek pupils could and did pick and choose between teachers and between institutions. They could and did attend the lectures of more than one teacher before deciding which group to join, or they could join different groups in succession, or they could go it alone and set up one of their own. Secondly, direct criticism of teachers is possible, and even quite common: this will lead us into the question of orthodoxy. Thirdly – the crucial question for this study – argument and debate take on two important roles; first they are one of the means of attracting and holding pupils, and secondly they serve to mark the internal and external boundaries of groups.

All three points should now be elaborated, even if very rapidly. It is true that our evidence for the first is partly anecdotal, from such sources as Diogenes Laertius' *Lives of the Philosophers*. But it is overwhelming. Theophrastus is said to have been taught first

29. On Coans and Cnidians, see Smith 1973, Lonie 1978: on the Hellenistic medical 'sects', see von Staden 1982, 1989, pp. 22ff, 58f, Frede 1987, chh. 12–15, Lloyd 1987a, pp. 158ff.
30. See Lloyd 1987a, ch. 2, pp. 56ff, on the individualistic and egotistical tendencies exhibited in Presocratic philosophy and Hippocratic medicine.

by one Alcippus from his home town of Eresus, then to have 'heard' Plato, but afterwards to have followed Aristotle, whom of course he succeeded as head of the Lyceum. Euclid of Megara (not the mathematician) is said to have associated with both Socrates and Plato, but then to have formed the group known as the Megarians (or Eristics or Dialecticians). The founder of the Stoa, Zeno of Citium, was taught first by Crates the Cynic, and then heard Stilpo the Megarian, as well as Polemo, who was head of Plato's Academy from around −314, before setting up his own school. The third head of the Stoa, Chrysippus, was taught by the then head of the Academy (Arcesilaus), but then went on to criticise him. He was also taught by the second head of the Stoa, Cleanthes, not that he agreed with all of his views either.[31] Those are examples from −4th- and −3rd-century philosophy, but they can be multiplied many times over, from other periods,[32] and from medicine.[33]

With so much movement between schools and criticism both between and within them, one is forced to ask what held any of these groups together at all. Some of the schools, at least, had an institutional basis, buildings, a library, an official or quasi-official head. They were perceived by outsiders as holding certain views in common and as having some kind of allegiance to whoever it was who was recognised as Founder.[34] These points, too, however, need qualifying.

Thus membership of a school may often have involved contributing to its upkeep, and pupils (however defined, and in whatever discipline) usually paid for instruction. However, the

31. For Theophrastus, see D.L. v 36, for Euclid of Megara, D.L. ii 106ff, for Zeno of Citium, D.L. vii 2 (where Timocrates is reported to have said that Zeno was also taught by Xenocrates for ten years: since Zeno was only about twenty when Xenocrates died, this may be thought unlikely), and for Chrysippus, D.L. vii 179, 183f.

32. Thus in the Academy, in the −1st century, there was a bitter dispute between Philo and one of his ex-pupils, Antiochus, in which Philo stood for the view of Plato that had been dominant since Arcesilaus, but Antiochus sought to revive the 'Old Academy'. The reaction of another who had been taught in the Academy, namely Aenesidemus, was to move away to inaugurate his own brand of neo-Pyrrhonian scepticism. The chief primary sources are Cicero's *Academica* i 13 and 43ff, Photius, *Library* 169b18ff, discussed by Long and Sedley 1987, i pp. 438ff, 468ff.

33. Thus the founder of the so-called Empiricist sect of medicine in the −mid-3rd century was Philinus, who had started out as a Herophilean: on the various affiliations of other Herophileans, see von Staden 1989, pp. 445ff. Galen's criticisms of some of his own teachers have already been noted, above at n. 8.

34. On the subject of philosophical allegiance, see especially Sedley 1989.

distinction between a regular pupil paying for regular instruction, in philosophy or medicine, say, and just anyone paying to hear a particular public lecture or debate, may have been no hard and fast one. Those associated with a particular school, whether as pupils or not, evidently felt *no life-long commitment* to it. Anyone could leave whenever they liked, and many did, whether to join another group, or to set one up for themselves.

It is true that when the question of the succession to the headship arose, more was at stake. It seems that heads were mostly elected by current members, though who exactly qualified to vote is unclear. But it is not as if the sole criterion for the new head was perceived doctrinal purity. Plato was succeeded first by Speusippus, then by Xenocrates, neither of whom agreed wholeheartedly with Plato's own philosophical positions.[35] When Chrysippus succeeded Cleanthes as head of the Stoa, we hear of a rivalry, and a debate, between Chrysippus (who had not been taught by Zeno himself) and Ariston (who had), as to who should represent Stoic doctrine in its disputes with its main rivals – a debate that Chrysippus won. Ariston, and two others, Herillus and Dionysius, are said by Diogenes Laertius to have 'differed' from the other Stoics, and it is easy to slip into thinking of them as heterodox. But we have to be careful, for that term may suggest that there was more of a fixed orthodoxy for them to diverge from than we are really entitled to suppose existed. Ariston's teaching may have 'differed' from Zeno's at more important points than did Chrysippus'. But Chrysippus too was recognised to have 'differed' from Zeno (Diogenes uses exactly the same word) as also from Cleanthes, whom he is said to have left while Cleanthes was still alive.[36]

While some allegiance to the Founder's view was expected, the question of what those views *were* was generally far more open, disputed and negotiable than was the case in China, even though

35. One extra factor that no doubt influenced the headship passing first to Speusippus was that he was Plato's nephew. Xenocrates, however, was no relation of either Plato or Speusippus, nor was it the general rule that the headship of philosophical or medical sects stayed within a family.
36. With D.L. VII 179 on Chrysippus (*diēnechthē*), compare D.L. VII 167 on Ariston, Herillus and Dionysius (*diēnechthentes*). Dionysius, however, was also called *ho metathemenos* ('the renegade'), and Ariston is described as a *hairetistēs* with his own followers. Long and Sedley 1987, I p. 359, go so far as to speak of Ariston's 'heresy', though that English term now has stronger connotations than those of the original Greek *hairesis*.

negotiation, as we have seen, happened there too. True, there is one principal Greek exception to what I have been treating as the general rule there, namely the Epicureans, who were much more conservative than most of their rivals, both in the sense that there was less doctrinal development from the teaching of Epicurus himself, and in the sense that there were fewer, indeed virtually no, defectors. However, with the other philosophical groups, and in particular with both the Academy and the Stoa, the point stands.[37] What the Founder himself stood for, could be, and quite often was, renegotiated from one generation to the next.

Argument and debate were thus essential to the activity of the Greek schools in their competitions with one another both for pupils and for prestige. I have illustrated the point from Greek philosophy, but it applies also to the learned medical groups of the Hellenistic period. While the actual extent of doctrinal uniformity between different contemporary members of a sect (let alone between different generations of those who passed as the *same* sect) varied, all sects acted as more or less stable, more or less well-organised and close-knit *alliances for defensive and offensive* argumentative purposes.

The Greek schools were there not just, and not even primarily, to hand on a body of learned texts, but to attract pupils and to win arguments with their rivals. They may even be said to have *r. led* their rivals, the better to define their own positions by contrast with theirs.[38] In those battles with the competition, you relied on your co-members for help, without necessarily being able to rely on them completely – for the possibility of their defection was always there.

Insofar as they were thus locked in dialectical disputes with

37. On the Academy, cf. above n. 32. As for the Stoa, it is customary to distinguish the so-called Middle Stoics, Panaetius and Posidonius, and Later Stoics, such as Seneca, from the three original heads, Zeno, Cleanthes, Chrysippus and their contemporaries. A note of caution is, however, in order, since for the Middle Stoics, especially, we generally rely on secondary sources, who can certainly not be counted on to be accurate on questions to do with agreements and disagreements between later and earlier members of the school.
38. This is particularly true of the Sceptics, who, as noted (p. 15), advocated suspension of judgement by way of the argument from *isostheneia* – the notion that for every 'dogmatic' view about underlying reality there is an opposing view of equal strength: cf. further below, p. 158.

one another, Greek philosophical and medical schools used, as
the chief means for the expression of their own ideas and theories, both lectures (public and private) and open, often public,
debates, sometimes modelled directly on the adversarial exchanges
so familiar in Greek law-courts and political assemblies.[39] The audiences they were aiming to persuade were first, a general public,
and then more particularly their own immediate rivals and colleagues and potential adherents or pupils. We may now turn to
our final topic, to consider what is suggested by the *prima facie*
contrast presented by the fact that in China, the preferred audience for much philosophical and scientific work was very different: the ruler or emperor himself no less.

The memorial to the throne is a standard vehicle not just of
Chinese philosophy but also of astronomy and even, to a lesser
extent, of medicine. Even when not actually presented to the
throne, texts were often written, according to a well-established
convention, in the form of such a presentation. Indeed this became increasingly the case for a time after the first great unification of China by the Qin around −221. Sivin (1995a and 1995c)
has recently argued that what eventually happened in the next
dynasty, the Han (from −202) − though it certainly did not happen
immediately − was the consolidation of certain key philosophical
concepts, those of *yin yang* and the five phases, in something approaching an orthodoxy that served two distinct but complementary purposes.[40] First it helped to legitimate the new Han rulers:
the claim was that the emperor was the sole mediator between
heaven and earth and as such the guarantee of the welfare of
the entire empire. Secondly, it helped to secure the roles of the
intellectuals who were themselves responsible for that elaboration
and consolidation. They thereby in part restored their own position, after the traumatic disruptions and destructions associated
with the wars leading up to the Qin unification and with the anti-
intellectual moves made by the first Qin emperor himself.

In this context, the appointment of official astronomers and
eventually the foundation of the imperial Astronomical Bureau
were no pieces of disinterested support for scientific research.

39. We shall be returning to this in Chapter 4.
40. Cf. further below, pp. 122ff.

The welfare of the empire itself depended on harmonious relations between heaven and earth for which the emperor himself was primarily responsible. In these circumstances he had a *personal* interest in calendar regulation, in eclipse prediction, in the interpretation of omens and so on.[41] New astronomical ideas and systems regularly take the form of memorials to the emperor, whether composed by officials on the imperial staff or by outsiders.

The position of doctors was in some respects rather different from that of astronomers, and not just because many of those who practised one or other type of healing were of low social status. At the other end of the spectrum we certainly hear of physicians who held official or semi-official positions at court, as the attendant doctors of kings or nobles (see Hucker 1985, pp. 478f on 太醫, *tai yi*, and 太醫令, *tai yi ling*). But there was no real equivalent to an Astronomical Bureau, empowered and obliged to advise the ruler on a regular basis on matters of cardinal importance to the state.

However, the *Canggongzhuan* in *Shiji* 105 illustrates how doctors too had occasionally to justify themselves to rulers or to those who represented them.[42] True, this is an exceptional case, since Chunyu Yi had been the subject of a denunciation and had only been pardoned thanks to the intervention of a daughter. But in answer to an imperial edict he later submits a detailed report in which he sets out explicitly to justify his own prognostic skills. In the series of exchanges at the end of the case-histories he undergoes a veritable cross-examination, answering a wide range of specific questions concerning his training, his pupils and his medical practice.

In contrast to the Greek experience, where public doctors were sometimes appointed by the Assembly and where doctors' standing in general was principally a matter of their reputation among their peers, what is striking about the Chinese evidence is that it shows that evaluating credentials could there be the responsibility not of other physicians, but of the emperor or of the bureaucracy acting on his behalf. We have other indications as well of imperial interest in medicine, in the role of the Yellow Emperor

41. See Sivin 1969 and cf. further below, pp. 167ff.
42. The importance of this material for our understanding of the situation of Chinese doctors, their training and practice, has recently been emphasised by Sivin 1995a at pp. 177ff.

in the *Huangdi neijing*. Although he is not always an interlocutor, several sections present dialogues between him and various respondents, Qi Bo, Shao Shi and the rest, where they generally make the running: in those cases, the Yellow Emperor often just asks pertinent questions, nicely illustrating how he needs his advisers.

However, even before the unification of China, the roll call of Chinese philosophers who sought to act, and indeed acted, as advisers to rulers, is impressive. It begins with Confucius, and proceeds with Mencius, the Mohists, Hui Shi, Gongsun Long and many more. The *Lüshi Chunqiu* is one of many classical texts that consist of advice to the prince. When the *Hanfeizi* considers the topic of persuasion, in the 説難 (*Shuo Nan* 'difficulties of persuasion') *pian*, 'chapter', (12), often cited as a prime example of a Chinese interest in what the Greeks called rhetoric, the chief focus of analysis is persuasion of the *ruler*. Han Fei and his followers did not have to concern themselves with persuading the *demos* in assembly, and naturally enough a number of the factors relevant to Greek-style rhetoric are simply not on his agenda (cf. further Chapter 4). The convention of addressing the ruler did not, of course, rule out criticising rival views, as we find happening often enough. But there is this difference, that that is criticism directed *to* a third party, whose views *had* to be deferred to, and that imposed certain restraints, not least because you did not know the extent to which the opposition had got to him before you.

Of course there are many exceptions from all periods. Chinese mathematics, for instance, does not take the form of memorials to the throne. In that very chapter of *Hanfeizi*, just quoted, although the topic discussed is persuasion *of* the ruler, the text is addressed primarily to those who had to do the persuading, ministers, not the ruler himself. But that said, there remains a marked penchant, in much extant Chinese philosophical and scientific writing, to take the ruler or emperor as the prime addressee. If you could attract his attention, that did wonders for your career. There were even distinct possibilities that the emperor, if persuaded, would implement the ideas you proposed, as with the case of the Astronomical Bureau.

But were not the Greeks also interested in persuading rulers? Has my earlier focussing on the debates in the schools not distorted the issue and exaggerated the contrast? Concessions must be made, for sure. First it is clear that some Greek philosophers were directly interested, and active, in politics. Some of the Pythagoreans evidently were, in the Presocratic period already, in Magna Graecia, a trend that continued down to Plato's contemporary, Archytas, the foremost statesman of Tarentum. Plato's own ill-fated visits to the court of Dionysius II of Syracuse were to try to persuade him to implement some of his ideas, and the Academy was, in part, a training-ground for statesmen. The list of Greek and Roman philosophers with political ambitions and experience contains some impressive names, not just Seneca, confidant of Nero, but the emperor Marcus Aurelius himself.

Greek works addressed to powerful statesmen are common enough, at least from the −4th century onwards, and they are not limited to those offering advice about political matters. Isocrates produces several examples of that last kind, addressed to Nicocles, Evagoras, Philip. But the Aristotelian Corpus contains a spurious *Rhetoric to Alexander* of more general scope. Among later technical treatises dedicated to rulers, there are Vitruvius' *On Architecture*, addressed to Augustus, and Oribasius' medical encyclopaedia, to the emperor Julian in the +4th century.[43]

The motives in some of these Greek and Roman cases are very similar to those that obtained in China. Vitruvius evidently sought the most prestigious patron possible − for his book and for his buildings. Yet first, access to powerful, let alone imperial, patronage was a comparative rarity: I take the Ptolemies' Museum to be the main exception, and even there the extent of the support it offered to scientists has often been exaggerated.[44] Secondly, there are fundamental differences in Greek and Chinese attitudes towards rulers, at least so far as our extant sources go. I shall have more to say on this topic in subsequent studies, but for now it is enough to note the chief point: where the Chinese were never in

43. This list could, of course, be much extended. At the same time Greek dedications to those who wielded little or no political power are also common. This would seem to be the case with the person to whom Ptolemy dedicates both the *Syntaxis* and the *Tetrabiblos*, the otherwise unknown Syrus.

44. The recipients of the Ptolemies' patronage included poets and literary critics among many others, as much as, perhaps even more than, those engaged in one or other branch of the inquiry concerning nature: see Fraser 1972. Their motivations were less a matter of seeking to foster science, than of boosting their own prestige, less a matter of sponsoring brilliant scientists, than one of sponsoring brilliance of any type.

any doubt that the wise and benevolent rule of a monarch is the ideal, the Greeks disagreed about the best political constitution as wholeheartedly as they did about every other topic in philosophy and science. Even when there was clearly no alternative to imperial rule – and Roman emperors at that – some of the philosophers contrived to maintain some sort of preference, in theory, for republican virtues: that even includes Seneca.[45]

So we often find Greek philosophers adopting a stance of fierce independence *vis-à-vis* rulers whom they might otherwise have been expected to have been keen to please. For every story of a philosopher toadying to a tyrant for a free meal, there is another that has the philosopher cocking a snook at the great. Aristippus at the court of Dionysius II illustrates the former (Diogenes Laertius II 66, 67, 70, 78), but Diogenes the Cynic, asked by Alexander to name a request, says 'stand out of my light' (Diogenes Laertius VI 38).

Yet with this independence came also a disadvantage. Compared with their Chinese counterparts, Greek philosophers and scientists had appreciably less chance of having their ideas put into practice. This was certainly the case in astronomy, where the increasingly accurate values obtained for the solar year and the lunar month in Athens by Meton and Euctemon around −430, and Callippus and others in the next century, *might* have led to a comprehensive reform of the chaotic luni-solar calendars used by different Greek states, but in practice had only limited and sporadic effect even in Athens itself (cf. further Chapter 8). The problem with the democracies, as their critics kept pointing out, was that they were fickle in their loyalties, inconstant in their decisions. Autocrats, too, could be just as arbitrary, for sure, but when – as in this instance in China – their own interests were at stake, they could and did move swiftly from theoretical approval to practical implementation. The chief case where Greek autocrats were similarly involved is such an exception that it tends to prove (that is, support) the general rule: I am thinking of the Ptolemies' reported concern to apply the ideas of Alexandrian engineers to improve military technology (Philo, *Belopoeica* 50.20ff, cf. Marsden 1971, pp. 106ff).

45. See, for example, Griffin 1976, p. 202, Schofield 1991, ch. 4. Similarly Dio Chrysostom combines advice to the emperor Trajan with a continued adherence to at least certain of his Cynical philosophical ideals: see Desideri 1978, 1991b.

The tendencies to internecine rivalry we find in much Greek philosophy and science may now be seen in a different light. In part, they may be seen as a reflection of the comparative lack of the kind of outlets that their Chinese counterparts enjoyed with patronage before the Han and often with stable official status afterwards. The superiority of theory to practice is a theme repeatedly taken up by scientists as well as philosophers in Greece: but that was sometimes to make a virtue out of necessity, since their work often had little chance of practical implementation. That point is valid, within limits, even for political philosophy,[46] and it is increasingly true in other domains, such as mathematics and astronomy.[47]

Let me now attempt to summarise the arguments I have presented. I began with a simplistic contrast between adversarial Greeks and irenic, authority-bound, Chinese, and then in a second stage pointed out some of the shortcomings of that opposition. Argumentativeness, and respect for authority, can both be found in both ancient societies, though not equally in both, nor uniformly across different disciplines and different periods. In a third part I have tried to identify some of the underlying factors at work in the social institutions within which philosophers and scientists operated.

First, schools, recruitment, and teacher–pupil relations. Talk of schools in Chinese and Greek philosophy and science conceals, or at least does not reveal, important differences. The prime duty of members of a Chinese *Jia* was the preservation and transmission

46. In the classical period, the possibility of implementing political proposals on the occasion of the founding of new colonies may have influenced such writings as Plato's *Laws* (if not also his *Republic*). The actual founding of Thurii in −443 is an enterprise in which Protagoras is reported to have been involved. However, to counterbalance this, we should bear in mind that the debate, reported in the first book of Aristotle's *Politics*, 1253b14ff, on whether slavery is 'natural' or 'conventional', is one that remained at the purely theoretical level, and had no impact nor outcome in terms of the policies recommended or adopted with regard to slaves in Greek antiquity.

47. Outside those fields, too, the insistence on the importance of 'philosophy' sometimes reflects a bid to upgrade a particular calling, by representing it both as disinterested (that is, not driven by the profit motive) and as based on a sound theoretical understanding. Both the doctor Galen and the architect–engineer Vitruvius represent the best exponents of their two callings as the philosophically inclined ones. Thus even with domains that certainly do have important practical applications, the orientation towards the theoretical in some Greek and Roman writers is pronounced.

of a received body of texts. In that context, pupils did not criticise teachers, and any given *Jia* did not see it as a primary task
to take on and defeat other *Jia* in argument. Criticism of others,
and innovation, both occur, to be sure, but in a very different
framework from that in which many Greek *sophoi* worked, where
their *haireseis* often fed off one another, where debate was one of
the chief ways in which individuals, and groups, made a name for
themselves (even among doctors), where dissent from what other
members of your own group believed, even those who had taught
you, was not ruled out and indeed quite common.

My second line of argument considers the differences that
may stem from the audiences addressed and from the relations
between those who produced the ideas and theories and those
who were in a position to put them into effect. Whom were the
writers concerned trying to persuade and what did they hope
to achieve by their persuasion – questions on which significant
diachronic differences come into play? Even before the Qin unification, rulers had been the target of much Chinese persuasion,
and, after that unification, the ambitions of emperors and some
of their intellectual advisers eventually meshed. Crucially there
was no apparent disagreement as to the political ideal, and a
clear sense that rulers could and did implement ideas put to
them by intellectuals, for instance in the context of the workings
of the Astronomical Bureau.

On the Greek side, not only were political ideals disputed, but
the prime target of persuasion was less often the ruler. It could
be the general public, or your own colleagues, rivals or potential
adherents. Though many Greek intellectuals admired Rome, the
unification of much of the Mediterranean world under Roman
dominion did not have the effect of getting Greek intellectuals to
rally behind Rome: they never rallied, exactly, behind anything.
This was not because they were particularly bloody-minded, but
rather because competitiveness was built into the institutional
set-up within which they operated. The suggestion would be that
Greek adversariality owes much to the internal dynamics of the
relations within and between their philosophical and scientific
sects.

Adversariality, and appeals to authority, can be and often were, in
both China and Greece, matters of etiquette and form. Etiquette,
as is well known, can *mask* agreements as well as disagreements,

just as well as it can be manipulated to *express* them, or more interestingly still be deployed to leave them – the agreements and disagreements – ambiguous. Reading ancient texts, we encounter the full range of such possibilities, and one of the chief challenges to interpretation is to study their varying exploitation. At the same time, beyond matters of politeness, there are institutional factors at work, in both societies, that underpin the conventions and establish or confirm them as the conventions they are. How certain institutional factors may help to throw light on the attitudes of adversariality and of respect for authority evinced in Greek and Chinese philosophy and science has been the topic of this first chapter. How far other aspects of the science produced in Greece and China may be related to other features of the social and political circumstances of their production will be explored in our subsequent investigations.

CHAPTER 3

Methodology, epistemology and their uses

Students of Greek philosophy and science are very familiar with the recurrent discussions, in the texts they study, of methodological and epistemological issues. In classical Chinese philosophy and science apparently analogous references to methods, rules and procedures are also common and the question of the origins of knowledge is sometimes discussed. Moreover the goal of philosophising is standardly represented as the *Dao*, the Way However, quite what roles such methodological and epistemological statements play, in the inquiries in question, is an issue that has never seriously been addressed in a comparativist perspective.

Do methodological and epistemological observations play similar or different roles in China and in Greece? What difference, if any, did it make when such questions were raised by ancient writers in one or other area of inquiry? Can we say why they did so, when they did, and even why they did not, when they did not? If you have what you believe to be the right method, then you need to *practise* it. But why, one might ask naively, would you need to state it? On what occasions and for what purposes would you do so? A similar point may be made about theories of knowledge, where from some points of view it might be remarked, naively, that what is important is *having* knowledge, not having a *theory about* it.

What follows is, of course, only a very small contribution to the study of a vast subject. What I have to say is limited to certain subject areas, and indeed, within those areas, just to certain texts, to be defined in a minute. My aim is to offer suggestions for an argument, and maybe at points a somewhat controversial argument, rather than anything approaching a comprehensive study. Controversial, since I shall argue that methodology and epistemology are not always quite what they seem, not always just the conscientious analysis of such issues as the roles of hypothesis, or definition, or observation and reason themselves – though they can be that, to be sure – but also, in addition or indeed instead, the basis of self-justificatory polemic. Why such polemics were needed, why they were engaged in, will take us back to some of the issues already broached in Chapter 2 and will enable us to elaborate some of the arguments there proposed.

First, it is essential to define the scope of my inquiry here. Chronologically, I have already specified that the chief target periods are the Greco-Roman world before the dominance of Christianity, China before the rise of the influence of Buddhism, but indicated that I shall need on occasion to go beyond +200. Then as to subject areas, I shall concentrate here on mathematics and medicine. The choice is, to some extent, arbitrary, but in both cases we have extensive corpora of primary texts on which to base our investigation. Within those corpora, I shall be concerned mainly, on the Greek side, with Euclid, Archimedes and the Greek mathematical commentators, and with certain Hippocratic treatises, together with the evidence for Hellenistic medicine in, for example, Celsus and Galen, and then with Galen himself.

On the Chinese side, we have first two classic mathematical treatises, the 周髀算經 (*Zhoubi suanjing*: 'Arithmetic Classic of the Zhou Gnomon' in Cullen's translation), assembled some time between the middle of the −1st century and the end of the +1st, and the 九章算術 (*Jiuzhang suanshu*: 'Nine Chapters of the Mathematical Art') compiled in the +1st century, with the commentary tradition on them, notably that of Liu Hui composed some time between +260 and +280. For Chinese medicine, our main extant early sources have already been mentioned (p. 00). Apart from the silk scrolls found at Mawangdui and elsewhere, we can draw on texts corresponding to the various recensions of the 黃帝內經 (*Huangdi neijing*: 'Inner canon of the Yellow Emperor'), namely the 靈樞, (*lingshu*: 'Divine pivot'), 素問, (*suwen*: 'Basic questions') and 太素 (*taisu*: 'Grand basis'), together with the *Canggongzhuan*, the biography of Chunyu Yi (who lived in the middle of the −2nd century) in Sima Qian's *Shiji* 105. The *terminus ante quem* for the Mawangdui scrolls is given by the date of the tomb in which they were found (−168): the Inner Canon recensions date mainly from the −1st century, and the *Shiji* itself dates, as noted, to around −90.

These works are nothing like the only extensive extant texts from Greek and Chinese mathematics and medicine that a fully comprehensive study would need to take into account. It has, too, to be borne in mind that we have indirect evidence for important traditions, in both China and Greece, that are *not* represented by substantial extant texts. Indeed some of these other practitioners, in both cases, do not belong to the circles of the literate elite. As remarked before (pp. 4f), just as the Greeks had their itinerant purifiers, their drug-sellers and root-cutters, and many types of women healers, very few of whom attempted, or were in a position, to compose treatises on their styles of medicine, so too Chinese medicine is not just a matter of what we read about in the *Inner Canon* (see Sivin 1995a, cf. Ngo 1976, Dewoskin 1983).

The arguments I have to propose here relate, then, only to parts, certainly not to the whole, of Greek and Chinese mathematics and medicine. Indeed the anti-generalisation caveats that I expressed in Chapter 1 are all the more relevant insofar as one outcome of my limited study of selected texts here will be to underline how difficult it is to see definite patterns, even in this restricted sample.

My final preliminary point concerns the distinction between implicit, and explicit, methodology and epistemology. Both terms can be used in looser or stricter senses. Epistemology can be taken to refer to whatever may be thought to imply a claim to know or whatever might allow us to investigate how such a claim, in a given context, might have been sustained. Again, any work of science or philosophy is more or less methodical and we can certainly examine the actual methods the writers use, whether or not they pronounce on them themselves. However, I shall be concerned more especially here with the stricter senses, where the terms are used of the explicit statements of the writers themselves on such matters as the correct methods to be used, or the criteria that have to be met for a claim to knowledge to be justified. We have to examine how such explicit statements, when they are made, relate to the actual methods used or the knowledge claims made. How far do such statements tally with those methods? Or are there discrepancies between methodological theory and practice? On what types of occasions, and with what aims, are such statements made, and what role do they play in the economy of the arguments presented?

Having said that as students of Greek thought we are all familiar with the recurrent methodological statements that punctuate many of the classic texts we study, I begin with a Greek writer who never once, in the substantial body of complete treatises that we have, uses the term *methodos,* namely Euclid.[1] In the *Elements* he never reflects self-consciously on the procedures he adopts, nor does he explain what the object of the exercise is. Nevertheless he proceeds with a self-confidence that certainly suggests that he knew exactly what he was doing, and there can be little doubt as to what that was. The *Elements* is the comprehensive systematisation and proof of more or less the whole of the elementary mathematics of his time.

To be sure, we can scarcely confirm that he indeed aimed at comprehensiveness. But such independent evidence as we have for contemporary mathematics (little enough, in all conscience), as well as the course of the development of Greek mathematics after Euclid, in Archimedes, Apollonius and so on, points in that direction. Evidently Euclid sought systematicity, and, most important, rigorous axiomatic-deductive proof. Book I sets out the definitions, common opinions and postulates he needs and further definitions are added in due course later. In principle, these are all the assumptions needed for the proofs he gives. In practice, for sure, there are terms that we might have expected him to define, but that he did not, especially the key term 'measure'. Conversely, some of the definitions included do not get to be used in the proofs. But such minor blemishes as these do not seriously call into question the overall strategy of the work.[2] The whole is a remarkably carefully articulated structure of

1. A search using Ibycus, the computerised index of Greek and Roman texts, reveals that the only occasion in the entire Euclidean corpus where *methodos* is used is in the fragments, VIII 236.6, and this is not Euclid, but Proclus, *In Euc.* 70.5.
2. Mueller 1981 provides an exemplary analysis of the deductive structure of the *Elements* and offers a number of telling criticisms of its strategies. My comments on Euclid's achievement in its historical context in no way gainsay the points that may be made when identifying the shortcomings of the work when judged from the stand-point of modern axiomatics: see, for instance, Suppes 1981.

demonstrations based on a small number of primary propositions and assumptions. The term 'elements' itself, as Aristotle
tells us,[3] was used of those propositions, the proofs of which are
implied in the proofs of all or most of the others.

We are faced, then, with an interesting phenomenon, a highly
methodical work, without any explicit methodology, but we can
gain a perspective on the matter by considering first some later
Greek mathematical texts, before turning back, later, to investigate the background to Euclid's *Elements* itself. One famous text
illustrates very clearly one type of context in which Greek mathematicians sometimes thought it necessary or desirable to introduce explicit methodological remarks. This is Archimedes' short
work called *ephodos*, conventionally translated the *Method*. This
opens by saying that he saw fit to write out and explain, for the
benefit of Eratosthenes, his addressee, the peculiarity of a certain way or manner (*tropos*) that is useful for the investigation
of certain problems in mathematics 'by means of mechanics'.
Archimedes makes it clear that the method is heuristic, not
demonstrative. The theorems discovered on its basis must thereafter be proved strictly, that is, by using the so-called method of
exhaustion. Nevertheless, as he puts it, the procedure is 'no less
useful even for the proofs of the theorems themselves. . . . It is, of
course, easier, when we have previously acquired, by the method,
some knowledge of the questions, to supply the proof, than it is
to find it without any previous knowledge' (*Method*, HS II
428.24ff).

As is well known, the 'mechanical method' depends on two
assumptions. The first is that a plane figure can be treated like
a weight with a determinate centre of gravity. Thus two plane
figures can be imagined as balanced around a fulcrum – and
similarly for solid figures too. Secondly, a plane figure can be
thought of as composed of the parallel line segments it contains
– and similarly a solid as composed of the planes it contains.

Now the method was and remained controversial, and both
assumptions are indeed open to challenge. First the idea of a
geometrical figure having weight appeared to apply physical notions to mathematical objects and thus to be guilty of a category

3. Aristotle, *Metaphysics* 998a25ff: for the use of the term in Greek physics, see above,
  pp. 9ff, 14f.

mistake. Secondly, the assumption that a geometrical magnitude is constituted by the indivisible line or plane segments it contains breached the principle of the continuum on which Greek geometry was based – for Greek geometers normally assumed that geometrical magnitudes are *infinitely* divisible.

In practice, Archimedes' use of the method yielded true theorems, which he sets about demonstrating independently. But it was easy to object that that was not guaranteed. It might, for example, have been objected that the application of a similar assumption to lines threatened to lead to the absurd conclusion that all lines are of equal length. In any pair of lines any point on one could be held to stand in one-to-one correspondence with a point on the other. But in that case, if the lines were thought of as made up of their indivisible elements, namely their points, they would all be of the same length. Whether Archimedes himself was perturbed just by the difficulty of applying mechanical assumptions, or just by those relating to the use of indivisibles, or rather by the combination of the two, is disputed.[4] However, his cautious recommendation was, as we have seen, that all the theorems discovered on the basis of the method had thereafter to be demonstrated strictly.

This illustrates one type of context – a defensive one – in which explicit methodological remarks may be made, namely as a response to the perceived controversiality of certain procedures. It is at least in part because the status of Archimedes' mechanical method might be called into question that he takes pains both to explain it and to give his view on its proper use.

In later Greek mathematics, the contexts in which explicit methodological discussions are introduced vary a great deal, but one recurrent motif is not just the description, but the justification or evaluation of a procedure. Thus both Hero (+1st century) and Pappus (+4th) frequently refer to the variety of methods that can be used to obtain the same result, and further add their own evaluative judgements about which, for example, is the more exact procedure (e.g. Hero, *Geometry* IV 290.6f) or which can be deemed to be sound. Pappus is not just responsible for our fullest, if still at points unperspicuous, account of

4. Among recent studies, see especially Knorr 1981, 1982, Sato 1986, 1987, Vitrac 1992, pp. 75ff, Roux 1992, pp. 151ff.

the general methods of analysis and synthesis in *Collection* VII 1,[5] but also several times lays down rules or sets out restrictions on the proper methods to be used in the investigations of certain problems.

One striking case is his discussion of the problem of finding two mean proportionals in *Collection* III. This opens with a lengthy account of a method of approximation used by an unnamed contemporary of his, which he criticises as inexact, before going on to report some correct methods including one for which he appears to claim some responsibility himself.[6] Similarly, in both III and IV he criticises those who ignore the methodological rule that each type of geometrical problem must be solved using the procedure appropriate to it, (1) plane problems by means of straight line and ruler constructions, (2) solid ones by means of conic sections, and (3) linear ones, where the solution required more complex curves, such as cochloids, cissoids or quadratrices (III 54.7ff, IV 270.1ff). At one point he even ventures criticisms of Archimedes and Apollonius themselves for breaching these category boundaries (IV 270.28ff, cf. 298.3ff).

In the next century too (+5th), Proclus comments extensively on mathematical methods, though less as a practising mathematician than for the philosophical lessons he wishes to draw. In his *Commentary on Euclid's Elements Book I*, he sets out the various component parts of a Euclidean proof and discusses in particular the distinctions between the different types of indemonstrables (*In Euc.* 75.27ff, 178.1ff, especially 178.9ff). It was the great achievement of Euclid to have presented irrefutable, *anelegktos*, proofs (e.g. *In Euc.* 68.6–70.18).

A comparison with the *Commentaries on the Republic* and on the *Timaeus* reveals, however, that one of Proclus' strategic aims is to set up an analogy and a contrast between the methods of

5. Controversy centres on whether or not analysis is confined to an examination of that from which a desired conclusion follows, or concerns also what can be deduced from the chosen starting-point. If the former, for the analytic procedure to be valid, the chain of inference has to be unconditionally convertible, though Pappus does not state as much in so many words. But analysis has in common with Archimedes' method that it relates not, or not just, to the deductive demonstration of certain conclusions, but to the heuristic investigation of theorems or problems. One recent study that summarises the controversy that goes back to Cornford (1932) 1965 and Robinson (1936) 1969, is Rehder 1982, cf. also Mahoney 1968–9, Szabo 1974–5, Hintikka and Remes 1974, Scolnicov 1975.

6. Pappus, *Collection* III 31.23ff, on which see Knorr 1986, ch. 8, and cf. Cuomo 1995.

geometry and those of philosophy. Developing a line of argument for which there were good Platonic precedents in *Republic*
VI and VII, Proclus praises mathematics as abstract and exact:
yet he claims, nevertheless, that it is inferior to dialectic and to
what he calls theology.[7] But if geometry, as using hypotheses, is
subordinate to theology, its great strength lies in the incontrovertibility of its proofs. For Proclus, as for so many other Greek
writers, geometry provided the model or ideal for strict demonstration, a model that was then extended to all sorts of other
fields. The title of Proclus' own metaphysical treatise, the *Elements
of Theology*, echoes Euclid, and in other writers proof *more geometrico* was sought even in such unlikely areas as medicine. We
shall come back to this.

Even this cursory glance at a selection of later Greek mathematical texts is enough to show that self-conscious reflection
on methods is by no means rare. Yet Euclid himself, as I remarked, offers no such comments. The *Elements*, we said, gives
every appearance of supreme self-confidence in the deployment
of demonstrative procedures. But where did that confidence come
from, and what gave him the ambition to attempt systematic
demonstrations in the first place? It may seem absurd even to
pose such questions, on two counts. Surely one needs no special
motivation to attempt demonstrations: and given Euclid's notorious self-effacement, how could one set about trying to answer
such questions, even if one thought it worthwhile asking them?

Now to the first objection we should remark that other mathematical traditions got along very well *without* attempting the
type of strict axiomatic-deductive demonstration favoured by the
Greeks. I shall have more to say on this later. As to the second,
it certainly has to be acknowledged that there are bound to be
large elements of conjecture in any attempted answers. In the
nature of our evidence, it is not as if the long-standing controversy over the extent of Euclid's debts, on the one hand to earlier mathematics, and on the other to philosophy, is ever likely
to be resolved. The best we can do is to identify and evaluate
possible influences and to broaden their scope in the light of the
exceptional nature of Greek-style demonstration.

7. On the intermediate status of mathematics, see, for example, Proclus, *In Euc.* 3.1ff,
   4.18ff.

First, so far as earlier Greek mathematics goes, let us consider those works of *Elements*, as Proclus calls them, that go back, he tells us (*In Euc.* 66.7ff), all the way to Hippocrates of Chios, active perhaps around –430. First it is not certain that that was their title. Secondly, so far as their contents and styles of argument go, we are reduced to guesswork in the main. In particular on one crucial point, for our concerns, we are in the dark. This relates to the question of whether, or how far, the notion of an *axiom* had been clarified and made explicit in the period before Aristotle. If we examine Hippocrates' own proofs of the quadratures of lunes, as reported by Simplicius, these are certainly rigorously deductive, but they are not based on *ultimate* primary premisses or axioms. Rather, they took as their starting-point (*archē*) the proposition that similar segments of circles have the same ratios as the squares on their bases. That proposition, so far from being primary, was one that Hippocrates *showed*, so we are told (Simplicius, *In Ph.* 61.5ff), by showing that the squares on the diameters have the same ratios as the circles – even though we are not told how he did that.

Of course any systematisation of a body of mathematical knowledge will involve discriminating between primary and derivative theorems, and Proclus' history suggests that attempted syntheses became increasingly complete and well-articulated in the period between Hippocrates and Euclid – the work of such men as Archytas and Theaetetus (*In Euc.* 66.14ff). Yet when all is said and done, the very limited evidence we have for pre-Euclidean mathematics does not yield any indubitable examples of demonstrations based on ultimate primary premisses clearly recognised *as such*. For the concept of an axiom itself, we have to turn to philosophy. So far as our extant evidence goes, it was Aristotle, as is well known, who first clearly defined and classified the various types of indemonstrables, that is, in his view, definitions, axioms and hypotheses. That demonstration must ultimately be based on primary propositions that are themselves indemonstrable is clinched, in the *Posterior Analytics* I 2, 71b9ff, I 3, 72b5ff, with arguments that show that this must be so, to avoid the twin problems of circularity and infinite regress.

But it is also well known that any claim that Euclid was simply following the *Posterior Analytics* will not do. First the match between his triad of indemonstrables and Aristotle's is not exact, notably in that Euclid's postulates do not tally with Aristotelian hypotheses. But then secondly and far more importantly, the *Posterior Analytics* insists that deductive reasoning should be cast in *syllogistic* form.[8] Euclid not only shows no signs of presenting arguments syllogistically in the *Elements*: his deductions cannot even be recast in syllogistic form without gross artificiality.[9]

Thus far the shape of my argument is familiar enough, though some of the details may, no doubt, be contested. But the point at which the comparativist will still legitimately be puzzled, and will press harder, but potentially more fruitful, questions, relates to the origins of the demand for the strictest style of demonstration, securing incontrovertibility. Here it is another part of the philosophical background that seems to me to be crucial, that relating to the definition of demonstration itself and to the analysis of what makes a demonstration a demonstration.

We must bear in mind that the terms that both Plato and Aristotle use for strict demonstration, namely *apodeixis, apodeiknumi* and cognates, had been, and continued to be, used extensively of a wide variety of more or less informal proofs and proving, showing, or exhibiting, outside philosophy, in such fields as historical writing,[10] political debate and forensic oratory. Greek orators and politicians, for instance, readily and repeatedly claimed that they had proved their cases, using those very same terms, *apodeixis, apodeiknumi,* and again *epideixis, epideiknumi, deiknumi,* as well as others such as *dēloō* and *apophainō.*[11] They spoke freely of proof when, for example, they had established, to their own satisfaction, what the facts of the matter were, or the guilt or innocence of the parties involved, or again when they had shown or at least

8. That is undeniably true of the *Posterior Analytics* as we have it, even if some scholars detect pre-syllogistic deductive modes of reasoning in the background, as also in such works as the *Topics*: see, for example, Solmsen 1929, Barnes 1981.

9. Attempts at such recasting have, indeed, been made, but they tend to confirm the artificiality of this: see McKirahan 1992, ch. 12.

10. Thus the uses of *apodeiknumi* in Herodotus include pointing to, as witness, I 171, bringing forward evidence, v 45, delivering (of accounts), VII 119, and showing by argument (*logos*), e.g. v 94, VII 17. The substantive, *apodeixis,* in its Ionic form *apodexis,* is used in relation to the presentation of his own history (Proem) and of displaying or proving, e.g. I 207, II 101, 148, VIII 101.

11. See, for example, the uses of *apodeiknumi* at Antiphon II 3.1, 4.10, IV 3.7, 4.9, v 64, 81, Lysias III 40, VII 43, XIII 49, 51, XV 11, of *epideiknumi* at Antiphon II 4.3, III 4.9, IV 2.7, v 19, Lysias IV 12, XII 56, XIII 62, of *apophainō* at Lysias XIII 51, and of *dēloō* at Antiphon II 4.8, 4.10, III 3.10.

declared that what they advocated was in the best interests of the state or of whoever it was they were addressing. Such informal notions – of proof beyond reasonable doubt – were very common, though what counted as reasonable was itself always open to challenge.

But one point at which Plato, for one, objected, with some virulence, was that all that the arguments of the orators and politicians could achieve was the plausible, the likely, the persuasive: they could not legitimately claim to secure the truth. In the *Phaedo, Gorgias, Republic* and *Theaetetus*, especially, a systematic contrast is developed between *doxa* (seeming/opinion) and *alētheia* (truth) and again between persuasion (*peithō, pistis, peithomai*) and proof (*apodeixis*), a contrast that draws, undoubtedly, on the previous use of many of these terms by the Eleatics and others, but that goes well beyond that use.[12] What the sophists, orators and politicians trafficked in, in Plato's view, was just opinion and the plausible. What persuaded audiences might or might not be true. It is the claim to yield truth and indeed certainty, and to be able to give an account, *logon didonai*, that marks out true philosophy, that is, *his* kind.

The conjecture, on this story, would be that it was the rivalry between competing claimants to intellectual leadership and prestige in Greece, that stimulated the analysis of proving and of proof. The first main challenge came from Plato, though it was not until Aristotle that we find an explicit *definition* of strict demonstration.[13] We should not imagine that those whose arguments and inquiries were thereby downgraded as being merely persuasive would have accepted the strictures of a Plato or an

---

12. I have discussed this in Lloyd 1979, ch. 2, especially pp. 100ff. It is notable that on two occasions, namely *Phaedo* 92d and *Theaetetus* 162e, the inadequacy of merely likely arguments is illustrated with an example taken from mathematics (Lloyd 1979, p. 116).

13. E.g. *Posterior Analytics* 71b17ff. Unlike Plato, for whom 'dialectic' is supreme among the branches of knowledge (e.g. *Republic* 534e), Aristotle treats what he calls 'dialectic' as inferior to the highest mode of demonstration, in that it proceeds from probable premisses or premisses that are generally accepted or reputable (*endoxa*), rather than from premisses that are true, primary and necessary (e.g. *Prior Analytics* 46a8ff, 68b9ff, *Topics* 100a25ff). But Aristotle follows Plato's lead in contrasting these with further, lower, in some cases deviant, modes of reasoning, peirastic, sophistic, eristic and the various types of rhetoric. For a first orientation on his distinctions, I may refer to my 1979, pp. 62ff.

Aristotle. On the contrary, there is no sign, in the −4th-century orators, of any inhibitions about claiming to prove their points.[14] But the effect of Plato's critique was certainly to *problematise* proof, and Aristotle's explorations of syllogistic and of causal explanation, combined with his classification of the indemonstrables, provided a comprehensive formal analysis of the axiomatic-deductive mode of demonstration, even though Aristotle himself was in some difficulty (as I have argued elsewhere, Lloyd (1990/1992) in implementing that ideal in practice in his own scientific treatises.

We must recognise that there is no evidence that Euclid or indeed any other Greek mathematician was directly concerned with the distinctions that Plato and Aristotle drew between the merely persuasive and the strictly demonstrative – let alone with their categorising of reasoners according to whether they delivered the one or the other. For all we know, Euclid *may* just have been following and developing earlier existing types of purely mathematical argument.

But we can certainly see, from those later writers we considered before, how, both for the mathematicians themselves and for others, geometry served as the model for demonstrations securing incontrovertibility. Some might imagine – many have assumed – that the internal dynamic of the development of mathematics itself would, somehow inevitably, eventually lead to a demand for strict axiomatic-deductive demonstration, and that there is accordingly no need to postulate any external stimulus such as I have conjectured to come from the philosophical preoccupation with the contrast between the merely persuasive and the rigorously demonstrated. Yet the difficulty for that view is the one I have mentioned: reference to other, non-Greek, ancient mathematical traditions – Babylonian, Egyptian, Hindu, Chinese – shows that they all got along perfectly well *without* any notion corresponding to axioms and accordingly without the particular notion of strict demonstration that went with it. It is time now to turn to the Chinese material in particular.

When we consult our earliest complete extant Chinese math-

14. This can be seen from the continued frequent use of *apodeixis, apodeiknumi* and so on, of informal modes of proof and proving. See, for example, Demosthenes XVIII 42, 59, XXX 4, XXXIII 37, LVIII 7, Aeschines I 44, 88, III 165, Lycurgus *Leoc.* 102, 129, Isocrates XI 30, XII 173, 251, XV 89, 118, XVII 28, XIX 16.

ematical texts, various contrasts with the Greek Euclidean tradition we have been discussing present themselves. But the first point worth remarking is how common explicit references to methods and procedures are, the key terms being 法 (*fa*, model, law, principle), 術 (*shu*, art, method, working) and 道 (*dao*, way) itself.

One passage in the *Zhoubi* makes large claims for what the way (*dao*) can achieve when someone follows it in mathematics, while it also brings out some striking features of the teacher–pupil relationship in this context.[15] The pupil, Rong Fang, opens by asking Chenzi (in Cullen's translation of *Zhoubi* 23–4): 'Master, I have recently heard something about your Way. Is it really true that your Way is able to comprehend the height and size of the sun, the area illuminated by its radiance, the amount of its daily motion, the figures for its greatest and least distances, the extent of human vision, the limits of the four poles, the lodges into which the stars are ordered, and the length and breadth of Heaven and Earth?' Chenzi replies: 'It is true.' Rong Fang then proceeds: 'Although I am not intelligent, Master, I would like you to favour me with an explanation. Can someone like me be taught this Way?' Chenzi replies: 'Yes. All these things can be attained to by mathematics, 筭術 (*suan shu*, the art or method of numbers). Your ability in mathematics is sufficient to understand such matters if you sincerely give reiterated thought to them.'

That is not as helpful, one might think, as it might have been. The master has his Way and the pupil strives to learn it. But this Way is not here thought of just as a means, but as an end, or one of them. Method is not here conceived so much as a means to facilitate the acquisition of knowledge: rather it is one of the items the pupil has to master to master the subject. What the teacher looks for, in the pupil, are signs that he has successfully internalised the procedures needed to carry out the investigation for himself, as well as the results themselves.

Rong Fang makes two unsuccessful attempts to work things out for himself at home. On each occasion he has to come back and ask again: 'I have exerted my powers to the utmost, but my understanding does not go far enough, and my spirit is not adequate. I cannot reach understanding and I implore you to

15. Cf. the discussion of this issue, above, Chapter 2.

explain to me' (*Zhoubi* 25). Eventually Chenzi does take him through the method, explaining, for example, how the height of the sun is to be got from a comparison of the noon shadow lengths of three gnomons located at distances exactly 1,000 里 (*li*: 'leagues') apart on a due north-south line. As for the dimension of the sun, given its distance, that is to be got by sighting it down a bamboo tube so that the diameter of the sun exactly fits the bore of the tube and taking the measurements of the bore and the tube. Given those measurements, the dimension of the sun is obtained by similar triangles.

Both procedures (I note in parenthesis) have analogues in ancient Greece, the latter with the technique Archimedes used to get the upper and lower limits of the angular diameter of the sun,[16] and the former with Eratosthenes' method of determining the circumference of the earth.[17] The difference, there, however, is that Eratosthenes assumed the earth to be spherical, and the rays of light from the sun to be parallel, while in the *Zhoubi* it is assumed that the earth itself is flat, while the sun's distance can be got from the difference in the shadow lengths. Without *some* assumptions, on either side, the data relating to shadow differences would not, of course, yield anything.

The *Zhoubi* sets out certain methods and procedures, labelled as such, for use in astronomical investigations. The *Nine Chapters* deals with a variety of problems in arithmetic and geometry, to do with the addition, subtraction, multiplication and division of fractions, for instance, and the determination of the areas and volumes of various rectilinear and curvilinear figures. The whole discussion is articulated in a highly formal style, first a question, then an answer, followed by the statement of the method to be used, this last section being introduced, standardly, by the expression 術曰 (*shu yue*: the method or the working states).

The 'workings' in question generally give what we might call algorithms to be used for the solution of the original problems. As already remarked, there is nothing that corresponds to

16. Archimedes, *Sandreckoner*, HS II 222.11ff. But Archimedes did not attempt to estimate the size of the sun by this method.
17. As reported by Cleomedes, *On the Circular Movement of the Heavenly Bodies*, I 10, 90.20ff, discussed, with reference to recent studies, in Lloyd 1987a, pp. 231ff. A similar investigation to that in the *Zhoubi*, but with different figures and results, is to be found in *Huainanzi* 3, the treatise compiled at the court of Liu An, king of Huainan until his execution in −122: see Cullen 1976.

the notion of axiomatic-deductive demonstration, not just in the *Zhoubi* and the *Nine Chapters*, but anywhere in Chinese mathematics until after the arrival of Western influences with the Jesuits in the sixteenth century. However, the algorithms of the *Nine Chapters* are the subject of self-conscious reflection. This is where Liu Hui's commentary is so interesting, as a series of studies by Karine Chemla, following work by Don Wagner, has shown (Chemla 1988, 1990a, 1990b, 1991, 1992a, 1992b, 1994, cf. Wagner 1979).

What Liu Hui does, in his commentary on several of the 'workings', is, in effect, to validate the algorithm, and indeed to do so, often, at a higher level of abstraction than the original. It is easiest to illustrate this with one of the simplest examples, to do with the procedure for the addition of fractions. He shows first that a fraction may be expressed in more, or less, simple terms: $\frac{a}{b} = \frac{ax}{bx}$. But then $\frac{a}{b} + \frac{c}{d} = \frac{(ad + bc)}{bd}$ is correct. Liu Hui attaches names to the two key procedures. 'Every time denominators multiply a numerator which does not correspond to them, we call this homogenize (齊, *qi*). Multiplying with one another the set of denominators, we call this equalize (同, *tong*).'[18] But $\frac{a}{b} = \frac{ad}{bd}$, and again $\frac{c}{d} = \frac{bc}{bd}$. So he now remarks that once cross-multiplication has been carried out, the addition can be effected, and 'the procedures cannot have lost the original quantities'.

There are two cardinal points of interest in this and other texts where Liu Hui offers explicit comments on the mathematical procedures in question. First there is what can be learned from them about Liu Hui's own concerns. Here and elsewhere he investigates the formal patterns that underlie the mathematical reasoning, indeed he looks for the *same* pattern in *different* contexts, thereby unifying the procedures used in those contexts. This may be compared with the aim stated in the *Zhoubi* itself (*Zhoubi* 24), namely to find methods that are 'concisely worded but of broad application'. Indeed Liu Hui himself draws attention to the point that 'homogenizing' and 'equalizing' are procedures that recur in different contexts in the *Nine Chapters*. What he aims to set out, as he puts it himself in the passage from which I have just quoted, are the 綱紀 (*gangji*), the guiding principles or key general features in the mathematical reasoning.

But secondly, if we confront Liu Hui's commentary with our

18. The text of Liu Hui comes at p. 96 of Qian's edition of the *Nine Chapters*.

comparative issues in mind, we can say this. What he does in the discussion of the addition of fractions and elsewhere is to *show* that the algorithms used are correct. Now that is as good a *proof* of the procedures as anyone could wish – provided, of course, that we do not limit our notion of what will count as a proof to axiomatic-deductive demonstration in the Euclidean style – provided, that is, that we do not stipulate that for a proof to be a proof, it has to be cast in that style. For what more should we expect of the proof of a procedure than an explanation of how and why it works, however that explanation itself proceeds?

So, first, if we are considering Chinese styles of proof, here are some excellent examples, but secondly, they are examples that occur in discussions that do not reflect any interest in axiomatic-deductive demonstration, but rather a concern to determine the patterns that underlie the mathematical procedures used.

The Greek preoccupation with proof *more geometrico* was certainly accompanied by notable efforts aiming to achieve, and often in fact achieving, clarity, exactness and rigour in the logical articulation of sequences of arguments. But that was not the only way in which sophisticated mathematics could develop: the Chinese texts show that, for in China there was no such concern, and yet not just the securing of complex results, but also a considerable, self-conscious interest in the analysis and verification of procedures and in the search for the underlying principles uniting different areas of mathematical reasoning.[19]

Moreover, the problem with proof in the Euclidean style was always that of securing an axiom set that would meet the demands of being both indemonstrable and self-evidently true. It has often been conjectured that Euclid adopted the parallel postulate as a postulate because he realised that it could not be proved without circularity.[20] But there is nothing to suggest that

19. The still prevalent notion that Chinese mathematics was exclusively practical in orientation cannot be sustained in the face of the well-developed theoretical interests in play already in the classical texts (Li and Du 1987 provide a general survey). Thus in his discussion of the determination of the volume of a pyramid – to which we shall be returning, pp. 152ff – Liu Hui uses a technique of indivisibles that has been compared with Cavalieri's theorem (Wagner 1978a, pp. 61ff) and he comments explicitly on the apparent lack of direct practical application of parts of his studies (Wagner 1979, p. 182).
20. This is the criticism that Aristotle levels at certain proofs about parallels in his own day, see *Prior Analytics* 65a4ff.

he did not also accept it as true.[21] Yet with the development of non-Euclidean geometries, our understanding of its status has, of course, been transformed. From the point of view of other mathematical traditions, that never sought axiomatic foundations, there is an evident irony in that one of the bases of the claims made for Greek geometry, that it yields what is incontrovertibly true, turns out to be a proposition that is anything but.

I turn now, inevitably much more briefly, to my second main field, medicine, and for the sake of even-handedness will start this time with some of the Chinese evidence. Once again, some of the principal sections in the various recensions of the *Huangdi neijing* take the form of dialogues. Often these are between the Yellow Emperor, who generally asks the questions, and his various respondents, such as Qi Bo and Shao Shi (cf. above, p. 40f). The Yellow Emperor is no ordinary pupil, nor do the answers take the form of an instruction to go away and work it out for himself. However, there is much play here, as in the *Zhoubi*, with the cardinal necessity to follow the *Dao*. The Way is the key, and not just as instrumental to an end, but as the end itself, at least in that the goal, sagehood, is its embodiment.

'Among the men of high antiquity', says Qi Bo in *Suwen* 1,[22] 'those who knew the Way took *yin* and *yang* as their model, harmonised themselves with disciplines based on what is regular (術數: *shu shu*, literally the working or art of numbers)[23]. . . . They were able to keep form and spirit intact, and were able to live out the span of years that Heaven allotted them, passing on at the age of several hundred years. The men of today are totally different . . .'

However, Qi Bo's answers do not always stay at the level of *obiter dicta*, for he also gives detailed explanations both with regard to the therapies to be adopted for particular complaints

21. Despite what has sometimes been claimed (cf. Tóth 1966–7), the possibility of alternative geometries was not entertained in Greek antiquity. When Aristotle mentions the idea of denying that the internal angles of a triangle sum to two rights (e.g. *Posterior Analytics* 93a33ff), this is never in connection with any proposal to construct an alternative geometry on the basis of such a denial.

22. *Suwen* 1.1, 7. I have had the benefit of extensive comments by Nathan Sivin on this and the texts referred to in the next paragraph. His translations, which I use, differ substantially from those offered by Unschuld 1985.

23. The interpretation of this phrase, and indeed the order of the two characters, vary. On the first, 術 (*shu*), see above, while on the range of meaning of the second, 數 (*shu*) – which may or may not modify the first – see Ho 1991.

and on techniques of diagnosis and prognosis. Thus at one
point, *Suwen* 12, he is questioned by the Yellow Emperor: 'When
physicians treat illness, they differ in their therapy for the same
disease, yet the patient recovers. Why is this?' Qi Bo's reply is
rather along the lines of the Hippocratic *Airs Waters Places*. 'The
disposition of the land makes this so.' In the five regions (East,
West, North, South and Centre), the varieties of illnesses reflect
the climate and diet of the inhabitants, and different therapies
have been developed to counter them (that is, stone therapy,
powerful drugs, moxa, needles, and exercise and massage respectively). Here, then, we have an account of the origins of certain
treatments, an account that, moreover, legitimates certain procedures in their use partly by according them ancient authority.
'Their therapies differed but the illnesses got better. That was
because they understood the real character of each disorder and
knew the great principles of therapy' (*Suwen* 12.1, 39).

The analysis of the *Huangdi neijing* recensions has suggested to
specialists that the various points of view represented correspond
to divergent literate medical traditions and can therefore yield
evidence for their interplay and development (see, for example,
Keegan 1988). If so, that interplay more often takes the form of
the claim that new ideas go further than older ones, or spell out
their message, than one of the rejection of earlier traditions. The
past is built on, not demolished.

However, the existence of overt rivalry between medical practitioners and practices emerges more directly in the other text I
proposed for examination, the *Canggongzhuan* of Chunyu Yi, in
Sima Qian's *Shiji* 105, which we have already cited extensively in
Chapter 2 (pp. 28ff). Chunyu Yi reports a series of case-histories
where his prognoses and diagnoses turn out to be correct, but to
justify them he refers repeatedly to what the Method of the Pulse
says. In some cases it is not clear whether these remarks relate to
texts or to a body of learning or to a combination of both: but
in his own account of his early training he certainly refers to
books on the pulse he received from his teacher Gongsheng
Yangqing.[24]

The way Chunyu Yi uses the Method can be seen, for example,

24. Sima Qian, *Shiji* 105: 2796, where the books are said to be those of Huangdi and
Bian Que.

in case 2 (*Shiji* 105: 2798–9). This is an illness of one of the grandsons of the King of Qi, which Chunyu Yi diagnoses as a *qi*-diaphragm-disorder.[25] The reason he knew that this was the case was that when he took the pulse, 'it was the heart *qi*: it was muddy and agitated in (reading *zai* for *er*) the cardinal tract (經, *jing*).' That allows the illness to be categorised as *yang* or to do with the *yang* vessels. The text then continues: 'The method of the pulse says: if the pulse comes rapidly and it leaves with difficulty and is not united, the illness is settled in the heart.'

Here we have a typical justification of what a pulse of a particular type can tell one about a patient's condition. In each case this confirms what Chunyu Yi had determined. However, although the Method sets out detailed correlations between pulse types and internal conditions, the question that might be thought to arise was *how* to recognise those types. The Method evidently could take you directly from the quality of the pulse to the diagnosis/prognosis of the complaint: but everything depended, clearly, on your being able to *feel* the pulse correctly. This was a remarkably comprehensive and systematic diagnostic technique, but the practitioner had first to have a good deal of knowledge and skill, in recognising the pulses he felt, in order to *use* the Method. Method was no substitute for knowledge, and indeed useless in its absence. rather it was a way both of systematising that knowledge and of justifying the conclusions it led the practitioner to draw.

As we have remarked before (Chapter 2), the evidence from the *Canggongzhuan* shows that it was perfectly possible, in classical Chinese medicine, for one doctor to criticise another openly, not just on a particular point to do with diagnosis or treatment, but more generally for their whole approach, for example for an uncomprehending use of earlier authorities.[26]

When we turn to the evidence for classical Greek medicine, however, the range and intensity of explicit methodological

25. I transliterate 氣, *Qi*, since neither a materialist rendering ('air' 'breath'), nor anti-materialist ones (e.g. 'energy') do justice to the range of sense and usage of the term. On the spectrum of uses of the term, its development and eventual association with *yin yang* and the five phases, see Sivin 1987, pp. 46ff.
26. As for example in Chunyu Yi's criticisms of the doctor named Sui, *Shiji* 105: 2810–11 (above, p. 29 at n. 19). That mere book learning is not enough to make someone a good practitioner is also a point that comes out of Chunyu Yi's account of his apprenticeship under Gongsheng Yangqing: 2794–6.

disputes are far greater than can be exemplified from Chinese medicine – or indeed than can be found in the Greek mathematical texts we reviewed earlier. The last main section of this study will attempt to explore the factors that may have contributed to this phenomenon. In particular, we shall see that on certain occasions methodology is not developed just to be applied in practice. Rather, it is elaborated for the sake of the polemical points to be scored on its basis. A claim to superiority in Greek medicine is sometimes based on having the right *justifications* for practices – not on having different practices.

In our classical Hippocratic texts criticisms of others' methods range from the correction of faulty techniques of bandaging[27] all the way to attacks where the whole conception of the nature and status of the art of medicine is at issue, where indeed the epistemological issues of the basis of any claim for medicine to be a branch of knowledge at all are at stake. One of the best known early examples where those general questions are debated is the work *On Ancient Medicine*, the principal aim of which is to expose the errors of what the author calls the new-fangled methods of his opponents, based on such 'hypotheses', or postulates, as the hot, the cold, the wet and the dry (ch. 1, *CMG* I 1, 36.2ff, chh. 13ff, 44.8ff).

Many points in the interpretation of this text are problematic, not least who precisely those opponents are.[28] But the gist of one major complaint is that they 'narrowed down the causal principle of diseases' (ch. 1, 36.4f). They appear to have attempted to base medicine on a very limited number of postulates from which the whole of medical practice could, somehow, be deduced. The author of *On Ancient Medicine* himself protests that that is completely to misconstrue the nature of medicine, which is an art (*technē*) with practitioners who vary in skill and judgement (ch. 1, 36.7ff), which has a principle (*archē*) and a method (*hodos*) through which many discoveries have been made and by means of which the rest too will be discovered if the investigator is up to the task and proceeds on the basis of these principles (ch. 2, 37.1ff). He does not himself deny that hot, cold, wet and dry are among the factors at work in the body and in diseases, but they

27. As for example in *Fractures*, ch. 25, L III 498.8ff. This feature of these Hippocratic texts is discussed in some detail in Lloyd 1987a, ch. 3.
28. See Lloyd 1991a, ch. 3. On the writer's own position, compare Hankinson 1992.

are, in his view, among the least important (chh. 13ff, especially ch. 16, 47.12ff).

This is a dispute not between doctors of the literate elite on the one hand, and radically different traditions of medicine, such as that of the itinerant purifiers, on the other, but *within* the groups of literate practitioners. The method of 'hypothesis' that the author of *On Ancient Medicine* attacks is one he associates with the investigation of meteorology and of 'things under the earth',[29] and at one point (ch. 20, 51.6ff) he explicitly resists the intrusion of philosophical methods into medicine in particular. On other occasions, too, there are signs of philosophical influence on −5th- and −4th-century Hippocratic texts, in relation not just to physical theories, but also to methodology. There are echoes, close to verbatim quotations, of Heraclitus, Empedocles and Anaxagoras in the treatise *On Regimen* I, for example.[30] As remarked before (p. 18 at n. 12), where Diogenes of Apollonia had opened his work (Fr. 1) with a methodological statement to the effect that the starting-point (*archē*) should be indisputable, the Hippocratic treatise *On the Art* states that the starting point of its *logos* is something that will be agreed by all (ch. 4, *CMG* I 1, 11.5f).

This might suggest as a hypothesis that these methodological forays in Greek medicine reflect contemporary philosophical disputes, where, ever since Xenophanes in the −6th century, debate on substantive physical or cosmological questions had been punctuated by second-order epistemological controversies.[31] Yet *just* to see here the effects of importations from philosophy would be too simple, even though the author of *On Ancient Medicine* writes of a tendency to 'veer towards philosophy' in his opponents (ch. 20, 51.9ff). On his own view of the matter, at least, his own positive methodology owes nothing at all to philosophy, but is, precisely, the traditional method of 'ancient medicine' (ch. 2, 37.1ff, cf. ch. 5, 39.6ff, ch. 12, 44.2ff).

29. *On Ancient Medicine*, ch. 1, 36.15ff. However it is not as if the author of this work approves of the use of 'hypotheses' outside medicine either.
30. *On Regimen* I, chh. 3–5, *CMG* I 2.4, 126.5ff, 126.20ff, 128.12ff, where many of the echoes or patallelisms are signalled in the footnotes in that edition (Joly and Byl, 1984).
31. As in Xenophanes, Frr. 18, 34, 35, 38, Heraclitus, Frr. 50, 54, 55, 101, 101a, Parmenides, Frr. 7, 16, Alcmaeon, Fr. 1, Empedocles, Frr. 2, 3, Anaxagoras, Frr. 21, 21a, Democritus, Frr. 6–11, 125.

The underlying preoccupations that exercise several Hippocratic authors emerge with some clarity when we examine two further related themes, the contrast between the (proper) practitioner and the lay person, and the role of chance in medicine. In both cases, it seems that the very existence of the – Greek – medical art was under threat and had to be defended in ways that have no Chinese parallel.

Thus the treatise *On Regimen in Acute Diseases* opens with a criticism of a rival work, the *Cnidian Sentences* (itself now lost), for merely giving an account of the symptoms that patients suffer from and the outcome of their diseases. But anyone, the writer protests, could manage that, if they questioned the patients. What requires real medical knowledge and skill turns out to depend on knowing the causes of diseases and on an appreciation of when precisely a change of regimen is needed. He points out that the same condition may arise from various causes (ch. 11, L II 314.12ff). Not recognising this, physicians often give the wrong treatment, and when someone else, maybe a lay person, suggests something different and the patient is cured, the original physician becomes a laughing-stock (ch. 11, 316.12ff) and medicine itself seems no better than divination (ch. 3, 242.3ff).[32]

As to the argument that medicine is just a matter of chance, three different treatises give three different reactions. The writer of *On the Art* (chh. 4ff, *CMG* I 1, 11.5ff) considers the objections (1) that patients can and sometimes do recover even without medical treatment, (2) that when they are treated, they do not always recover, and (3) that when they are treated and do get better, that is not necessarily because of their treatment. To this, the writer counters that there are *causes* at work, in recovery and indeed also in death, in any event. Even when medical practitioners do *not* intervene, the reasons for the patients recovering, or dying, are not a matter of chance. 'Everything that happens will be found to have some cause, and if it has a cause, the spontaneous can be no more than an empty name' (ch. 6, 13.2ff). The positive argument is that medicine, based on reason and experience, can identify the causes and can achieve cures.

In *On Affections* (ch. 45, L VI 254.9ff) the writer concedes that

---

32. Lloyd 1979, p. 39 and n. 152, sets out a variety of Hippocratic evidence relating to the contrasts between the physician and the lay person, and between the true physician and the quack.

some remedies are discovered by chance and that lay people might stumble on them just as much as doctors. But he too insists on the contrast between what comes about by chance, and what belongs to medical reasoning, which he asserts can only be learned from those who can distinguish what belongs to the medical art.

A third work that exhibits a similar defensiveness but produces a very different solution to the problem is *On the Places in Man.* Chapter 46 (L vi 342.4ff) opens with the extravagant claim that the whole of medicine has already been discovered. The doctor who understands has least need of chance: indeed what passes as good fortune and bad really reflects the knowledge or ignorance of the practitioner. Successes just reflect the doctor's knowledge and ability, and the author accepts the corollary, that failures also stem from the doctor's lack of understanding.

Fighting for the right of medicine to call itself a branch of knowledge, and disputes over what status it could claim, continue and intensify in the Hellenistic period, where again the question arises of the nature and extent of the philosophical influences at work. The notion that there were three clearly defined schools, of Dogmatists, Empiricists and Methodists, has – as we have remarked before (p. 35 at n. 29) – been much exaggerated, in some ancient as well as many modern commentators. However, the disputes on such questions as whether underlying causes or hidden reality can be investigated – or on whether, or in what circumstances, anatomical dissection is a valuable or a justifiable procedure – these disputes, reported in such texts as the Proem to Celsus' *On Medicine* and Galen's *On Sects for Beginners*, are real enough. Evidently some of the issues in question are the *same* issues that were discussed in the Hellenistic philosophical schools, particularly those concerned with the various types of sceptical challenge to the existence of stable criteria of knowledge – though whether the influence was always from philosophy to medicine, or sometimes also in the reverse direction, is a matter of controversy.[33] But just as evidently, the issues to do with dissection are, at points, specific to medicine and to the life sciences.[34]

Galen's polemic with the Methodists[35] combines several of the

33. See, for example, Barnes 1982, Sedley 1982, Frede 1987, chh. 12–14, Matthen 1988, Allen 1993.
34. We shall be returning to this controversy below, pp. 197ff.
35. See especially Frede 1985, 1987, chh. 14–15, Hankinson 1991a, De Lacy 1991.

features we have mentioned so far and enables us to pick up themes from our earlier discussion of method in Greek mathematics. Galen is critical of all the chief medical groups he identifies, but the nature of his criticisms varies in a revealing manner. First he outlines the debate between the Empiricists and those he calls Dogmatists. He attacks the former on the chief grounds that while relying on experience, they have no theoretical underpinning to explain why they adopt the therapies they adopt. Accordingly they are at a loss to deduce what should be done when they are confronted with a new disease. The Dogmatists are criticised for the converse failing, not of relying on experience too much, but of not paying sufficient attention to it in the first place.

But this disagreement, as Galen reports it, was *just* about the account to be given of medical *method.* The Empiricists and Dogmatists did not, in general, according to Galen, differ in the *actual* therapeutic measures they used. It emerges here, then, that explicit methodology, in their hands, merely supplied a different justification for *agreed* practices. This was methodology for that, polemical, purpose, not to validate different medical procedures and therapies.

But in his attacks on the Methodists, Galen has opponents who diverged not just in methodology, but also in medical practice. Their techniques of diagnosis and treatment centred on the idea of the *koinotētes*, common conditions, but these were not disease entities as normally understood in Greece, but, as their name implied, characterisations of the general state of the patient, whether 'lax' or 'restricted' or a mixture of the two. Therapy was, then, a matter of countering the lax with the restricted or vice versa.[36]

The general background to the disputes, in Hellenistic medicine, on the relative importance of reason and experience as criteria of knowledge, is, to be sure, philosophical, though the debate had ramifications throughout the inquiry into nature, including in the mathematical branches of physics, as we can see from Ptolemy's *Harmonics*, for instance.[37] But the applications to medicine were distinctive, as also was the Methodists' version of

36. I have given a short account of Methodist medical theory and practice in Lloyd 1983, Part III, chh. 5–6. Cf. also Frede 1987, ch. 14.
37. See, for example, Ptolemy, *Harmonics* I 1, 3.1ff, III 3, 93.11ff, among many other passages, and cf. Barker forthcoming.

an alternative. For Galen, what they considered the proper method was a travesty, and, as he never tires of saying, they are the most unmethodical of medical practitioners:[38] in his view, after all, they rejected the whole of what he considered to be the essential theoretical basis for medicine.

By contrast, Galen's own idea of method included the ambition to give, wherever possible, demonstrations in the geometrical manner.[39] Here we come back full circle to Greek mathematics, for the existence of that goal, in that field, had a catalytic effect in other domains of inquiry. While the sceptical doctors resisted even limited knowledge claims, the most aggressive anti-sceptics, such as Galen, claimed to be able to deliver certainty, via the deployment of proof *more geometrico*. Galen's onslaught exhibits at its most vituperative a debate in which rival practitioners sought to undermine one another not just in terms of their therapies or diagnoses, but in terms of the underlying conception of the nature of the medical art itself.

I return, then, in conclusion, to my original questions, to do with the roles that methodological and epistemological statements of various types play in China and in Greece. Even such a selective survey as this serves to show one negative point rather clearly, namely that no straightforward generalisation, contrasting the Chinese data as a whole with the Greek, will do, any more than one attempting to set up a simple opposition between mathematics (in both cultures) and medicine (in both) We have, rather, a spectrum of uses, and differences of degree rather than of kind.

Thus both in China and in Greece, and in both mathematics and medicine, methodological statements have certain pragmatic and defensive roles. They are used to introduce and describe particular techniques in particular contexts (algorithms, or formulae of other types, or statements of the method to be used in medical diagnosis or treatment), and the introduction and description of a procedure easily shade into the validation and justification of its use (as in Liu Hui with the rewriting of algorithms) or the explanation of its status (Archimedes on his method).

38. E.g. Galen, *On the Therapeutic Method* (*Methodus Medendi*) 1 3, K x 27.2ff. It is striking that, in the *Shiji* 130: 3292, 5, the *Dao Jia* is, in effect, *commended* for having a law or method (法, *fa*) that is no method.
39. Cf. further below, pp. 199ff.

However, explicit methodological statements may also have a further, more overtly polemical, function. True, self-conscious methodology and epistemology often *present themselves* as the neutral analysis of second-order questions, of how to conduct an inquiry and on the status of the inquiry itself. Focussing on such questions may, and did, bring to light important features to do with observation, experience, hypothesis, definition, proof, explanation, understanding and much else besides. More attention is paid to epistemology as such in our Greek sources than in our Chinese ones, but we should bear in mind that some of the classical Chinese philosophers who were most interested in such issues are particularly badly served in our extant sources: that is true especially of the Mohists (Graham 1978, especially pp. 30ff). Besides, such topics as the need for experience in understanding are referred to commonly enough, for example in Chinese medicine (cf. above, pp. 28f on Chunyu Yi on this point).

But if methodology can and does play a justificatory role, the next question is what kinds of justification it offers, and directed at whom? One contrast that our analysis of the medical materials surveyed may suggest relates to the starting assumptions of those to whom methodology is addressed, those to whom it is supposed to be useful.

Chunyu Yi was undoubtedly concerned to justify his medical practice, and for this he refers quite often to the Method of the Pulse. Yet that method itself presupposes the ability to discriminate the different qualities of the pulse. *That* is not the subject of further argumentative justification. Rather, it is a matter of the practitioner being able to *feel* the pulse, a matter of experience not of theory.

But several of the Greek medical texts we considered start, as it were, further back. They have in mind an audience who may be inclined to deny that there is such a thing as the medical art at all, or who have a totally different view of what that art consists in from the writers of the texts in question. Here there is a radical vulnerability on no less than three scores. As we saw from Galen's remarks on his predecessors and contemporaries, there was not just a rivalry between Greek doctors who shared agreed medical practices but offered a different justification for their use: there was also bitter dispute about what practices to adopt, what a disease is, what the doctor had to treat. To that had to be added the threat, mostly from outside medicine itself, of the denial of the claim that medicine is based on *knowledge* at all.

We discussed in Chapter 2 the nature of the rivalries that existed between intellectuals of different types in China and in Greece, and I argued there that in Greece, dispute and argument were fundamental to the ways in which individuals or groups recruited adherents and won intellectual prestige. We can now see what a potent, and potentially self-destructive, weapon methodology provided in such disputes.

On the one hand, it laid the basis for claims of superiority – of one inquiry or discipline over another, or of one style of conducting the same inquiry over another style: you undermined your opponents with the argument that their study or practice must be wrong, since their methods were.

On the other hand, foundational disagreements, in the Greek manner, tended to problematise the very viability of any inquiry itself. It was not just that an inquiry might be deemed to be flawed or inferior if it did not yield certainty, though the high ground was captured by those who could sustain *that* claim. In the case of medicine, the question was whether it could be said to be any more than just a matter of chance. If it did not yield certainty and was not exact, how could it be defended against the accusation that it was mere guesswork?[40]

I have conjectured that one of the factors in the background to those Greek preoccupations with the demand for certainty was the need that some of the philosophers felt to distance themselves from those whom they generally considered to be no more than mere opportunistic purveyors of the plausible. Our next study will tackle some of the issues from the point of view of those whom those philosophers tried thus to marginalise, that is, from the side of rhetoric and the development of the techniques of persuasion.

40. For further discussion of alternative Greek models of medicine, I may refer to Lloyd 1991b.

CHAPTER 4

The techniques of persuasion

Every scientific work aims to persuade, though that goal generally remains implicit and is not spelt out by the author. Ancient
scientific works in China and in Greece are no exception, and in
both societies some explicit attention is given to the question of
the techniques of persuasion in general. In China, for instance,
the 戰國策, *Zhanguoce*, contains a variety of anecdotes retailing
strategems and devices, including argumentative devices, that
enabled their users to get their way, influencing people, winning
them over, overcoming their objections or resistance, getting them
to do what was wanted. Moreover, 韓非子, *Hanfeizi*, 12 – the *Shuo
Nan* 'chapter' to which we have already referred – provides a
classic analysis of the theme of, as its title puts it, the 'difficulties
of persuasion'.

In ancient Greece, both the practice and the theory of rhetoric
underwent rapid development in the −5th and −4th centuries.
Treatises on rhetoric go back to the (now lost) works of Corax
and Teisias, and Aristotle's *Rhetoric*, in three books, refers frequently to his predecessors' treatment. The occasions for the
practice of rhetoric included the extensive political and legal
debates, in the assemblies, councils and law-courts, that were
such a prominent feature of the life of Greek citizens. This was
especially true of the democracies, and one democracy in particular, Athens, provides us with the bulk of our extant evidence of classical political and legal speeches. But we should not
underestimate the extent to which the oligarchies, too, engaged
in political debate, even though the decisions there lay in the
hands of a smaller group, the 'few' rather than the 'many'.
True, the Spartans prided themselves, and were admired by
others, for not wasting words, and the Athenians, conversely,
had a reputation not just for argumentativeness but also for

litigiousness. However, techniques of persuasion are certainly not confined to just one type of Greek city-state, let alone just to Athens.

I have suggested before that the negative reaction of some philosophers, primarily Plato and Aristotle, not just to the practice of rhetoric, but also to the way it was taught – by rival intellectuals ('sophists') – was an important part of the stimulus to formulate and define the strictest mode of demonstration, one that would secure far more than the persuasive, indeed not just truth, but certainty, incontrovertibility. I have also pointed out that certain features of that concept of demonstration – notably its axiomatic basis – are peculiarly Greek and have no counterpart in the notions of proof developed in classical Chinese thought, whether in mathematics or elsewhere. There, as we have seen in Chapter 3, what we have is, rather, proof procedures used for the verification of algorithms and associated with an interest in the correspondences between the features of mathematical reasoning deployed in different types of problems.

This suggests as a further question for investigation, the comparisons and contrasts in the theories and practices of persuasion in general. In part, this is interesting for its own sake: what are the important similarities and differences first in the contexts of Chinese and Greek persuasion, and then in its modes or techniques? But in part, too, this should help to throw light on that further issue of the background to the Greek contrast between the merely persuasive and the certain. I shall begin with a rapid survey of a selection of the Chinese materials before turning to the Greek ones.

The *Zhanguoce* is a compendium of nearly 500 anecdotes compiled during the Han in most cases from earlier materials. These anecdotes set out how advisers of different types – ministers, courtiers, visitors, even rulers themselves – tried to get certain courses of action adopted. The overwhelming majority of the stories take the ruler or some person in power as the target. In the course of the highly diverse stories themselves, many general dicta appear, about human nature, about the vagaries of fortune and so on. The techniques of persuasion used are allowed to speak for themselves and are not the subject of explicit general analysis. But much attention is paid to such matters as establishing the *bona fides* of the adviser and undermining that of anyone countering his advice.

Two recurrent argumentative strategies are, first, the use of dilemmatic arguments, and secondly, analogies. Dilemmatic arguments take different forms.[1] In one type, a course of action is recommended both positively and negatively – the latter via an exploration of the consequences of its non-adoption. But in another, advocacy of a scheme proceeds by an argument that *whatever* the outcome, the scheme is advantageous. Thus in *Zhanguoce* Zhao 205: 107, 3ff, permission to allow the troops of Wei to pass through Zhao to attack another state is advocated on the basis of the argument that *whether or not* Wei succeeds in its attack, Zhao will gain an advantage. Conversely at Eastern Zhou 10B: 4, 20ff, a ruler about to attack Qi is warned against an alliance with Qin on the grounds that *whether or not* the attack on Qi is successful, it will be Qin that will be strengthened.

Analogical arguments, in *Zhanguoce* as elsewhere in classical Chinese texts,[2] appear in a vast variety of guises. In *Zhanguoce* sometimes the analogue is a historical precedent or otherwise similar set of actual or reported events. But often too the comparisons are drawn from further afield, from folk-tale or fable, involving, for example, the real or imagined behaviour of animals. Thus in the famous story of the tiger and the fox (Chu 154: 81, 3ff), the fox saves his own life by claiming that the other animals are afraid of him. To persuade the tiger that this is so, he gets the tiger to follow him into the forest, whereupon indeed the other animals retreat out of fear, though not, of course, of the fox, but of the tiger following behind. In the case to which it is applied, an adviser can accept a report that a certain part of the country is afraid, but reinterpret who is the real object of that fear.

There need be no explicit analysis of the points of similarity claimed between the two cases compared (the positive analogy) let alone of where they differ (the negative analogy), and the conclusion to be drawn is often left implicit – either when it is obvious, or in order to exploit the analogy's open-endedness.

1. Cf. Crump 1970, pp. 17ff, on 'doubled persuasions'. Cf. more generally Knechtges 1976, p. 25, Kroll 1985–7, p. 124.
2. There are full analyses of the role of analogical reasoning in Chinese thought in Reding 1985 and 1986b.

However, we also find cases where analogical arguments are countered: either the original analogy is reinterpreted, or an alternative analogy is proposed.

A sequence of arguments in the controversy involving Gaozi, Mencius and Xunzi can be cited to illustrate that last point. Gaozi, it will be recalled (cf. p. 28), is said to have held that human nature is indifferent, Mencius that it is good, Xunzi that it is bad. But Gaozi, as reported by Mencius, starts off with a comparison between our nature and willow wood, from which cups and bowls can be made, while Mencius countered by pointing out that that involves cutting and carving, violating the wood indeed. Gaozi then offers a second analogy, with a whirlpool: 'if you open a channel for it in the East, it flows eastward, if you open a channel for it in the West, it flows westward. Man's nature has neither good nor bad allotted to it, just as water has neither East nor West allotted to it.' But that is countered by Mencius by pointing out that water does have a tendency to flow downwards. It can be forced off its course, but that natural tendency remains, just as (Mencius would have it) a person can become bad, but by nature humans are good (Mencius 6A/1, 6A/2, translations from Graham 1989, pp. 120f).

Interestingly, in the continuation of the dispute, in *Xunzi* 23, the comparison with wood reappears – though now with the emphasis on the human intervention necessary to make it useful. Human nature, he argues, has to be forced straight – like crooked wood: 'hence crooked wood inevitably requires steaming and bending with the arrow-straightener to straighten it . . . ; and granted that human nature is bad, it inevitably requires teachers and standards to correct it.' (*Xunzi* 23: 5ff, translation adapted from Graham 1989, p. 246).

The *Zhanguoce* provides a series of models of arguments that can be adapted to the various problems that any adviser would be likely to face. But it does not set out an explicit general analysis of the persuasive techniques involved. *Hanfeizi* 12, the *Shuo Nan* 'chapter', offers just such an analysis, tackling head on the difficulties the adviser will encounter both in recommending courses of action and in protecting his own position.

The key to success, according to the opening arguments, lies in knowing the mind of the person one is trying to persuade. 'If the person you are trying to persuade is out to establish a reputation for virtue, and you talk to him about making a fat profit, then he will regard you as low-bred, accord you a shabby and contemptuous reception, and undoubtedly send you packing. If the person you are trying to persuade is, on the contrary, interested in a fat profit, and you talk to him about a virtuous reputation, he will regard you as witless and out of touch with reality, and will never heed your arguments.' Han Fei then introduces the possibility that the person you are dealing with conceals his real motives, though in this case only one of the two types is considered.

If the person you are trying to persuade is secretly out for big gain but ostensibly claims to be interested in a virtuous name alone, and you talk to him about a reputation for virtue, then he will pretend to welcome and heed you, but in fact will shunt you aside; if you talk to him about making a big gain, he will secretly follow your advice, but ostensibly reject you. These are points that you must not fail to consider carefully. (*Hanfeizi* 12: 221, translation adapted from Burton Watson 1964, p. 73)

The object of this exercise is not just positive – to get your recommended course of action approved – but also defensive. The situation envisaged is not just one of opportunity, but also one of danger. 'Undertakings succeed through secrecy, but fail when the talk is divulged. Although the ruler himself has not yet divulged his plans, if you in your discussions happen to hit upon his hidden motives, then you will be in danger.' This section of the chapter proceeds by itemising no less than six other ways in which the person offering advice may be at risk. Thus 'if some great person gets hold of a good scheme from somewhere and plans to use it to win merit for himself, and you happen to know where he got it, then you will be in danger'.

The important thing in persuasion is to learn how to play up the aspects that the person you are talking to is proud of and play down the aspects he is ashamed of. Thus, if the person has some urgent personal desire, you should show him that it is his public duty to carry it out and urge him not to delay. If he has some mean objective in mind and yet cannot restrain himself, you should do your best to point out to him whatever admirable aspects it may have and minimize the reprehensible ones (*Hanfeizi* 12: 221–2, translations from Burton Watson 1964, pp. 73ff).

What emerges from this subtle and eminently pragmatic

analysis is a picture of the extremely delicate position in which Chinese advisers were often placed *vis-à-vis* those whom they were trying to advise. The principal situation envisaged is one where the adviser has to deal with a ruler or otherwise with a person with power and authority.[3] Their needs to maintain their reputation and not lose face have to be taken into account: their whims have to be humoured, and there is no question of the adviser attempting to be too idealistic in winning the ruler round to a course of action that was 'virtuous' but went against his intentions. The main thrust of the discussion is to advise the adviser to study the ruler's character, to play on his emotions and his vanity, to exploit his weaknesses, to beware of the differences between his real and his expressed intentions – and to do all this, so far as possible, without himself being revealed as a manipulator. The whole is a masterly analysis of the *psychology* of persuasion.

Greek orators, statesmen, advisers were also faced, from time to time, with autocrats who had to be humoured to be won round. But the more typical target audience envisaged in Greek rhetoric is some group of fellow citizens. In Greek law-courts (*dikastēria*) the decisions rested with the 'dicasts': they are conventionally translated 'jurors', but they combined the roles of both judge and jury. There were no 'professional' judges to advise them on points of law. Rather, they were themselves responsible for judging matters of law as well as of fact, deciding on guilt or innocence and delivering sentences as well as verdicts. In the democracies, the dicasts were chosen by lot – a key institution that ensured the wide diffusion of responsibility and experience, in political as well as legal matters. At Athens, a further important development, in the −5th century, was the introduction of pay for service in the dicasteries, a move that was hailed by the friends and the foes of democracy alike as having radical repercussions. Since there could be as many as 5,001 dicasts serving in a single court, participation was widespread: Socrates, for example, we know, was tried by a court numbering 501. Once pay was introduced, the poor were certainly not disadvantaged

3. The target of persuasion is often left unspecified or described merely as a 貴人, *gui ren*, a 'person of eminence', but he is imagined as being in a position to decide policy and to implement it on the highest issues. At the end of the chapter reference is made more clearly to the ruler or master of men, 人主, *ren zhu*.

– and some, to be sure, complained that they exerted an undue
influence in the courts.

The political institutions of the democracies exhibited many of
the same features. In principle all citizens were equal. Any citizen
could attend, and address, the Assembly, and the numbers that
did so attend, at Athens, again ran into thousands. The Athenian constitution underwent certain changes between the –5th
and –4th centuries, notably in the distinction between laws and
decrees – between *nomoi* and *psēphismata* – the former permanent,
the latter of only limited effect.[4] But the people continued to
exercise ultimate sovereignty, in, and through, both the Assemblies and the law-courts. We shall have more to say about the
radical revisability of Greek constitutional arrangements in our
final chapter (pp. 216f).

Moreover the key principle on which democracy rested was
one man, one vote. To be sure, in the democracies, as far more
obviously in the oligarchies, some individual citizens were more
influential than others: the rich, the well-born, the well-connected,
enjoyed a disproportionate share of elective offices, tendencies
that the democracies attempted to counter by extending the
principle of a prior selection of candidates by lot and by severely
limiting eligibility to re-election to the same office. But while
actual political practice, at Athens and elsewhere, did not tally
exactly with the constitutional ideal of equal rights for all citizens, the direct involvement of large numbers of citizens in the
political process, from deciding constitutional questions and
affairs of state, to dispensing justice in the courts, was very considerable judged by the standards of most other societies, ancient
or modern. If that is especially true of Greek democratic constitutions, the point has, as already noted, some validity with
regard to Greek oligarchies as well, insofar as their workings
too involved the active participation of a substantial group of
individuals, even when those with full political rights were the
'few' or the rich, rather than the 'many' including the poor.

Greek citizens thus had ample opportunities to assess others'
attempts at persuasion and indeed to attempt it themselves.
They could address the Assemblies: they *had* to speak on their

---

4. A full analysis of these changes is given by Hansen 1991 with references to earlier
   literature.

own behalf in the law-courts in civil cases. Although from the late
−5th century on, litigants could employ a speech-writer to prepare their cases (indeed some of the extant speeches of Lysias
were written for others to deliver), the litigants themselves gave
the speeches in court. When Greek citizens were not themselves
engaged in forensic or political persuasion, they often found
themselves in audiences evaluating the tactics that others used in
those contexts. They had, indeed, to exercise their critical judgement on that question whenever, as so often, the decision on the
legal or political issue in hand rested with them.

All of this is significant for the development of both the practice and the theory of Greek rhetoric. While, as we shall be elaborating shortly, many of the techniques used in persuasion in
China and in Greece are very similar, at least in general terms,
the contexts of their use vary both in nature and in extent. In
Greece, the people to persuade were your peers, in public meet-
ings of a variety of kinds, including political assemblies and law-
suits. In China, as we have remarked before, the overwhelming
concentration of interest, in our extant texts at least, is in persuading the ruler. The occasions on which people other than
the ruler's immediate entourage would need to develop skills
in speaking were, accordingly, by comparison very rare.

The explosion of interest both in the practice and in the theory of rhetoric that occurred in Greece from the mid −5th century occasioned a good deal of comment, some of it neutral or
favourable, but much of it adverse. First as to origins: Corax and
Teisias, mentioned by Plato and by Aristotle, are, as noted, the
first we hear of to have written treatises on rhetoric, called simply
Arts, technai. Cicero quotes an account he attributes to Aristotle
concerning the circumstances.[5] Both Corax and Teisias were based
in Syracuse which in the mid- −5th century enjoyed a half century or so of democratic rule between earlier, and then later,
tyrannies. In this account, the particular stimulus to these early
rhetorical theorists came from the help sought in litigation by
returning exiles attempting to recover their property which had
been appropriated when they had been expelled by earlier tyrants. That serves to symbolise the connection between rhetoric

5. Cicero, *Brutus* 46f, which probably refers to a now lost work of Aristotle, the *Collection of Arts.*

and litigation, even if (1) we have no grounds for supposing that rhetoric was confined to the democracies, and (2) it is clear that its eventual use was not limited to litigation. For Aristotle, for instance, there are three main branches of rhetoric, namely forensic, deliberative and 'epideictic' (the rhetoric of praise and blame).

Certainly some of the early practitioners evoked an admiring reaction. We hear that when Gorgias came as an ambassador for his home state of Leontini to Athens in −427, his performance caused a sensation. We have two of his epideictic speeches, the *Helen* and the *Palamedes*, from which to judge both the elaborateness of his style and the artfulness of his persuasive tactics. In the *Helen*, in particular, he comments directly on the power of *logos* (the term covers 'word' 'speech' and 'argument'). The aim of that speech is to exonerate Helen of Troy from wrong-doing. If she did what she did because she was persuaded by *logoi*, then she is not guilty, for such is the power of *logoi* that to be persuaded by them is tantamount to being *forced* to do what you do.

This can be seen, the speech continues, in the arguments/ speeches of the philosophers and the 'meteorologists' (those who studied things in the heavens or things under the earth – the inquiry concerning nature, in other words) as well as those engaged in forensic contests. The very speech that invites us to accept its arguments about Helen, plays on the ambivalence of speech and argument itself, for they do violence to the hearers and exploit mere seeming as opposed to the truth. It is particularly striking, in view of later developments, that for Gorgias, forensic, philosophical and (broadly) scientific discussions *all* exemplify the same power – and the same ambivalence.[6]

Gorgias and others evidently enjoyed considerable success. We are told by Plato that Hippias especially made large sums of money with his teaching.[7] Yet many saw the new techniques of speaking, and those who taught them, as dangerously subversive. The objections took a variety of forms, with charges of immorality, corruption, irresponsibility, overlapping with the apparently lesser complaints that the new rhetoric traded in the merely

6. See Lloyd 1979, pp. 82ff, with reference to earlier studies, and cf. most recently Wardy forthcoming b.
7. Plato, *Hippias Major* 282de. The theme of the sophists' pay is a recurrent one in Plato, cf. *Protagoras* 349a, *Hippias Minor* 364d, *Theages* 127e f.

plausible. While the grounds of the objections varied, so too did the individuals or groups objected to. While the term 'orator' (*rhētōr*) was neutral, the term 'sophist' came to be used, on occasion, with marked pejorative undertones, when applied to various representatives of the new learning. Those so labelled taught a variety of subjects – and did so for money – but pre-eminent among those subjects was rhetoric or skill in public speaking.

One recurrent charge was that the sophists taught people how to make the worse, or weaker, cause appear the better, or stronger. It is not just Plato and Aristotle who made the accusation – Aristotle naming Protagoras in particular in this connection, *Rhetoric* 1402a23ff – but also, for example, Aristophanes, who produced an elaborate competitive debate between the Just and the Unjust Logos in the *Clouds* 889ff. We can certainly verify that some teachers of rhetoric composed model speeches arguing both sides of a case. The *Tetralogies* of Antiphon provide some extant examples, with paired speeches arguing first the prosecution's, then the defence's, case. Again the anonymous treatise known as the *Dissoi Logoi*, or Double Arguments, develops antithetical theses in a more general, and not specifically forensic, context. Yet the idea that any of these were direct incitements to immorality was clearly an exaggeration: their purpose was, rather, to train the speaker to appreciate what, on any occasion, his opponents might say.

For Plato, as is well known, the chief culprits were those he labelled 'sophists', though these ranged from those such as Protagoras, Gorgias, Hippias – for whom he has a certain respect – to a variety of lesser figures, such as the logic-chopping Euthydemus and Dionysodorus, by way of the dangerous immoralists represented by Thrasymachus and Callicles. But for Aristophanes, for instance, the prototype of the new subversive learning was Socrates himself – later to be tried and convicted for, among other things, corrupting the youth. The Aristophanic image of Socrates made Plato's task all the more urgent, since for Plato, Socrates was the model of the true inquirer into wisdom, a genuine educator, concerned with the soul's welfare, not with monetary gain, indeed an educator who, according to Plato, never taught for money.

The relations between 'philosophy', 'sophistic', 'rhetoric', 'politics', thus became a veritable battlefield. Where Gorgias, as we found, runs philosophical, scientific and forensic arguments together, we see from a passage in Thucydides that in the political debate there were those who tried to distance responsible political argument from the kind of rhetoric they associated with the sophists.

An episode in the Mytilenean debate (Thucydides III 37ff) brings out the *actual* overlap between the styles of persuasion used in different contexts. Cleon is there made to rebuke his audience – the Athenians in Assembly – on the grounds that they are easily misled. Everyone, he says, wants to be an orator, and is reluctant to yield to anyone else in quickness of wit, praising sharp remarks before they are out of someone's mouth. The trouble is that they do not treat serious matters sufficiently seriously, but rather behave more like those spectating at a performance of sophists than like people deliberating on affairs of state. Gorgias had indeed asserted that one should destroy one's opponents' seriousness with laughter, and their laughter with seriousness (Aristotle, *Rhetoric* 1419b2ff), and we may be sure that such a tactic was used in both political and other debates. But there is, of course, a particular irony, in Thucydides, in that it is Cleon – otherwise represented as an irresponsible demagogue and a dangerous manipulator of the Assembly – who should accuse the Athenians of not discharging their responsibilities in their political debates and of being too easily manipulated.

It is now time to turn back to the more purely philosophical reaction to the development of the practice and theory of rhetoric. Plato, as we have pointed out before, insisted on the contrast between true philosophy on the one hand, and both rhetoric and sophistic as currently practised on the other. That contrast, in his view, corresponded to a contrast between a concern for truth and certainty, on the side of philosophy, and one for the merely plausible and for persuasion, on the other side – contrasts that were to prove a significant stimulus, so I argued, to the development, in Greek thought, of the ideal of strict demonstrative proof.

Where Aristotle, in turn, agrees with Plato, and where he diverges from him, are alike important for our concerns here. He is as keen as Plato to contrast merely probable arguments with strictly demonstrative ones. In the strictest acceptance of the term, demonstration, *apodeixis*, must meet very rigorous criteria.

First, the inferences must be valid deductions: indeed Aristotle supposes that these will be syllogistic in form. Then secondly, the ultimate premisses of such deductions must be true, necessary, primary, and explanatory of the conclusions. The kind of arguments used in rhetoric – and indeed also in dialectic – are bound to be inferior, since *their* premisses are merely probable. They are the generally accepted opinions or the opinions of respected authorities, the *endoxa*, or whatever views your partner or opponent accepts.

But if strict demonstration, in Aristotle as in Plato, has as its goal incontrovertibility, Aristotle explicitly allows a more positive role to rhetoric than Plato did. Indeed Aristotle even permits another type of demonstration, labelled, precisely, *rhetorical* demonstration. He is prepared to use the very same term, *apodeixis*, that he employs of the strictest axiomatic deductive demonstration defined in the *Posterior Analytics*. From one point of view, this should not surprise us, when we recall that there were plenty of orators and others, before Plato and after him, who used that term of their own arguments (cf. above, pp. 56ff at n. 11 and n. 14). They *claimed* to have *proved* their cases, that is not, of course, by means of axiomatic deductive demonstrations, but by methods that established the conclusions beyond reasonable doubt.

But Aristotle's notion of rhetorical demonstration differs from the actual demonstrations we find in Greek orators in one fundamental respect, namely that the analysis he offers of the topic takes syllogistic as its standard of comparison. There are two main types of argument used in rhetoric, so we are told at *Rhetoric* 1356a35ff, namely the 'enthymeme' and the 'paradigm'. But the enthymeme, in Aristotle's view, is the counterpart, in rhetoric, of the syllogism, while the paradigm is the counterpart of induction.[8]

The way in which Aristotle thereby scores a multiple victory over a variety of opponents is truly remarkable. On the one hand, he complains that earlier writers on rhetoric had only dealt with a small part of the art (*Rhetoric* 1354a11ff). They omitted political

8. On the meaning of the term 'enthymeme' and the background to Aristotle's use of it in his rhetoric, see Burnyeat 1994. While Burnyeat successfully shows what Aristotle owes to earlier practice, it remains the case that Aristotle's is the first fully elaborated *theory* of the enthymeme that we have.

oratory and discussed only forensic (1354b22ff), Moreover, most of what they had to say was on what is 'outside the subject-matter', that is, not to do with the substance of the cases in question. As Aristotle explains, 'prejudice and pity and anger and such-like affections of the soul are not to do with the subject-matter, but are directed at the dicast' (1354a15ff). In particular earlier writers said nothing about the enthymeme, which is the 'body' of proof (1354a14ff).

It is certainly possible that Aristotle has here exaggerated the limitations of earlier rhetorical treatises for his own polemical purposes. Later, when he deals with apparent, or fallacious, enthymemes in *Rhetoric* II ch. 24, he concedes that the *Art* of Corax concentrated heavily on the topic of the likely or probable (*eikos*) (1402a17ff, cf. Plato's *Phaedrus* 266e, 267a, where Teisias, Gorgias and Theodorus are mentioned in the same connection). However, to the extent that Aristotle's diagnosis of the limitations in his predecessors' treatments is valid, it would have the striking implication that those, pre-Aristotelian, treatises on rhetoric were appreciably closer to Chinese discussions of persuasion than Aristotle's own work was. The fundamental respect in which that would hold is that, concentrating on prejudice, pity, anger and so on, they focussed on the psychological aspects of persuasion – and in that would be comparable with the discussion of 'the difficulties of persuasion' in *Hanfeizi* 12 – even though there is still this difference, that the contexts of the imagined use of persuasive techniques varied, in China and in Greece, in that the chief Greek targets were, as Aristotle says, the dicasts, not the ruler.

But if Aristotle claims superiority over earlier Greek writers on rhetoric because he included what they omitted, namely the analysis of rhetorical proofs, the *actual* analysis that Aristotle gives enables him to score a second victory, over rhetoric itself judged from the stand-point of strict, axiomatic-deductive, demonstration.

Rhetorical demonstration falls short of strict demonstration on three main counts. First, the enthymeme does not necessarily make all its premises explicit, for when a point is well known, it is omitted (*Rhetoric* 1357a16ff). Secondly, and more fundamentally, it does not use necessary premises, but rather merely probable ones or signs (*Prior Analytics* 70a10ff, cf. *Rhetoric*

1357a22–32). Thirdly, where demonstration is needed, in rhetoric, is on unclear or disputed points: when something is clear, there is seldom need to demonstrate it (*Rhetoric* 1417b32ff). If indeed a forensic orator had premisses that were true, primary, immediate, better known than, prior to, and explanatory of, the conclusions – as the *Posterior Analytics* demands – the last thing he would dream of needing to do is to proceed to a demonstration.

The second main type of rhetorical argument identified by Aristotle, in addition to the enthymeme, namely the paradigm, also exhibits certain differences from induction outside rhetoric. Induction in general aims to establish true *universal* propositions – the premisses that will be needed in deductive syllogisms. Indeed Aristotle's discussion of induction, in *Prior Analytics* II ch. 23, 68b15ff, envisages complete induction, the review of *all* the particulars exemplifying a universal, precisely because he there has in mind what induction contributes to syllogistic.[9]

Paradigms, by contrast, proceed by the direct comparison of two similar cases. The three main types of such analogical arguments that he describes in the *Rhetoric* II ch. 20, 1393a22ff, are (1) the appeal to historical examples, (2) *parabolai* ('illustrations' – exemplified here by the kinds of comparisons Socrates used) and (3) fables (as in Aesop's animal fables). All three types are indeed much used by Greek orators. Moreover, as our earlier survey showed, plenty of examples of analogical arguments, of these very same general types, are found also in classical Chinese writers. The first point of contrast there, however, is that the Chinese do not analyse or classify them *as such*: and the second that there is certainly no suggestion that they should be judged inferior from the stand-point of another mode of argument, induction, the stricter review of particulars brought into play in relation to syllogistic.

Let me now recapitulate the main points that our investigation has brought to light. First, it is clear and important that in both ancient civilisations, Greece and China, techniques of persuasion were not only widely deployed, but were also the subject of explicit, self-conscious reflection.

However, secondly, as to the contexts of their deployment, the

9. Some aspects of the relationship between Aristotelian 'induction' (*epagōgē*), paradigms, and analogical reasoning in general, are discussed in Lloyd 1966, pp. 405–14. Cf. McKirahan 1992, ch. 18, with references to recent scholarship.

existence of such institutions as the dicasteries and the popular assemblies, in the Greek city-states, ensured both an extensive interest in, and a familiarity with, the topic of what is effective in persuasion among large numbers of Greek citizens. Some Greek and Roman writers connected the rise of teachers of rhetoric to such institutions, particularly well-developed in the democracies, though neither the theory nor the practice of Greek rhetoric was solely confined to democratic constitutions. The emergence of those who sought to teach the subject contributed, however, to the attention paid to how persuasion worked, the attempt to formulate its rules, to present it as an *art* – where the teachers themselves evidently vied with one another to give the most persuasive account of the techniques of persuasion. The Chinese, too, as we saw, developed analyses of persuasion, but *Hanfeizi* 12 concentrates on persuasion of a single individual, the powerful man or ruler, and is directed at those who sought to influence such. Thus both the extent, and the contexts, of persuasion, in the two ancient societies, differ.

So too, thirdly, do the types of analyses offered. The great strength of the *Shuo Nan* discussion in *Hanfeizi* 12 is the subtlety it brings to the diagnosis of motivations. What Plato had to say on that subject in the *Phaedrus*, 271d, for example, is thin by comparison.[10] The *Shuo Nan* exploration of the interplay between pretended, and actual, intentions, and of how the adviser's exploitation of that interplay has sometimes itself to be concealed, offers an analysis of the psychology of persuasion that goes beyond anything to be found in the early Greek handbooks, even though they are certainly aware of the emotive effects of certain tactics and discuss such matters as how to win sympathy, appear responsible or create prejudice. Part of the reason for the contrast is obvious. Evidently when the target of persuasion is a single person, the question of his real or pretended motivations has a sharp focus. While the crowded court or assembly could be swayed, capturing their individual motives was necessarily more complex.

The extra element, fourthly, that comes to be introduced into

---

10. Again, when in the *Rhetoric* II chh. 12–14, 1388b31ff, Aristotle offers an analysis of the characters of the different types of audience that an orator might face, he does so in terms of very broad distinctions between 'young', 'old' and 'men in their prime'.

Greek analyses is the attempt to classify and evaluate the argument schemata that the rhetorician uses or should use. The particular reasons for this development are no doubt complex, but we can pin-point some of the factors in play, at least where Aristotle is concerned. His claim was that earlier writers had, on the whole, omitted such an analysis. It is not that arguments were not always part of persuasion: but the attempt to generalise their various types coincides, in his case, with the further ambition to establish the similarities, and more especially the differences, between rhetoric as a whole, and a higher, purer, style of reasoning in philosophy.

Like Plato, we said, Aristotle drives a wedge between persuasion and strict demonstration, the former dealing with the probable or the plausible, the latter with what is incontrovertibly true. Yet unlike Plato, Aristotle is prepared to allow demonstration of a kind in rhetoric also. Rhetoric aims at persuasion, to be sure, but it uses arguments among its many resources. The analysis of rhetorical argument is then represented as an important part of the *Art* – the basis of one of Aristotle's claims to outdo his predecessors on that subject. But the kinds of argument rhetoric uses are analysed in terms derived from Aristotle's account of the strictest form of demonstration, and this has the immediate effect of downgrading those arguments when compared with philosophical ones.

In our earlier chapter on adversariality (Chapter 2) we identified certain similarities and differences in the modes of rivalry found *within* Greek and Chinese philosophy and science. The focus of our discussion there was chiefly the rivalry between groups of individuals engaged (broadly) in the same inquiries, philosophers, say, or mathematicians, or doctors. Our study of the development of techniques of persuasion enables us to say more on the modes of rivalry *across* groups.

One strikingly prominent feature of the interrelations of intellectuals of different kinds in –5th and –4th-century Greece is the controversy over the relations between rhetoric and philosophy. For some, such as Gorgias, the arguments deployed in forensic contexts, in philosophy and in science were on all fours with one another: all dealt in persuasion. But then first Plato and then Aristotle insisted that true philosophy is utterly distinct from rhetoric, in its aims, its motives and its methods.

Yet their views, in turn, achieved far less than universal acceptance. Isocrates, for one, Plato's contemporary, was to call his
own, largely rhetorical, educational programme 'philosophy'.
Many Stoics, too, accepted a positive role for dialectic within
philosophy. Chrysippus, for example, acknowledged that those
who wished to inculcate knowledge should instruct their pupils
not just positively but also negatively, surveying the arguments on
the opposite side and destroying them 'just as is done in the
dicasteries'.[11]

As we have seen, Chinese philosophers and scientists disagreed
strongly with one another on all sorts of issues and there is no
lack of variety among those who engaged in persuasion. But while
different modes of persuasion can certainly be exemplified in different contexts in Chinese mathematics, medicine, philosophy,
politics, no one style of reasoning attempts explicitly to distinguish
itself from the others by contrasting its own modes of argument
with those of its rivals. Just as law-courts did not supply positive
models for adversariality, no more were they the source of negative ones of a style of argument that philosophy should avoid. No
Chinese group attempted to mark itself out as different from,
and superior to, all others, on the grounds that it could deliver,
what no one else could, more than just what is persuasive, namely
the incontrovertibly true.

For that to occur in Greece, the philosophers in question had
to envisage an alternative audience to the general public gathered
in the assembly, in the law-courts, or indeed to hear sophistic
exhibition lectures and debates. Those philosophers shuddered
at the idea that the outcome of a discussion should be settled
by majority vote. Their preferred audience was their fellows,
their colleagues or followers. Yet they did not *put aside* their

---

11. The evidence for this comes chiefly from admittedly hostile sources. Thus Chrysippus'
view is reported and criticised by Plutarch, *On Stoic Self-Contradictions* 1035f ff. For
Plutarch himself, anything that savoured of arguing both sides of a question – *in
utramque partem* – was abhorrent, no doubt because of the associations that had with
the practices of the sophists that Plato and others had anathematised (see above,
p. 83). But further than that, Plutarch objects to anything that might seem to assimilate or confuse philosophy with forensic advocacy – the former contending for truth,
the latter for victory, 1036ab. So it is clear that Chrysippus' point of view, as Plutarch
reports it, represents what Plutarch would consider a damaging admission. However
Plutarch's own further remarks, 1036d ff, suggest that Chrysippus himself had his
own reservations about arguing both sides of the question, when that undermines
correct apprehension.

experience as citizens when they attended lectures in the philosophical schools. Aristotle as good as admits as much in two telling passages. At *Rhetoric* 1354a4ff he remarks that both rhetoric and dialectic are *universally* practised, at least up to a point. 'Everyone' – all Greeks, that is – 'tries to some degree to examine and uphold an argument, to defend themselves and to accuse.' That, to be sure, is in the context of his own discussions of rhetoric. But in his cosmology as well, at *On the Heavens* 294b7ff, he concedes that 'we are all in the habit of relating an inquiry not to the subject-matter, but to our opponent in argument'.

The intra- and cross-disciplinary rivalries that permeate Greek intellectual life are often just below the surface even among those who protested that they were above the fray of competitive debate. But the final irony has yet to be mentioned. The key claim in the Platonic and Aristotelian conceptions of high philosophy was that it could yield strict demonstration, incontrovertibility and truth. Yet appeal to the truth is recognised as a technique of persuasion.

In fact, of course, Greek orators too claimed that the truth was on their side with great regularity, just as they frequently announced that they had proved their cases. Aristotle indeed recognises the strength of the appeal to the truth in argument (*Rhetoric* 1355a20ff). But that comes in a passage where he had just said that the truth, and what is like the truth, come under the purview of the same faculty. The problem was, of course, to discriminate them, to distinguish what is true from what merely appears as such.

The riskiness of the Aristotelian claims becomes apparent. Rhetoric and dialectic, the claim is, argue both sides of the question, but philosophy is one-sided and seeks the truth alone. But as the later sceptics were to argue, the problem was to define the criteria that could be invoked to uphold the claim to have indeed secured the truth and not just what appears to be true. In the Aristotelian theory of strict demonstration the self-evidence of the primary premisses is crucial, and yet also crucially problematic.

As we have said before, the Greek ambition to deliver incontrovertible conclusions was no sooner expressed than it tended to be controverted. The highest style of philosophy owes more to rhetoric than it lets on, even at the point where it strives to distance itself from rhetoric. For, after all, it does not escape its own rhetoric. The claim was that it was not merely persuasive: it was demonstrative. But demonstration based on the truth was the supremely persuasive kind of argument.

The form of the claim was clear enough. Demonstrations proceeded by valid deductive arguments from premisses that are true and necessary. Rhetoric, with its use of the probable, its appeal to the feelings or the emotions of the audience, was bound to have to accept that its rhetorical demonstrations failed by the standards set by philosophy. Yet while the structure of the philosophical claim is clear, the problem there was to exemplify and practise what it preached, and as Aristotle's scientific treatises themselves amply illustrate, the actual securing of those primary indemonstrables was bound to prove elusive.

For the classical Chinese, formal logic, and the type of analysis of argument schemata that depends on it, were quite alien, and so the attempt to analyse rhetorical arguments in terms of their formal validity would, no doubt, have seemed a distraction from the exploration of the pragmatic, inter-personal aspects of persuasion. Moreover, as we have seen, for Aristotle at least, the classification of rhetorical arguments was not undertaken *just* for its own sake, but also for the polemical purpose of distinguishing them from his own style of high philosophising. Of course, Chinese thinkers, for their part, were not always engaged in persuasion, of the ruler or anyone else. But for them, the alternative was not another style of discursive reasoning – that could somehow claim to outdo all the others – but rather a matter of practising wisdom. Cleverness in speaking was suspect in China, as it also was in Greece, but far more radically so in China, in that what merely plausible speaking was there contrasted with was not another mode of speaking or reasoning at all, but a matter of being, that of the sage, the living embodiment of the *Dao*.

CHAPTER 5

Causes and correlations

One might assume that the, or a, notion of cause is universal. Given that humans are intentional creatures, surely some concept of agency is presupposed by all humans whether or not it is precisely the same concept, and whether or not that idea serves as the basis for a more general understanding of causal relations. That may or may not be true of implicit human beliefs or assumptions.[1] However, as soon as we focus on the *explicit* vocabulary available to discuss notions of causation in different societies, wide cross-cultural diversity becomes apparent. The study of ancient Greece and of ancient China, in particular, reveals certain striking differences both in the extent of the theoretical interest in the topic of causation and in the forms that interest took.

The Greeks were evidently preoccupied by the question, and not just in philosophy and science. The ancient Chinese, by contrast, did not develop elaborate theories of causation, though of course in many contexts they engaged in discussion and analysis of what causes or brings about what. Much Chinese theoretical effort was devoted not to establishing cause-effect relationships, but rather to setting up schemas of correlations. Correlative thinking, so it has been argued,[2] is their forte, as distinct from, and indeed opposed to, causal theorising.

The aim of this chapter is to assess the hypotheses that these preliminary observations may suggest. First, how far does a contrast between a cause-oriented Greek culture and a correlation-oriented Chinese one hold water? Second, if we find differences and contrasts here, can we even begin to say why?

1. Sperber *et al.*, ed., 1995 contains a collection of studies analysing many of the problems primarily from the point of view of developmental psychology.
2. See, for example, Needham, 1956, pp. 253ff. One of the earliest systematic Western analyses of Chinese correlative thinking or use of correspondences was Granet 1934, pp. 375ff. Cf. also Henderson 1984, Schwartz 1985, ch. 9, Graham 1986, 1989, pp. 319ff.

I shall begin with an analysis of some of the varieties of Greek ideas about causes. I shall then attempt a brief survey of some Chinese notions of causes and of the forms that correlative thinking took and the purposes it served. That will lead me back to the Greeks, for they, for sure, were no strangers to correlative thinking, though not necessarily primarily of the types that flourished in ancient China. The picture that emerges from even a highly selective discussion is appreciably more complex than my initial characterisation allows. As to the underlying factors that might be held to account for such similarities and differences as we find, the tentative nature of the suggestions that I have to propose should once again be emphasised at the outset.

In approaching the ancient Greek concern with causes, one difficulty lies in the potential for muddle in our own, philosophical or lay, concepts – on such questions as the relations between causes, motives, reasons and explanations – muddles that have often been diagnosed as the source of misinterpretations of ancient Greek ideas. Our best tactic is to revert to the Greeks' own terminology, and if that gives our discussion an air of unfamiliarity, there may be advantages as well as disadvantages in that.

Their primary terms include *aition, aitia, prophasis*. The first two cover what is responsible, what is to blame, and the cognate masculine *aitios* can be used of the guilty party. The third, *prophasis*, is more complex and disputed. It can be used of an excuse or pretext, offered as justification for certain behaviour, but it has been suggested (Rawlings 1975) that the term is used in medical texts of the –5th century for the precondition of a disease, useful to the doctor in predicting it. In that context it is close to *sēmeion* (sign) and contrasted with the necessary or primary cause, *aition*. However, both in other medical texts and elsewhere, *prophasis* is often used as a synonym for *aition*, that is to say as 'cause' (Rawlings 1975, cf. Lloyd 1979, pp. 53f).

The prominence of this whole nexus of ideas, both in classical texts and in later Greek literature, is striking. The historians of the –5th century, for instance, are concerned to identify the *real* causes of historical events, as opposed, that is, to what the parties involved may have alleged. One famous example is Thucydides' discussion of the true causes of the Peloponnesian War (I 23), where he uses, indeed, a contrast between *aitia* and *prophasis* for this purpose. Again, contemporary medical writers are frequently exercised over the distinction between the causes of an illness and merely concomitant factors. Thus the author of *On Regimen* III ch. 70, *CMG* I 2 4, 202.11f, remarks that 'the sufferer always lays blame on the thing he may happen to do at the time of the illness, even though this is not responsible (*aition*)'. In *On Ancient Medicine*, too, ch. 21, *CMG* I 1, 52.17ff, the writer observes that doctors as well as lay people tend to assign the cause of a disease to something unusual that the patient has done near the onset of the complaint, such as 'taking a bath or going for a walk or eating something different'.

Similar preoccupations continue, and with a richer conceptual framework in which to talk about and analyse them, in Plato and Aristotle, and thereafter in Hellenistic philosophy and medicine. It is not just that a great deal of attention is paid to aetiologising, that is, to giving substantive answers to substantive questions about the causes of different types of things or events. A considerable effort was also expended to clarifying the notion of *aition* itself, or rather to justifying one interpretation of it against others, one framework for the aetiologies against rival frameworks.

Among the areas of ancient Greek dispute that complicate our task of matching their concepts against our own ideas of causation and of explanation are the following (cf. Frede 1980). Should *aition* and *aitia* be thought of as entities, substances, bodies or whatever? Or are they events? Or are they predicates, or do they correspond to statements, propositional items? Some Greek writers appear to use the two terms more or less interchangeably, but Chrysippus, for instance, is reported by Stobaeus (I 139) to have distinguished an *aitia*, as the statement (*logos*) of an *aition*, from the *aition* itself. That view would tend to make *aitia* approximate to 'explanation', *aition* rather to 'cause'.

Again, are the effects activities, or events, or objects, or the bringing about of a certain change in the *being* of a thing? There is a distinction, in some of our sources, between an Aristotelian view, where the effect is described by a noun (for example, a ship, a liquefaction), and a Stoic view, where the cause is a cause of a predicate's being true of something, where the effect is expressed by a verb (for example, something's coming to be a ship, or something being liquefied). Sextus Empiricus reports those views, in order to cast doubt on both of them from his own, sceptical, position (*Outlines of Pyrrhonism* (*P*) III 14). A quotation from Clement's *Miscellanies* (VIII 9 26) serves to illustrate both the sophistication of some Greek discussions and how far away they are from some of our own supposedly basic intuitions:

Hence becoming, and being cut – that of which the cause is a cause – since they are activities, are incorporeal. It can be said, to make the same point, that causes are causes of predicates, or, as some say, of sayables (*lekta*) – for Cleanthes and Archedemus [two Stoics of the late –3rd and –2nd centuries respectively] call predicates 'sayables'. Or else, and preferably, that some are causes of predicates, for example of 'is cut', whose case [i.e. substantival form] is 'being cut', but others of propositions, for example of 'a ship is built', whose case this time is 'a ship's being built'. (Translation from Long and Sedley 1987, I pp. 333f)

Thus there was controversy both about what an *aition* is, and about what would count as an *aition*, however construed. What types of *aition/aitia* are to be sought or investigated? Aristotle arrived at his systematic and would-be comprehensive analysis of the four types (material, formal, final and efficient) by claiming that they subsume, and go beyond, all his predecessors' thinking on the subject.[3] The matter corresponds to what a thing is made of, the form to the characteristic features that make it the thing it is, the final cause is its function or the good it serves, and the efficient picks out what brings it about. Thus in the case of an object such as a table, its matter may be wood, say; its form is what makes it a table (rather than any other wooden object, say a chair); its final cause corresponds to the function of a table, and the efficient cause is the craftsman who made it. But Aristotle would offer the same type of analysis not just of objects, but also of events.

It is clear that of these four, only the efficient cause looks like a *cause* in any ordinary English sense – even though the convention to speak of all four as causes is still deeply rooted in those who specialise in ancient Greek philosophy. Aristotle maintains, however, that all four correspond to different, but equally valid, questions, asking, in relation to things or to events, 'because of what?', *dia ti*. The answers to all four may tell us something relevant to the full account of what the thing or event is. But it

3. Some of the problematic features of Aristotle's theory of causation are discussed in Moravcsik 1974, Sorabji 1980 and Waterlow 1982.

is not the case that all four types of question will be given positive answers in every case. In particular, not everything has a final cause. Thus residues in the body serve no good, and are just the end-products of natural processes. The residues themselves have no final cause, though the natural processes (for example digestion) certainly do (*On the Parts of Animals* 677a11ff). Again, having eyes of a particular colour serves no purpose, though *having* eyes certainly does (*On the Generation of Animals* 778b16ff).

Moreover, Aristotle also insists that in any type of inquiry there is a distinction between an account merely of the fact, and one that gives the explanation (the reasoned fact). To take one of his examples, one can conclude that planets are near because they do not twinkle, but a strict demonstration proceeds via a middle term that sets out the cause, i.e. it concludes that they do not twinkle because they are near. This means that there is no mere constant conjunction, but an important *asymmetry*, between causes and effects (*Posterior Analytics* I ch. 13, 78a22ff, II ch. 16, 98a35ff).

In this area the Hellenistic philosophers went far beyond Aristotle, offering a variety of overlapping and competing schemata, with Stoic views being particularly influential (Frede 1980, Barnes 1983). How far they were, originally, reacting directly to Aristotle is not clear: the treatises by which we know him were not generally available in Athens in the generations immediately following his death.[4] However, our chief sources for the Stoic view, such as Galen, Alexander, Clement and Stobaeus, were all aware of the broad contrasts between the Aristotelian and the Stoic taxonomies of causation.

For one of the fuller accounts we may go, again, to Clement (*Miscellanies* VIII 9 33). 'When preliminary (*prokatarktikon*) causes are removed the effect remains, whereas a sustaining (*sunektikon*) cause is one during whose presence the effect remains and on whose removal the effect is removed. The sustaining cause is called synonymously the complete (*autoteles*) cause, since it is self-sufficiently productive of the effect.' This makes the sustaining/complete cause a sufficient condition, but then Clement proceeds to other types of cause, auxiliary (*sunergon*) and joint (*sunaition*).

4. For a careful analysis of the direct evidence on the question of the availability of Aristotle's treatises in the decades following his death, see Sandbach 1985.

The difference between the joint cause and the auxiliary cause lies in the fact that the joint cause produces the effect along with another cause which is not independently producing it, whereas the auxiliary cause, in creating the effect not independently but by accruing to another, is acting as auxiliary to the very cause which *is* independently creating the effect, so that the effect is intensified.[5]

Though Clement does not there elaborate on preliminary (*prokatarktikon*) causes, we find a further distinction between them and antecedent (*proēgoumenon*) causes attributed by Galen to a Stoic-influenced medical theorist called Athenaeus (+1st century). Preliminary causes, on this view, are external factors whose function is to produce some change in the body, whatever this change may be.

If what is thus produced in the body belongs to the class of what causes disease, then, while it has not yet actually given rise to the disease, it is known as an antecedent cause ... Often, he says, the sustaining cause is produced directly from the preliminary cause without an intermediary, though sometimes it comes through the medium of the antecedent cause (Galen, *On Sustaining Causes*, 2, *CMG Supp Or.* II 54, cf. 55.16ff, translation from Long and Sedley 1987, I pp. 334f).[6]

We do not know how far this view was shared by the Stoics as a whole, and elsewhere we find other uses of the same term here translated 'antecedent'. But we can see the relevance, in medical theory, of the distinction between external factors and the alterations they produce inside the body. We shall be considering other more general contexts, in which the internal/external contrast is crucial, in due course.

Three general remarks may be made at this stage. First, in the Hellenistic period, the idea that an *aition* is *active* gains ground. We can see this, for instance, in Sextus' general characterisation (*P.* III 14) that 'in the broad sense cause is that by whose activity the effect comes about'. It would appear, therefore, that Aristotelian 'efficient causes' looked to *them* – to Hellenistic philo-

---

5. Translations from Long and Sedley 1987, I p. 336: cf. p. 342 where auxiliary causation is illustrated by the prolonged pushing which will make an already rolling cylinder roll faster, and joint causes – where there is no sustaining cause – by the example of a choir, where the cause of our hearing a harmony is not any one voice, but the combined effect of all.
6. Galen wrote a treatise on preliminary causes (*De Causis procatarcticis*) which is extant only in a Latin version (*CMG Suppl.* II): see Hankinson forthcoming.

sophers – more like *aitia,* just as they look to *us* more like 'causes'
too (Frede 1980, p. 218).

Secondly, two of the major philosophical debates between
Stoics and Epicureans focus on issues to do with causation. First
there was the question as to whether 'final causes' form any valid
part of the proper explanation of things and events. Teleology
and providence were asserted by the Stoics, but just as emphatically denied by the Epicureans. Secondly, there was the issue of
fate and determinism. Is everything determined, and if so, in what
sense? According to some reports, Chrysippus made fate a preliminary, not a complete, cause, though anti-Stoic commentators,
such as Plutarch (*On Stoic Self-Contradictions* 1056b) just countered
that that made him inconsistent. But if the Stoics were certainly
determinists in some sense, the Epicureans defended free will
with the notorious postulate of the 'swerve', a minimal deviation
in the trajectory of an atom that is, by definition, *uncaused.*[7]

Thirdly, in connection with the determinism issue, the distinction between internal and external factors comes to the
fore, and the relative importance of each is fiercely disputed. Our
principal sources, Cicero and Gellius, attribute to Chrysippus a
famous analogy between human action and the rolling of a cylinder. A cylinder does not move without being pushed, but once
pushed, the way the cylinder rolls is due to its own *nature* (sic).
So in human agency, we can distinguish between two factors. An
'assent' does not occur unless prompted by an 'impression'.
But

just as the person who pushed the cylinder gave it its beginning of
motion but not its capacity for rolling, likewise, although the impression encountered will print and, as it were, emblazon its appearance on
the mind, assent will be in our power. And assent, just as we said in the
case of the cylinder, although prompted from outside, will thereafter
move through its own force and nature.[8]

There are, to be sure, many problems connected with the details of the taxonomies on offer, with what they owe to different
thinkers coming to the issues from philosophy or from medicine,

7. Much of the ancient evidence for these debates is assembled by Long and Sedley
1987, I Sections 20, 55 and 62, pp. 102ff, 333ff, 386ff.
8. Cicero, *On Fate,* 42f: *suapte vi et natura* is the expression in 43, *suapte natura* in 42.
Translations from Long and Sedley 1987, I pp. 386ff.

and with the shifts in emphasis that occurred between the classical and the Hellenistic periods, none of which can be broached, however cursorily, here. But enough has perhaps been said to enable me to identify two central and overlapping questions about Greek notions of causation, even if attempting to answer them will involve a good deal of speculation.

First, we may ask what sustains all this concerted interest, in ancient Greece, in *aitia*? Second, what are the principal models or paradigms that the Greeks appealed to: in other words can we identify the chief sources of *their* primary intuitions in this area? I shall try to use the study of the latter question to help answer the former.

The first and fundamental point is a simple one. As has often been remarked, the original connotations of the terms *aition*, *aitia* and their cognates connect them firmly not just with the domain of human behaviour in general, but with what we may broadly call the 'legal' context in particular. *Aition*, I noted, picks out what is 'responsible' for something. *Aitios*, in the masculine, is used of the 'guilty party'. *Aitia* is 'blame' or 'guilt' or the apportioning of such or an accusation imputing blame. These terms *come from* the 'legal' domain, and, I shall claim, the original associations with responsibility *stay* with them to a remarkable degree.

True, other paradigms are also influential. Ideas drawn (1) from the arts, (2) from living creatures, and (3) from the broader political sphere not only permeate particular explanations of specific phenomena,[9] but also provide the basis for the main Greek cosmological theories. Thus ideas based on the arts and crafts are common in Aristotle and others to illustrate final causes, the good or the function that things serve. Even without an explicit concept of final cause, the Presocratic philosopher Empedocles already compared the workings of his cosmic principle *Philia* (love) with metal-working, wood-working, even baking. Living creatures, too, often provide models for goal-directed behaviour. Again, the commonest Greek term for principle and starting-point, namely *archē*, also means seat of authority, rule, even magistracy, and these political notions remain in the background in many of the more general uses of the word.

9. There is an analysis of a selection of the primary evidence for this in Lloyd 1966, Part II ch. 5, pp. 304–83.

The three types of models in question are also the sources of general cosmological doctrines, representations of the world as a unity and as a whole (cf. Lloyd 1966, Part II, ch. 4, pp. 210ff). Several of the Presocratic philosophers already pictured the cosmos as a political state, even though they diverged on the type of state in question. Some, such as Anaximander (–6th century), saw it in terms of a balance of opposed equal powers – and Empedocles represented the relations between his equal cosmic principles as being governed by a 'broad oath', that is, a kind of contract between them. But others (Xenophanes, Anaxagoras, Plato, Aristotle) saw the cosmos as a monarchy, under a single divine ruler: while Heraclitus saw the world in terms of strife or anarchy. As for technological and vitalist images, Plato, for instance, represents the divine ruler as a craftsman, Demiurge, and he speaks of the world itself as a living creature. All three ideas, the world as state, as artefact and as living creature, can be found combined in various Stoic thinkers (e.g. Diogenes Laertius VII 137–143, Eusebius *Evangelical Preparation* XV 15).

This cosmological application of these types of models shows how ready the ancient Greeks were to attempt *unified* explanatory accounts that *start* with causal ideas that seem to us domain-specific, but that *end with* grand generalisations in which the cosmic order as a whole is apprehended on the basis of one or more domain-derived ideas. We shall have more to say on this when we come to consider systems of correspondences and correlative thinking.

The examples so far considered do not exhaust all the types of models used in ancient Greek causal explanations. Let me mention two of the factors that complicate the picture. (1) In various versions of Greek atomism, the changes for which the atoms are responsible are construed in what we may call mechanical terms, though some of the associations of that term should not mislead us. The most complex machines the ancient Greeks knew were the compound pulley, the screw press, the corn mill and the ballista. The interactions of the atoms are typically a result of their colliding, pushing, rebounding, interlocking. That was the way every atom behaved, including the spherical atoms with which the soul was identified. Psychological properties, like all other secondary phenomena, have their ultimate ground in the only real existents, atoms and the void.

(2) Again, various instances of what has been called (some-what anachronistically) 'action at a distance' occur in connection with the Stoic doctrine of 'sympathy'. From the time of Posidonius (−1st century), at least, the lunar cycle and the tides were known to be linked, but in Stoic continuum theory, everything is con-nected with everything else, and systems of resonances play an important role in cosmic relations and in organic ones.[10] In both astrology and medicine, the idea that there are so-called indicat-ive signs provided the basis for inferences and predictions con-cerning the unknown, the internal condition of the body or factors influencing future events.

It would certainly be rash to attempt generalisations across all the disputed areas of Greek causal thinking. But let me now attempt to illustrate some of the contexts in which the notion of *responsibility* remains at, or near, the centre of preoccupation. First, it is evident that it is *the* key question in the debate between free will and determinism, for that whole argument revolved, precisely, around what *we* can be held responsible for, what is 'up to us' (*eph' hēmin*), and in what sense it is up to us.

That is only to be expected, no doubt, given that free will versus determinism is primarily an ethical/moral debate. But the distinctions between external and internal factors, between 'preliminary', 'antecedent' and 'sustaining' causes, are not ones limited to what can be called narrowly moral questions. The roll-ing of Chrysippus' cylinder (p. 99 above) may be an analogue for human behavior, but it is an analysand in its own right. The interest in drawing the distinction between the role of the push, and the role of the nature of the cylinder itself, remains, to some extent at least, an interest in apportioning divided, if impersonal, responsibilities, that is, their relative importance in bringing about the effect produced.

Equally, when the doctors deployed the same general distinc-tion, they were intent on identifying the factors that needed coun-tering to secure a cure. They examined the individual case, or the general epidemic, to try to find out what was principally to blame (though, to be sure, medical aetiology is not always a matter of apportioning blame, since some of the effects investigated are

10. However, the use of the notion of the 'sympathies' between things is certainly not confined to Stoics. Lloyd 1983, pp. 171f, 177ff, discusses, for example, its use in the Methodist medical writer Soranus.

desirable). True, sometimes an *external* cause was perceived as primarily responsible, but it was often assumed that it operated *via* producing some change in the *internal* condition or state of the patient. Doctors sometimes concentrated on removing external causes, when these were not irremediably past or otherwise beyond control. But it says much about the style of Greek medicine that far more often they were concerned to try to induce the opposite *internal* condition in the patient – to return, that is, to *nature.*

The Stoic and the medical uses of the contrast between external and internal causes are not the only contexts in which causation and nature are deeply intertwined. But as I have already pointed out (p. 6), there was nothing natural, in the sense of given, about the Greeks' conception of nature. Rather, that concept was developed in the context of a hard-hitting polemic between rival claimants to knowledge and prestige. It was *the* concept that both so-called 'natural philosophers' (*phusikoi*) and medical theorists invoked to identify a domain of the investigable – *their* area of expertise, in other words. The contrast was with the miraculous, the magical, with, precisely, the 'supernatural'. Yet what nature included was, and remained, intensely controversial. Aristotle's twin claims, cited before, that humans are by nature city-state-dwelling animals, and that slavery is a natural institution, illustrate that point eloquently enough.

Thus, long before the Stoics and the Hellenistic doctors, Aristotle was already preoccupied with the natures of things and their essences, what makes them the things they are, as opposed to their accidental characteristics. To be sure, he contrasted 'natural' locomotion with 'forced', and nature itself with *technē*, art or craft. But in both cases nature is the primary domain. He even says that art imitates nature (e.g. *Physics* 194a21f, 199a16f), doing so indeed in the context of final causes. *We* might have thought that they are better observed in art, where they correspond to intentions and purposes on the part of human agents. But Aristotle takes a different view. For him, the final cause does *not* depend on intentions: rather, it is the good served.

Moreover, in Aristotle and others, nature is all the *aition* you need, and that can tell us a lot about 'nature' and perhaps even more about *aition*. Once some effect has been successfully traced back to an origin in the nature of the thing in question (for some philosophers, its essence), that is all the explanation you require, indeed all you can give: your inquiry is at an end. Thus, whereas in some of our modern intuitions about causation, causes can be tracked back indefinitely – if A is caused by B, we can ask what B in turn is caused by – that is importantly not true of much Greek thinking about *aitia*. Conversely, objections that were later raised about the circularity of explaining the effect of opium in terms of a *vis dormitiva* do not bother an Aristotle or a Galen at all. They were confident, after all, that there *are* natures and essences, however difficult they may be for *us* to ascertain correctly. These natures and essences are the *aitia* of the effects that we observe, whether or not we have independent evidence relating to those essences over and above the very effects themselves.

At this point it might be objected that, whatever may be said on behalf of the thesis of the ongoing connections, in Greek thought, between the notions of responsibility, cause and nature, the thesis runs into two major difficulties. The first is that in the legal context, the notion of *aition* is often, though certainly not exclusively, used in apportioning blame, often by way of a distinction between the voluntary and the involuntary. But *aition* in Greek 'physics' is even-handed, indeed, in the teleologists, weighted in favour of a focus on the good produced. As just noted, for Aristotle, the good is not a matter of intentions.

Then the second and more fundamental objection might go like this. Granted that the natural philosophers are interested in giving causal accounts, is it not the case that their accounts differ, precisely at the point at issue, from those that carry the associations of blame and personal responsibility that are central to the legal context? Was it not by offering a quite new idea about *impersonal* causation that they developed the new inquiry into nature?

Both points have some validity, but the thesis should be refined, not abandoned. It is true and significant that the vocabulary of *aitios* and *aitia* antedates the development of the inquiry into nature and is indeed shared by the naturalists and their opponents. Thus the author of the Hippocratic work *On the Sacred Disease* sets out to refute the 'purifiers', whose accounts of the different types of 'sacred disease' refer these to various gods: they, according to the purifiers, are the responsible agents or

aitioi (the term repeatedly used in this connection in chh. 2f).
Against them, the Hippocratic writer himself insists that the disease, like all others, is natural and has a natural cause, where he uses *aitios*, *aitiē*, along with *prophasis* and *phusis*, nature, for *his own* view (see Lloyd 1979, ch. 1, pp. 15ff, 26ff).

It is not that, in the naturalists' view, *all* causes are natural, of course. I have remarked that Aristotle contrasts natural to forced motion. Nor are all *regular* causes natural ones (the view of the opponents of *On the Sacred Disease* might well be that Poseidon is regularly responsible for cases of the disease where the patient 'snorts like a horse': he is usually also responsible for earthquakes). However, the claim was that, where natures have been identified as causes, they are the ones that count.

Thus the naturalists did not invent an entirely new, custom-built, vocabulary to apply to causation specifically in the physical domain. Rather, they adapted the terminology that had applied, and that continued to apply, primarily to human behaviour. But this use of a shared terminology makes the competition between alternative accounts, the naturalists' and the traditional, all the sharper. The naturalists could claim not just that their accounts are superior, but that they *superseded* alternatives. 'What is responsible' must now be located *not* in the domain of personal agency, but in that of species-specific essences.

So the Greek naturalists' idea of what counted as causal did indeed differ from many traditional stories, in that the factors to be invoked are not personal. Nature is certainly not wilful, and the vocabulary of blame is inappropriate (though the *praise* of nature is, in fact, common in the teleologists,[11] and we should not imagine that, even for the non-teleologists, the study of nature is entirely value-free). But they thereby secured an area to be investigated, and at the same time prescribed the manner of its investigation. In this programme, natures are the goals of inquiry: yet the idea of responsibility is still present, since this is now the area over which, in a sense, nature itself is responsible. Moreover the programme shared with the original contexts of responsibility that, once you have identified what counts as such, as what is responsible, your inquiry is at an end.

But what can the foregoing analysis tell us about the second of

---

11. Galen's *On the Use of Parts* is devoted to this theme and waxes eloquent on the subject.

my two initial interrelated questions, namely *why* there appears
to be such a concerted interest in causation in ancient Greece in
the first place? Evidently even to suggest an answer here, we have
to be a good deal more speculative than we have been already.
Certainly traditional lines of interpretation should not be lost
from view. Aristotle himself spoke of curiosity and wonder as the
primary sources of (Greek-style) philosophising – not the same
thing, to be sure, as an interest in causation, but, for him, closely
related to it. However, that suggestion is not as helpful as might
appear, since curiosity and wonder themselves may be as much
a part of the *explananda* as of the explanations.

The admittedly tentative argument that our earlier analysis suggests is that one factor influencing the general Greek preoccupation with causation lies in the very extensive experience of the
legal process that many ordinary Greek citizens of the classical
period had. The frequency and variety of that experience have
been indicated before (pp. 79ff). Greek citizens had repeated
opportunities, indeed obligations, not just to participate in political debate in mass Assemblies and in councils: when not themselves litigants (which, it seems, they often were), they regularly
served as *dicasts* (judge/jury) in the law-courts and as such were
responsible for deciding questions of guilt and innocence, and
for adjudicating between the opposing points of view expressed
by prosecutors and defendants. We have discussed before the
inflence of this legal/political experience on Greek styles of rhetoric (Chapter 4) and more generally on Greek modes of adversariality, the tendencies not just in law and politics, but also in
philosophy and science, to set thesis against antithesis, and to
advocate one point of view *via* the refutation of alternatives (Chapter 2).

The suggestion that our earlier analysis prompts is that this
deep-seated experience and involvement in the law helps to
throw light not just on the styles of causal inquiry favoured by
the Greeks, but also on the prominence of the interest in such
inquiries themselves. We have remarked on the ongoing underlying associations of the notion of cause, *aition*, and that of responsibility. But there are other ways, too, in which typical Greek
scientific and philosophical causal investigations carry traces
of the influence of ideas drawn initially from the legal sphere.
It is well known, for instance, how much the general Greek

vocabulary for evidence, for testing, even for proof, owes to the legal sphere.[12]

Thus two of the principal general terms for evidence, namely *tekmērion* and *marturion*, relate primarily to witnessing. Again, one of the regular terms for the testing or evaluating of ideas or theories, used in philosophy as elsewhere, *dokimazein*, has a technical sense in connection with the testing of a candidate's eligibility for office. Another, *basanizein* (originally associated with the touch-stone, *basanos*) is used of the torture to which slaves were, in principle, subject, when called as witnesses. A third that is also commonly used, in philosophy and science, for testing an idea or hypothesis, namely *elegchos*, is a standard term, in the classical period, for examining, and more especially refuting, a witness or an opposing speaker. As for words for proof, we have pointed out before (pp. 13f, 56 at n. 11) *both* how concerned the philosophers and scientists were to *contrast* their styles of demonstration with the proofs claimed by orators in courts of law, *and* that the *vocabulary* of proof and proving used by orators and philosophers alike is substantially the same.

It would be absurd to suggest that Greek philosophers and scientists were either directly or indirectly reacting to, or reflecting, Greek experience of the law in *all* their theoretical analyses of the notion of cause and in all their practical applications of the idea: we have seen how multifaceted their interests were. But that experience certainly appears to exercise a pervasive influence on many aspects of Greek intellectual life as well as of Greek culture. It is not just that *who* is responsible is, for obvious reasons, the dominant concern in the discussion of human agency, whether in forensic, or political, or philosophical contexts, or again in the writing of history or even tragedy or epic. *What* is responsible is often the way the key question in science is framed in attempts both to understand what happens and to effect change – as, for instance, in medicine, both in the diagnosis of a complaint and in its treatment.

A way of testing some of those conjectures concerning the Greek data is to turn now, though much more briefly, to some of the Chinese evidence relevant to the problem. No doubt to try to generalise about classical Chinese thought is as foolhardy as

12. Some of the principal evidence for what follows is set out in Lloyd 1979, pp. 252ff.

it is to do so with Greek. There are important differences both as between different periods, and as between different fields of inquiry, on issues that are relevant to our investigation. Moreover, the point made earlier, about the distortions that may arise from the application of our own modern concepts of causation to ancient materials, is as relevant to the Chinese as to the Greek case. The problem is exacerbated because there is a relative dearth of explicit discussion, in classical Chinese texts, of the key terms in question, notably 故 (*gu*, reason, cause), 使 (*shi*, send, command, cause), 原 (*yuan*, spring, source, origin), 因 (*yin*, rely on, because), 由 (*you*, to proceed from, source), and 本 (*ben*, root).

This very lack of explicit analysis points to one immediate difference from the Greeks. Where the Greeks develop, as we saw, elaborate rival taxonomies of *aitia*, the classical Chinese discussions of terms to do with causation are comparatively rare. There are, for instance, some elliptical passages in the Mohist canon, dating from between the late −4th and the late −3rd centuries. There, in *Canon* A 1, 故, *gu*, is said to be what something must get before it will come about, and this is followed by a couple of explanations. In Graham's translations (1978, p. 263): 'minor reason: having this, it will not necessarily be so; lacking this, necessarily it will not be so.' 'Major reason: having this, it will necessarily be so; lacking this, necessarily it will not be so.' Graham's comment on this is that 'the minor reason is the necessary condition, the major the necessary and sufficient condition'. For 使, *shi*, in *Canon* A 77, we are given two 'definitions', namely 'to tell' and 'a reason', with the explanations (Graham 1989, p. 162, cf. 1978, p. 324): 'to give orders is to tell: the thing does not necessarily come about. Dampness is a reason: it necessarily depends on what is done coming about.'[13]

Now the Mohists were not exactly in the mainstream of Chinese philosophy and their influence after the end of the Warring States period was negligible. It is possible, indeed likely, that there was a good deal more to their analyses of *gu* and *shi* than emerges in our extant texts, though just how far their views corresponded to general Chinese perceptions is not clear. Graham himself remarked of *gu* (1989, pp. 161f) that it is 'in the first place what is at the origin of something; the word can

---

13. See further Graham 1989, pp. 161f, cf. Peterson 1989, pp. 207f, Reding 1993.

also be used of a thing in its original state or of the fact behind a statement', and of *shi* that it is used primarily of employing a person – which corresponds to the first of the two Mohist explanations, namely to give orders. We can see that in both cases the human domain provides one of the sources for Chinese thinking about reasons and causes. However, the points taken from that domain relate, in the case of *gu*, to the fact underlying a statement, and in that of *shi*, to the context of commanding. In neither case do they relate directly to the context of legal responsibilities.

But there is a fundamental difference in the actual experience of the law, between ancient China and ancient Greece, that bears on our problem. First and foremost, far from delighting in private litigation, as the Athenians did, the Chinese generally considered any case that came to law as a failure, a breach of good order (Hulsewé 1986, p. 525). There was, in any event, practically speaking no civil law. Differences between individuals or groups that might well have been the subject of appeal to litigation in Greece were generally settled by discussion, by arbitration, or by the decision of the responsible officials. The Chinese had, to be sure, no experience that remotely resembled that of Greek dicasts, nor, come to that, that of Greek public participation in open debate of political issues in the Assemblies. As we have remarked before (p. 90), the forensic context was not an important source, for the Chinese, of either positive or negative models, defining the techniques of persuasion to be imitated, or acting as a foil to the development of modes of philosophical demonstration set up in contrast to those styles of persuasion.

Yet Chinese interest in the explanation of events is certainly highly developed in such contexts as history and medicine. Sima Qian's *Shiji* frequently comments on the reasons for the successes or failures of individuals, rulers, dynasties, often remarking not just on their strategy and tactics, their skilful plans or miscalculations, but also on their moral strengths and weaknesses. Similarly, in the context of persuading the ruler to adopt a course of action, the *Zhanguoce* uses the diagnosis of why events turned out favourably or disastrously in the past as a source of recommendations or warnings, encouragements or remonstrations. Besides *gu* and *shi*, such explanatory accounts use such term as 原 (*yuan*, source) and 本 (*ben*, root) for the origins of a sequence of events, or 由 (*you*) or 因 (*yin*) for the source from which an effect stems, the

means by which it is achieved or the factors relied on in order
to bring it about.

That causal vocabulary is common, too, in the medical treatises. The *Huangdi neijing* often offers accounts of the origins of
diseases, both in general and in particular cases, distinguishing
especially, as Sivin 1987, pp. 100ff, 273ff, has shown, between
internal and external factors (*yin*). Again Chunyu Yi's case-
histories, in *Shiji* 105, which we have cited before, can be used
both to exemplify the different types of explanatory accounts
included and to suggest the limits of the explanations offered.
Thus Chunyu Yi often has remarks to make about how the illness was contracted or 'caught', 得 (*de*), mentioning, in this context, such factors as over-eating, drunkenness, over-indulgence in
sex, a bad fall and so on. These trigger the onset of the illness,
though they are not generally linked to the specificities of the
complaint as set out in Chunyu Yi's diagnosis.

In that second context, Chunyu Yi uses precisely the same
formula, repeatedly throughout the twenty-five case-histories, to
introduce how it was that he came to understand the illness in
question, namely 所以知。之病者 (*suo yi zhi . . . zhi bing zhe*).[14]
Rendered literally, this means: 'as for that whereby I knew so-
and-so's disease'. The account that is then offered often refers to
a disorder that Chunyu Yi has inferred from some sign or characteristic of the pulse. In case 1, for instance, we are told: 'When
I, Yi, took his pulse, I got the liver *qi*. The liver *qi* was turbid but
calm. This is an illness of the 內關 (*neiguan*, literally "inner"
"connection" or "pass").'[15] He cites the 'Method of the Pulse'[16]
as his authority for a connection between a 'long' and 'strung'
or 'vibrant' pulse and a liver disorder. But it is striking that he
neither explains how it is that one recognises a 'long' or a 'strung'
pulse themselves, nor does he attempt any further justification of

14. The importance of this point was rightly stressed by Hsü 1987.
15. *Shiji* 105: 2797, 6–7. Problems to do with the translation of *qi* have been noted
    before (p. 65 n. 25): the term does not necessarily signify a substance ('breath'), as
    opposed to an activity, process or manifestation of energy. The interpretation of
    illness terms and of those for the parts or aspects of the body affected (not necessarily
    anatomical structures) is also in many causes problematic and disputed. See in gen-
    eral Sivin 1987. On the various medical senses of the term *neiguan* in particular,
    much debated in the commentaries, compare Bridgman 1955, p. 67 n. 78, with Sivin
    1987, p. 314.
16. Whether the Method of the Pulse refers to a text, to lore, or to a combination of
    both, is sometimes unclear: cf. above, p. 64 at n. 24.

why such a pulse relates to the liver disorder in question. As we have remarked before (p. 65, p. 72), *how to feel* the pulse is evidently not considered to be something that can be, or needs to be, explained *verbally*. It is rather a matter of what any doctor will have learnt from long experience: nor, as we shall see, is that the only mode of implicit knowledge that these accounts presuppose.

The term *gu* is frequently deployed, in this and other medical texts, both in relation to what happened and with regard to the doctor's own diagnoses or prognoses. In the former type of usage, it picks out the cause of what happened, in the latter the reason for the given diagnosis, though these two are sometimes run together. Thus in case 1, again, the patient himself had reported, at the start of the complaint, that he suffered from a headache. Chunyu Yi comes back to this at the end. The hot *qi*, he explains, had ascended to the upper parts. It had reached the head and was moving around and causing disturbances there. Hence (*gu*) the head ached (*Shiji* 105: 2797, 12f, picking up 2797, 4).

But elsewhere *gu* relates not just to what happened, but to why Chunyu Yi said it would. In case 6, a case of wasting of the lungs of some kind,[17] the prediction is insanity after three days, death after five. The usual complex analysis of the signs of the pulse is given to explain the diagnosis/prognosis. At the end of the account he first attributes the madness on the third day to an injury to the 陽明 (*yangming*: this is the name of one of the three main *yang* 'warps' or circulation tracts in the six-warp system, Sivin 1987, pp. 8off) and then says: 'as for death after five days, the liver and heart [pulses] were distant from one another by five degrees:[18] hence I said, on the fifth day, exhaustion, and after exhaustion, death.'

Again in case 18 (2808) Chunyu Yi first picks up the reason (*gu*) why he had said that in the female patient in question 'there was no descent of the menses' and then why he had also remarked – again on the basis of his pulse examination – that the underlying reason for her contracting the illness was that she desired, but could not have, a son.

17. *Shiji* 105: 2801–2. It would once again be foolish to attempt too determinate a diagnosis of the complaint in question.
18. *Shiji* 105: 2802, 6. The correlation between five days and the five degrees or parts, 分 (*fen*), is, no doubt, important, however the latter are to be measured.

Case 15, similarly, is a case where the diagnosis is an injured spleen and the prognosis the blocking of the diaphragm when spring comes, followed by the passing of blood and death in the summer (*Shiji* 105: 2806–7). After some criticism of the faulty diagnoses of other doctors, Chunyu Yi comments that the reason for the fatal illness developing in the spring was that the stomach *qi* was yellow. 'As for its being yellow, that is the *qi* of earth. The earth does not overcome wood. *So* [in that case] when spring comes, one dies' (2807, 4). However, when the patient is contented and fat, he lasts another season: and in this instance, that was the case, and the patient in fact died, as predicted, in the summer.

Here is one of many cases where the background assumptions involve a set of correspondences, between colours, organs, and 'phases'. Yellow is here associated with the spleen, the injured organ in this case ('he had the complexion of an injured spleen: when I looked at him, he was a deathly yellow', 2807, 3), and yellow was regularly correlated with earth. In the mutual destruction cycle of the five phases, water overcomes fire, which overcomes metal, which overcomes wood, which overcomes earth, which overcomes water. So there is no way in which earth can overcome wood (often correlated with spring). Reference to other texts that develop these ideas gives us the background information necessary, but it is assumed in the account Chunyu Yi gives, and needs and receives no explication there.

It is correspondences of this type that have led some scholars to suggest that there is a more concerted interest, in China, in correlative thinking than in causal explanation. That elaborate correspondences were proposed is well known. Needham offers a systematisation of such material that sets out in tabular form the correspondences found between the five phases and no fewer than twenty-nine other types of factor. These include seasons, cardinal points, tastes, smells, numbers, musical notes, star-palaces, heavenly bodies, planets, weather, rulers, ministries, colours, instruments, classes of living creatures, domestic animals, 'grains', sacrifices, viscera, parts of the body, sense-organs and affective states.[19]

19. Needham 1956, pp. 262ff. One may contrast Graham 1989, pp. 340ff, who pays more attention to the difficulties of correlating five-factor analyses with four-factor ones. Cf. also Unschuld's alternative reconstruction, based on the materials in the *Huangdi neijing*, Unschuld 1985, pp. 67ff ('The Medicine of Systematic Correspondence') at p. 95.

The first problem here has to do with the origin and dating of the attempt at *comprehensive* correlations. Eventually, indeed, elaborate schemata were proposed in classical Chinese texts. That was where one of the great strengths of the Chinese bid to establish a systematic world-view undoubtedly lay. But the texts in which they are to be found do not, in general, antedate the –3rd century, and they represent a considerable and well-motivated effort at providing a comprehensive framework within which much social, political and cosmological thinking could be organised. Evidently this effort drew on much earlier ideas, but *their* systematicity and comprehensiveness should not be exaggerated.[20]

However, the hypothesis that sets up a simple opposition between Chinese correlative and Greek causal thinking suffers from further severe limitations both on the score of what it asserts and on that of what it denies. As we have seen, it is far from being the case that there was a total lack of interest, in China, in identifying the causal factors at work in a whole variety of practical contexts. In the examples we have considered, different types of causal explanations are given, though, to be sure, they presuppose a lot of background and implicit knowledge, much of which is evidently thought neither to require, nor even perhaps to be capable of, verbal explication.

One text that can be used to confirm that the pursuit of causal explanations beyond a certain point seemed futile is the negative comments made in *Zhuangzi* on the inquisitiveness of the *Ming Jia* philosopher Hui Shi (–4th century). The *Ming Jia*, or 'Lineage of Names', like the Mohists, were certainly not in the mainstream of Chinese philosophising of their own time, and their influence from the Han on was negligible. Hui Shi, in particular, was frequently criticised for his paradox-mongering (cf. below, p. 152, pp. 163f). But he also was for his curiosity, his almost Greek-style pursuit of the causes of things. This evokes in the *Zhuangzi* the sardonic comments:

There was a strange man of the South called Huang Liao, who asked why heaven did not collapse or earth subside, and the reasons (*gu*) for wind, rain, and thunder. Hui Shi answered without hesitation, replied without thinking, had explanations (説, *shuo*) for all the myriad things, never stopped explaining, said more and more and still thought he had

---

20. This point has recently been emphasised by Sivin 1995a, pp. 190f, and 1995c, and cf. above, p. 39 at n. 40, below, pp. 122f.

not said enough, had some marvel to add. (*Zhuangzi* 33: 81–3. Translation after Graham 1989, p. 77)

This speaks eloquently to a realisation of the futility of seeking causes beyond a certain point or in relation to certain subject-matter, but that of course is not to deny that up to that point, or on other subject-matter, they can and should be given. While much of the understanding that Chinese philosophers and scientists sought was indeed of the relations of similarity, interdependence, complementarity between things – that is, of their correlations – rather than of sequences of causes and effects, the former interest certainly did not exclude the latter.

The converse is also manifestly true of Greek speculation. The second main objection to the contrastive characterisation of Chinese correlative versus Greek causal thinking is that it ignores or underestimates the well-developed Greek interests in correlations. The most famous early example of that is the Pythagorean Table of Opposites (*sustoichia*) reported by Aristotle in the *Metaphysics*, 986a22ff. This sets out ten pairs of opposite terms where it is, precisely, the analogy in the relationships between each pair that the Table exhibits. Thus on the side of limit, there are odd, one, right, male, at rest, straight, light, good, square: on the side of the unlimited, even, plurality, left, female, moving, curved, darkness, evil, oblong.

True, we do not know precisely when the Table in the form quoted by Aristotle was worked out, and whenever that was, those who were responsible clearly did not invent all the correlations proposed but in several cases drew on much earlier beliefs. The assumption that right is good, left evil, for instance, is one for which it would be foolish to suggest a historical origin.[21] But more importantly, although Aristotle, for one, does not himself adopt the Pythagorean Table in the form set out in the *Metaphysics*, he certainly redeploys the basic idea of columns of correlated opposites for his own purposes. Thus the belief that right is to be associated with male, front, upper, hot, and conversely left with female, back, lower, cold, is given explanatory work to do in a wide variety of contexts in his cosmology, in his embryology

---

21. The Greek pre-philosophical background is explored in Lloyd 1966, pp. 41ff, and the continued philosophical use at pp. 51ff. For a cross-cultural analysis of comparable material, see Needham, (ed.), 1973.

and elsewhere in his physics. It is better, he repeatedly says, for the more honourable part to be in the more honourable position, and nature has achieved this 'where no greater purpose prevents it'.[22]

We should certainly not assume that merely because we find tendencies to use correspondences in both China and Greece, the underlying perception of the correlata is necessarily the same. The questions of the presuppositions made concerning pairs of opposites and oppositions, in particular, will occupy us in the next chapter. However, for now the basic point may stand, that a concern for the correlations between things can be found in both ancient societies.

But if it is clear that in this matter, as in so many others, to contrast ancient China and ancient Greece as polar opposites flies in the face of considerable counter-evidence, what positive results, we may now ask in conclusion, may be suggested – however tentatively – on the basis of our study?

First as to some of the similarities we have observed. It is not at all surprising that one of the commonest areas *to* which causal reasoning is applied, and one that serves as a model *for* causal accounts in other fields, is the human domain, comprising, *inter alia*, the ordering of people, the identification of motivations, the making of artefacts. Causing is often a matter of commanding, often one of human creativity. A second common motif in both ancient societies is the concern for the origins or sources of things, not just their chronological starting-points, but that in virtue of which they acquire their principal characteristics. Just as the Chinese were interested in the roots, *ben*, of things, so Empedocles described his elements as roots, *rhizōmata*, and the terms for seeds and seed-mixture, *spermata, panspermia*, figure in Greek physical theories as well as in specifically biological ones. In many different contexts, in both societies, processes are described or understood in terms drawn from the experience of living organisms.

Yet even at this level of generality, differences begin to emerge as soon as attention is paid to the specificities of the organic, technological or socio-political models used. The last group presents

22. See, for example, *On the Parts of Animals* 665b18ff and other texts cited in Lloyd 1966, pp. 52ff.

a particularly complex case. The idea of the importance of what governs, rules, orders, is extremely common in both ancient societies. The Greek term *archē*, as we noted (p. 100), covers seat of authority, rule, even magistracy, as well as beginning or principle. Yet the additional resonances of responsibility (even blame) that we detect in the Greek causal vocabulary are, we argued, peculiar to, and reflect, the particular, and particularly intense, Greek experience of the law and of litigation. We shall have more to say on the various modalities of the notion of hierarchy, in China and in Greece, in Chapter 6.

But Greek socio-political experience may also be relevant, we suggested, to the most important difference that we identified at the outset. Chinese philosophers, unlike Greek ones, did not devote much effort to proposing elaborate explicit theories of what a cause is, and *a fortiori* did not do so to defend one such theory against rivals or competitors. Here is another instance of the lack of unanimity on basic questions that we encounter so often in Greek culture. They did not agree with one another even on what counts as a cause and on which types of cause are valid subjects of inquiry. Rather, different individuals and groups proposed different taxonomies with their own metaphysical and sometimes moral agenda in view. As we noted with methodology, so too with causation, one way Greek intellectuals sought to put down rivals was to argue that their theories must be wrong, since their whole idea of the nature of the issues was. As in the adversarial disputes of the law-courts, not much attempt at compromise, at finding the common ground, is to be seen.

Certainly, as we have noted before, there were plenty of disagreements among Chinese intellectuals too, and explicit criticisms made by philosophers, mathematicians, doctors, of other philosophers, mathematicians, doctors. But unlike in classical Greece, indeed in Greco-Roman antiquity as a whole down to its eventual Christianisation, the bid to consolidate a comprehensive unified world-view was largely successful in China. To be sure, this was an achievement of the Han period, stimulated by a yearning for orthodoxy that, as Sivin has pointed out (1995a, pp. 190f: and cf. further below, pp. 122f), reflects the particular circumstances of the post-Qin situation. But it was not that the Han thinkers *introduced*, but rather that they *systematised*, the schemata of correlations that provided the main articulating framework for that world-view.

The Greeks too, we said, had their penchant for correlations, not just their Tables of Opposites, but more grandiose theories (as in Aristotle) in which nature and art, *phusis* and *technē*, were held to exhibit the same basic causal structure. Yet not even the latter led to *general* agreement, among the Greeks, as to the framework within which either causes or cosmological correlations should be discussed. The ambition to give new aetiologies, and indeed to propose new analyses of causes, was seemingly unending, and although those who demanded strict demonstration required also strict indemonstrables as their *ultimate* primary premisses, the goal of such demonstration was elusive, for, as we have remarked, Greek incontrovertibility claims were repeatedly controverted. If the case of Hui Shi certainly shows that Chinese philosophers too could, on occasion, exhibit well-developed speculative tendencies in the matter of the causal explanations of phenomena, the reaction he provoked exemplifies a key point, in that it reflected not any demand for argumentative closure by way of demonstration based on self-evident premisses, but rather a pragmatic sense of the limits of what can be given such explanations.

CHAPTER 6

Greek and Chinese dichotomies revisited

Since I wrote at some length, several decades ago, on Polarity as a mode of argumentation in early Greek thought (Lloyd 1966), a word of explanation is in order for my return to this topic. A lot of work has been done, since *Polarity and Analogy*, on the subjects it broached, some with, some against, the grain of its arguments.[1] If I return to the topic of dichotomies now, it is not to go back over old disputes, but rather first, in the hope that a new comparativist attack on the issues will lead to new insights, and secondly, to investigate what this study can tell us about *how to go about* comparing Greek and Chinese thought. There will be lessons to be learnt both about substantive issues and about methodological ones. I shall proceed, in the first instance, by way of a critique of some common assumptions in an effort to clear the ground for a better targeted and more securely grounded discussion of the problems.

Ancient Greek and ancient Chinese ideas on opposition have been juxtaposed on innumerable occasions. Sometimes it is with some sense of the difficulties of generalisation on either side, with some awareness of the problems of the lacunae and bias of our sources. But whether or not reservations and qualifications are expressed, one very often finds one or other of two diametrically opposed theses being argued for – thereby exemplifying, one might say, one of the types of polarising argument that are themselves under discussion. *Either* the claim is that we are dealing with the same or very similar patterns of thought, in both China and Greece, maybe even ones of universal applicability. *Or* (less often) that the similarities are superficial and mask underlying

1. I have summarised some of the principal reactions and commented on what I have learnt from them in Lloyd 1992c.

radical differences that reflect the fundamental contrasts between the two ancient civilisations.

It will be useful first to outline briefly some points in connection with each of those two theses. Students of early Greek philosophy do not usually have to progress very far into their subject before they are confronted with comparisons with China. Thus the interplay of opposites and the notion of continual flux in Heraclitus may be compared with Chinese ideas of process.[2] Or again the Pythagorean Table of Opposites, the *sustoichia*, may be compared with Chinese ideas based on *yin* and *yang*, and with what is correlated with those two principles – often set out, in just the way in which Aristotle reports the Pythagoreans, in the form of a Table of opposed pairs (see, for example, Guthrie 1962, pp. 251ff).

It used to be common for such comparisons to be the starting-point for a search for *origins*. Who first had the idea that (as Alcmaeon put it) 'all things go in pairs'? This type of question was often answered by the suggestion that perhaps it was neither the Greeks nor the Chinese themselves, but someone in between, the Indians, the Iranians, or whoever. Quite what the intermediaries in question were supposed to have originated was generally left indeterminate – as between, for example, explicit Tables of Opposites, and implicit ones: that is, ideas that *we* can, if we try, represent as such.[3] Indeed a cynic might remark that the ideas at issue *have* to be left very vague for any talk of origins to have even the slightest claims to plausibility.

Such grandiose speculations about origins have, for some time, been on the decline. To start with, any such hypothesis has to be *massively* speculative. In the absence of solid, reliably dated, evidence, the argument that what we have is *compatible* with whatever grandiose hypothesis is propounded does not cut much ice:[4] for the evidence, such as it is, is so meagre it is compatible with widely divergent speculations and cannot be said to discriminate

2. See, for example, Needham 1956, pp. 37ff. Attempts to compare Heraclitus with Zoroastrian ideas are outlined in West 1971, ch. 6.

3. The important distinction between explicit, 'actors'', categories and those categories only made explicit by outside 'observers', has been brought to bear on the use of opposites by Goody, especially 1977, ch. 4, who argued that many of the Tables of Opposites reported in modern anthropological fieldwork are the artefacts of the ethnographers doing the reporting.

4. Cf., for example, many of the arguments used by Renfrew 1987.

in favour of any one. But the more widespread the use of opposites is believed to be, the less urgent, the less sensible indeed, the attempt to specify some particular spatio-temporal and cultural origin.

The way that argument leads is to a view that has also often been expressed in connection with the appeal to opposites, namely that we are dealing with a *universal* phenomenon, not just a phenomenon common to many different cultures, but one embedded in thought, language, communication themselves. That effectively removes the need to pursue the Holy Grail of an origin: but only at the cost of leaving most of the major problems in place. For if we are dealing with a universal phenomenon, just how the distinctive forms it took in different cultures are to be accounted for is anything but clear.

Of course, with care it is possible to identify certain basic features of all communication. As linguistics pointed out many years ago, all meaning depends on contrast, on difference. Terms signify thanks to the fact that they occupy a more or less determinate place in a contrastive network. Phrases and sentences bring terms into collocations that again signify something – though not necessarily some *one* thing – by not signifying everything. Propositions assert or deny some predicate of some subject and imply the negation of their contradictories, though well-formed propositions are the tools of formal logicians, not the normal currency of communicative exchanges in natural languages.

But it is equally obvious that to locate the similarities between Greek and Chinese oppositions at that level is vacuous. If the varied uses of opposites in both societies merely reflect a universal feature of communication, that blocks further questions just as effectively as the lack of historical data does the pursuit of the question of origins.

Some extravagant talk of the similarities between Greek and Chinese polarities has been countered, on occasion, by just as dogmatic an insistence on their contrasts. *Just* to describe them as polarities, and to think of them, thereby, as somehow equivalent, is, on this second view, entirely to miss the significance of the fundamental differences in the ways they were used and in the very nature of the polarities in question.

A typical example of this second view would be that which makes use of a contrast we have already discussed in Chapter 2, namely the supposition that the basic contrast between Greek and Chinese cultures lies in the aggressive adversariality – the agonistic spirit – that animates the first, and the sense of compromise and the avoidance of confrontation that guide the second. In the sphere of the use of opposites, the point would be that the Greeks very much stressed the *opposition* between them, the warfare that Heraclitus thought of as father of all and king of all (Fr. 53), the strife that he said *is* justice (Fr. 80), the antagonism and confrontation that seem to be implicit in much of the very vocabulary in which opposition is expressed, in Greek, starting with the terms *antios* and *enantios* themselves.[5]

By contrast, on the Chinese side – so this second point of view would have it – the relationship between *yin* and *yang* is one of mutual interdependence and reciprocity. Even when *yang* is at its strongest, *yin* begins to reassert itself: conversely, at the moment of maximum *yin*, *yang* already starts to reemerge. *Yin* and *yang* are opposites, for sure, but they are correlatives defined in terms of one another. They are aspectual and relational: what is *yin* in one regard may be *yang* in another. So far from mutually excluding one another, neither exists in isolation from the other.[6]

The second view would have to concede, no doubt, that there is an idea of reciprocity in some Greek talk of opposites. Anaximander's cosmic fragment (Fr. 1) speaks of the penalty (*dikē*) and recompense (*tisis*) paid to one another by certain unnamed, but evidently opposed, forces; in Empedocles the relationship between Love and Strife is governed by a 'broad oath' (Fr. 30); there are many mundane references to the orderly cycle of the seasons; and in Greek medical theory, health is frequently identified as a matter of the balance between opposed factors, whether those factors are thought of as qualities or substances such as elements or humours. But – the argument would be – they are not the central, nor the most characteristic, uses of oppositions in Greek thought. With many Greek pairs of opposites, particularly those that underpin some of their deepest ontological assumptions, the relationship is anything but one of reciprocity and interdependence. Thus, becoming depends upon being, but *not* vice versa. Appearance depends upon reality, but *not* vice versa.

5. Analogous points have been made in connection with the English term 'opposition' by Rodney Needham 1987, for example at pp. 27ff.
6. With Needham 1956, pp. 232ff, and Graham 1986, compare Sivin 1987, pp. 59ff.

Again, according to some Greek thinkers, in living creatures body depends upon soul, but not vice versa, and again the changing upon the unchanging, and potentiality upon actuality. The examples could be multiplied – though, as this multiplication proceeds, so the extent to which the ideas in question could be claimed to be typical, let alone universal, in Greek thought tends to diminish.

At this point, the opposition between the first, and the second, point of view – between one that emphasises similarities, and one that stresses differences, as between Greek and Chinese polarities – leads very quickly to an impasse. It is obviously futile merely to chalk up points on either side. Rather, the questions that we should be asking have themselves to be rethought. The suggestion I now wish to pursue is that it is not the question of whether this or that type of opposition is more prominent or more central that we ought to focus on, so much as the issue of what *work* the talk of oppositions does in either culture. *How* are they used to make sense of experience, *what* sense are they expected to make, *how* are they deployed in debate, *how* (to adapt a famous expression of Lévi-Strauss) are they 'good to think with'?

But to tackle this nexus of questions it is essential to have a much closer look at some of the data, the actual uses of opposition in China and in Greece.

We may begin with China, where we should not be taken in by what used to be standard professions of the great antiquity of *yin* and *yang*, and the concept of the five phases, *wu xing*, with which they are associated. The latter used to be called 'elements', but they are not substances, but processes, phases, indeed, in the perpetual transformations of *qi*.[7] As already remarked, the elaboration of *yin yang* and *wu xing* into complex systems of correspondences is, as Sivin (1995b and 1995c) has demonstrated, in large part a product of Han thought, that is, not earlier than the end of the −3rd century. Of course that is not to deny that certain uses of these and related ideas go back much earlier. *Yin* and *yang* originally refer to the shady, and sunny, sides of a hill,

---

7. Needham already raised objections to translating *wu xing* as five elements, but persisted in that usage himself. Needham 1956, pp. 242ff, gives an account of the cycles in which the five, water, fire, wood, metal and earth are related, with comparisons with Greek and other element theories at pp. 245f. Compare Sivin 1995b, 1995c.

or the banks of a river. Indeed that is their main usage until the end of the −4th century. There are references to 五德, *wu de*, the five virtues or powers, antedating the Han, and it is in all probability as five activities, indeed as a set of moral standards, that the concept of 五行, *wu xing*, itself first appears. But what is missing from the extant evidence are good, reliably datable, texts from the Warring States period (−480 to −221), let alone from earlier times, presenting a *cosmological* use of *wu xing* as five phases. That is the use familiar from the elaborate systems of correlated factors, phases, colours, tastes, seasons, cardinal points and so on, on which we have already remarked in Chapter 5 (pp. 112f).[8] The complementarity of members of opposite pairs, father and son, ruler and minister, male and female, can certainly be exemplified readily enough in pre-Han texts: but what cannot, are syntheses based on a cosmological understanding of the five phases.

It is true that there are considerable problems of source-evaluation here, where the work of Graham (1978, 1981, 1986), Shaugnessy (1983), Keegan (1988), Loewe (1993) and others, besides Sivin himself, has taken scholarship a stage beyond that secured by Needham's pioneering forays. Many of the principal classical texts, philosophical, mathematical and medical, that, in the days before Needham, used to be believed to go back several centuries before the Han, or at least to represent faithfully ideas that did, are now seen in a very different light, and many are, in any event, compilations consisting of several distinct strata.

The key question, for the five phases, is the evidence for the work of 騶衍, Zou Yan, active around −305 to −240, whom Needham considered to be the founder of what he called the Naturalist school.[9] Sivin's close analysis of all the admittedly limited direct evidence for this thinker leads to the conclusion that he was, indeed, responsible for important and original ideas. These include an account of the earth that starts with a catalogue of China's contents, including its institutions, and proceeds outwards to encompass parts of the world that no one had seen – or indeed could ever see. But, to quote Sivin's verdict (1995c), 'there is no cosmos. The stars in their courses, the rhythms of the seasons . . . play no

8. See Needham 1956, pp. 253ff, Graham 1989, pp. 340ff, though both scholars resist attempts to push back the dates of such correlations to long before the Han.
9. With Needham 1956, pp. 232ff (where Zou Yan is dated to between −350 and −270) compare Sivin 1995c.

part' in this expansive scheme. Zou Yan's Five Virtues (*wu de*, not *wu xing*) imply a mutual conquest system, but that is a story of dynastic change, a 'philosophy of history', and ultimately ethical and political in character.

All of this may seem rather scholastic from the point of view of our understanding of Chinese opposites. After all, someone might ask, what difference does it make *when* precisely the elaboration of *yin yang* and the five phases into a fully fledged cosmological system took place. After all, it was certainly *one* of the most important Chinese systematic theories that (everyone must agree) antedates the end of the Han (+2nd century) at the latest, and it certainly draws on, even while it develops, much earlier ideas, not least with regard to the complementarities of opposed pairs.

But that objection would miss the key point. The date and circumstances of the development of this cosmology *are* significant. To quote Sivin again (1995c): the 'association [of the concepts of *yin yang* and the five phases] with cosmology and science came about, not because they were pulled by the demands of science or technology, theoretical or practical, but because they were fitted into various doctrines that (among other aims) legitimated the workings of the unified and centralised Qin-Han state as a model of Nature's processes. The Han did not spawn a single tightly integrated orthodoxy. Nevertheless, its rulers and intellectuals learned to yearn for one. This drive ensured that the more or less convergent world view that informed the eclectic philosophies of the time also pervaded the sciences as they gradually emerged.'

There were special reasons for this 'yearning', both from the side of the rulers and from that of the intellectuals. First, from the side of the rulers. The first Qin emperor (Qin Shi Huang Di) had unified China by conquest. When his dynasty collapsed, soon after his death in –210, the legitimacy of the warlords who tried to establish themselves as his successors was anything but assured. The new, Han, dynasty needed, one might say, all the support it could muster.

As for the intellectuals, they were reacting to what Sivin (personal communication, cf. 1995a, pp. 190f) has called the 'multiple traumata of the Qin-Han transition'. 'First [there] was the contempt of the First Emperor [viz. Qin Shi Huang Di], the slaughter of scholars, attempts to burn books in private hands. Next was the enormous attrition of books in the warfare that ended the Qin. The upshot was that scholars considered their canons threatened. Transmission was problematic. When in the Han they were offered court protection for their teachings, they jumped at it.'

On this view, the cosmological synthesis of *yin yang* and the five phases served a particular function at a turning-point in Chinese history. The key feature of the system is the unity of the political and the natural orders, with the emperor serving the role of mediator between heaven and earth. The human or social order, the due, properly hierarchical relationships that apply all the way from emperors and their ministers, to fathers and sons, was naturalised as a mirror image of the cosmic order, the reciprocity of heaven and earth themselves. As we have said, some of the ideas thus synthesised reach far back into earlier Chinese thought: but what was new was the synthesis. That very neatly served the dual functions, of helping to underpin the emperor's position, and of contriving to provide a *raison d'être* for the literati who helped to secure that underpinning.

Of course, not all the literati joined in; and not all were in favour with the emperors. Not all worked away at, or even applied, some version or other of the *yin yang* five-phases synthesis. Some were notably idiosyncratic characters, such as the sceptic Wang Chong of the +1st century (an admittedly marginal figure). Yet even he, in the *zi ran* chapter of the *Lun Heng* (18: 365–71), has heaven and earth, high and low, balance one another in a reciprocal relationship parallel to that between male and female. Again, of the technical mathematical treatises, the *Nine Chapters* at least offers no explicit grand cosmological framework.

While reservations must, no doubt, be entered, the crucial point for our understanding of the Chinese use of systems of oppositions remains that they often serve political purposes: or rather they are, in a broad sense at least, themselves political. We can distinguish, for analytic purposes – as I have just done – between the natural and the social order, but they are parts of a single seamless whole. The emperor's role is not *just* political in the narrow sense. To be sure, his rule directly secures social order: but he has a further more important cosmic function to fulfil. The welfare of the empire as a whole depends on the harmonious relationship between Heaven and Earth – which the emperor's own behaviour, his virtue, has to guarantee. One consequence of this is the direct concern that the emperor had for the study of the heavens (astronomy, as we say) which we shall be analysing further in Chapter 8.

The balance between Sivin's two points, that there was no single orthodoxy under the Han, and yet a strong desire for one, must be respected. Divergences, between individuals and between groups, remained, both within each broad field, medicine, mathematics, astronomy, and between them. Chinese medicine, in particular, was not just a matter of the styles of theory and practice cultivated by the authors of the *Huangdi neijing*, any more than classical Greek medicine was just a matter of the views of the authors represented in the Hippocratic Corpus.

Nevertheless the consensus among Chinese intellectuals, and the sense that they operated with a common conceptual framework and spoke, as it were, the same theoretical language, are far greater than is the case with ancient Greece.[10] But that is understandable, given the relationship between the Chinese literati and the imperial authorities, the role the former played in legitimating the emperor's position, and conversely the direct support that the emperors could and did provide for members of the literate elite.[11] In that general socio-political situation, the stress on reciprocity, interdependence, complementarity, that we so often find in Chinese references to pairs of opposites, could be seen as reflecting what were perceived as the prerequisites of social order. That was an idea that gained momentum with the gradual consolidation of the imperial order under the Han, even if the ideal of complementarity in human relations was one that received eloquent expression already in Confucius.

In this view the emphasis was not so much on the *opposition* of

---

10. This remains true, even though, as noted before (p. 24 at n. 9), Greek uses of arguments appealing to past authorities grow during the Hellenistic period. Which authorities were the ones to follow, and what they stood for, remained disputed.

11. This was not limited to support for those appointed to posts in the Astronomical Bureau, on which see below, pp. 168ff. As noted (p. 41), the tradition of philosophers advising rulers goes back to Confucius and was extensively cultivated both by groups (the Mohists) and by individuals (Hui Shi, Gongsun Long) both in the Warring States period and later. On the rulers' side, the attempt to gather around themselves impressive entourages of 'guests' can be documented, though the role of what are sometimes called, quite gratuitously, Academies, such as the 稷下, *Jixia*, one, founded by prince Xuan, is controversial. With Needham 1956, pp. 234f, compare Sivin 1995c.

hierarchically distinct but complementary functions, as on the *mutual support* they could provide one another. What might be thought to be a major exception to this attitude towards opposites, in Chinese medicine, turns out rather to confirm the underlying notion at least as the ideal. Chinese pathology makes much use of the idea of the body attacked by hostile forces from without, the sources of many disorders within.[12] Yet here too the ideal for *health* is often viewed as a matter of balance, and the hostility of the hostile forces is evidently to be deplored as well as controlled.

Our tendency, with the still common Western insistence on the separation of the political and the physical (or scientific) domains, may well be to wonder whether there were not plenty of oppositions in classical Chinese thought that strike a very different note, in the sense that they do not overtly, nor even covertly, reflect that implicitly political emphasis on the importance of harmony and reciprocity. No doubt there were, for there were indeed many different types of opposition and many more applications of *yin* and *yang* than we have indicated here. Yet if we are looking for scientific uses of opposites that are quite uncontaminated (as we might be tempted to say) by the social and political, we are bound to be disappointed. That very search would, in fact, be deeply anachronistic, and indeed runs counter to the Chinese sense of the seamlessness of the whole constituted by the social and cosmic order. Given that *yin* and *yang* themselves have an inherently human and social dimension, as well as a cosmic one, that seamlessness has to be respected. This is not to apply human *analogies* to the cosmic situation, *nor* vice versa: but rather to see heaven and earth, ruler and minister, father and son, old and young, male and female, as all, ideally, embodying the same reciprocal relationship.

If we turn back now to Greek opposites, what chance have we of making better sense of them? Certainly there is no analogue to the dual functions that, in Sivin's interpretation, the *yin yang* and five phases synthesis served in the crises of legitimacy (both political and intellectual) under the Han. Rather, as I have already said, there was far less consensus among the Greeks in their references

12. See Sivin 1987, pp. 95ff, cf. Kuriyama 1995.

to opposites – as in other matters, including in particular a lack of agreement on the question of the ideal, or even the acceptable, political order. Whereas for the Chinese, throughout their history until modern times, there seems never to have been any serious doubt about the political ideal, namely the wise and benevolent rule of a single king or emperor, the Greeks, as is so well known, engaged in more or less constant argument, from the –5th century until long after they had lost their independence to Rome, about the merits and demerits of democracy, oligarchy, monarchy, and about their varieties, deviations and true types.

I shall come back in due course to explore the possible connections between the uses of opposites and political preferences in ancient Greece, but the first and fundamental point is the very diversity of such uses that we find. Not only are they deployed in every kind of inquiry, in metaphysics, cosmology, the exact and natural sciences (as we call them), medicine, ethics and politics: the nature of the relationship between different pairs is quite diverse, as Greek theorists of opposites, such as Aristotle, themselves pointed out. There are, in his view,[13] (1) contradictories (pairs of propositions of which one or other must be true), (2) contraries – which themselves come in two main kinds, those that do, and those that do not, exclude intermediates (as odd and even, and black and white, respectively), (3) correlatives (such as double and half), and (4) privations (such as sighted and blind). This type of analysis certainly did not prevent generalisation about opposites: Aristotle himself said (*Physics* 188b27ff) that all his predecessors adopted opposites as principles. But it helped to draw attention to the varieties of relationships in play. Oppositions between statements are one thing: oppositions between things another.

Given this great diversity, it is not at all surprising that examples can be found to suggest both similarities with, and differences from, the uses we have considered from China. There are Greek opposites where the relationship is one of reciprocity and mutual interdependence, and others where the relationship is one of incompatibility, including relationships between pairs of items that belong to different orders or levels of reality. So each of the two, simplistic, viewpoints that I mentioned at the outset

---

13. Lloyd 1966, pp. 86ff, gives a summary account.

– that which sees a basic similarity between ancient Greece and China with regard to polarities, and that which stresses the differences between them – can be said to have some evidence in its favour. But that, of course, does not get us anywhere.

To make some progress in understanding, on the Greek side, we must first press harder on the question of the underlying reasons for that diversity – though no doubt with little hope of encompassing it all. Domain by domain, however, a recurrent feature of much Greek speculative thought at all periods is a certain theoretical free-for-all, as rival 'masters of truth'[14] set out claims and counter-claims on any number of obscure issues in a bid to make a name for themselves.

It is repeatedly the case that the starting-point for a new Greek theory, in cosmology, physics, medicine, is the denial of an existing one. To the view that the world came to be is opposed the assertion that it is eternal, to the view that there is just the one world, the idea that there is a plurality, an indefinite or unlimited number, separated from this one in time or space or both, to the view that matter, space and time are infinitely divisible, the theory that they are constituted by indivisibles. Even when the theories in contention do not take the form of pairs of strict contradictories, they are nevertheless implicitly opposed to one another, in competition with one another as the one true account of the problem at issue. Opposition here, then, one might say, is a product of rivalry.

Now, that rivalry is already a feature of the second of the two views I sketched at the outset, namely that which – in the manner familiar since Burckhardt – stresses the adversariality, the agonistic spirit, that pervades Greek culture (cf. above, Chapter 2). But the move we now need to make, to help make better sense of more of our data concerning opposites, is to see that adversariality as not just a *first-order* matter – of the attitude that emphasises the hostility between certain pairs of opposites – but a *second-order* one as well, of the relationships between different types of theories (and their proponents), including *some* that stress (at the first order) harmony and reciprocity, as well as *others* that emphasise hostility.

14. This term, originally used by Detienne 1967 of the early Presocratic thinkers as opposed to later, systematic philosophers such as Plato, captures a recurrent feature of Greek intellectual life and may usefully be applied to the contending claimants to intellectual prestige throughout the classical period.

It seems possible to relate this variety of modes of opposition broadly to the circumstances in which Greek intellectuals operated, where we may now pick up and elaborate some of the themes of our earlier discussion in Chapter 2. In the classical period, at least, those circumstances were evidently very different from those of their Chinese counterparts. Early Greek philosophers had no emperors to impress. Some certainly found their way to the courts of tyrants, where analogies with the courts of Chinese rulers of the pre-Qin Warring States are not too far-fetched.[15] Some Greeks did so to enlist the tyrant's support for a political programme (as Plato seems to have tried with Dionysius II), others just in search of a living. But many more operated in one or other of the more or less democratic, or more or less oligarchic, city-states, whether their own, as citizens, or in others, as metics or resident aliens, or simply as visitors. In the −4th century, Athens became the centre of philosophy and home of all the main philosophical schools, Plato's Academy, Aristotle's Lyceum, Zeno's Stoa, Epicurus' Garden. Some of these received some support from the political powers of the day: Aristotle's Macedonian connections were enough to get him into trouble with those who thought they saw a political opportunity on the death of Alexander in −323. But it was not until Roman times that these schools had stipendiary heads. Throughout the classical and early Hellenistic periods, they were mainly self-supporting, relying on the wealth of their members and (as much and sometimes even more) on fee-paying pupils.

From the −4th century onwards the competition among Greek philosophers can be said to be not just for prestige in general, but also for those pupils. We know that the prospective pupils often 'shopped around', attending different schools before becoming more firmly attached to one – and even then not so firmly attached that there was no possibility of defection (cf. above, pp. 35ff). Dialectical debate was, in Greece, the essence not just of philosophical activity, but also of philosophical recruitment. While this point is especially true of philosophy, it has relevance also throughout the history of Greek medicine. It was not just their patients who paid Greek doctors, but also their pupils.

15. I have, however, expressed my reservations about finding any analogue to the Greek city-state structure in archaic China, Lloyd 1990, p. 125.

Analogies may be suggested with some Chinese teachers and their institutions, but also disanalogies, notably in that the entry of pupils into the imperial Academies came to be controlled by examination. There was no need there, then, for the members of rival schools to advertise themselves – as many Greeks did – by attempting to outdo one another in public debate on the issues of the day.

So the first argument we might offer is that some Greek uses of opposites reflect a rivalry that was endemic in Greek intellectual life for identifiable *institutional* reasons. But can we go further? Is there a Greek analogue to the political argument mounted by Sivin for China? Again, we must be careful to distinguish between the levels at which we look for connections.

Thus at one level, we certainly find the relationships between opposites described in terms that are directly drawn from the political sphere. The medical theorist Alcmaeon, in the −5th century, speaks of health as the *isonomia* (equal rights) of various opposed factors in the body – wet, dry, cold, hot, bitter, sweet and so on – and of disease as the *monarchia* (sole rule) of one of them (Fr. 4). The term *isonomia* is often associated with democratic ideals – not that we should necessarily infer from his use of that language that Alcmaeon was a democrat or was covertly advocating democracy: we simply have no evidence of his political leanings whatsoever.

But then there is a further complication, namely that talk of equality (*isotēs*), at least, is not confined to democrats. The oligarchs, too, thought that rights should be distributed 'equally', but by that they meant what Aristotle calls 'proportional' equality,[16] where the share any individual was entitled to reflected differences in birth or wealth. Some people were, according to the oligarchs, definitely more equal than others.

However, the more appropriate level at which to conduct our analysis is deeper: we should focus not on the points where Greek constitutions differed, but on what they all had in common. The topic we should now investigate is the *hierarchical* structures that are present in Greek city-states of every type, a particularly promising subject since it affords the possibility of a direct confrontation with Chinese hierarchisations.

16. Aristotle sets out competing views about 'the equal' in the *Politics*, e.g. 1280a7ff.

Let us begin with an obvious Greek example. It would be an exaggeration to see Plato's entire metaphysics as just a cover for his political programme – the ideal of philosopher-kings, the insistence that moral and political decisions (like all others) should be left to 'experts'. However, there are connections that Plato himself points out between his recommendations for the welfare of the state and those for the welfare of the individual. Both depend on the due observance of the fundamental contrast between *what rules* and *what is ruled*, or rather between *what should rule* and *what should be ruled.* A similar idea finds echoes also in the justification that Aristotle offers for his notorious view that slavery is a natural institution (*Politics* 1253b14ff, 1254a17ff). It is natural since it exemplifies the natural contrast between what rules and what is ruled, one found also in the relationship between male and female, and even in that between soul and body. His doctrine of slavery is just one of the most striking instances of an authoritarianism that permeates much of his thought, including his natural science. We shall come back to that at the end of the chapter.

But while, unsurprisingly, hierarchical notions are prominent in certain authoritarian political philosophies, we may once again dig deeper. A consideration of the ancient Greek perception of the democratic ideal brings to light some important and unexpected points. Decisions, on the democratic view, should be taken by majority vote. But while those in the minority were obliged to concur in that decision, it was not that they were expected to be happy with it. On the contrary, it was often assumed that they would continue to hold their different view, and might well continue to advocate it in the hope of reversing the decision at a subsequent vote.

Thucydides provides several examples of such reversals, even within the space of a few days, at Athens during the Peloponnesian War. One of the most famous instances is the pair of Assemblies held on consecutive days, in the first of which the Athenians voted to have all the citizens of Mytilene put to death for having revolted from Athens, but in the second of which, seized with remorse, they rescinded the vote and spared them (Thucydides III 36ff). While the institutions of the democracy guaranteed free speech – that is, the right to address the Assembly – and therefore to try to persuade the majority, it was not imagined that this procured *unanimity*. So the democratic ideal was not one of total agreement, so much as one of the due management of disagreement (cf. Loraux 1987).

This already brings to light one point where, from a Chinese perspective, what the various Greek political constitutions of the classical period had in common is as striking as where they diverged. The anti-egalitarian, oligarchic, Greek ideal was that good order depended on the differences between rulers and ruled being duly observed. Not much is said, by those who promulgated such a view, about the complementarity or interdependence of those two. Some writers emphasise, to be sure, that the good state is for the sake of the whole, not for the good merely of a section:[17] but in that context not much is generally said about the 'whole' including slaves. Rather, the stress is on the need for those ruled to obey.

But in the egalitarian, democratic, Greek ideal, too, the potential hostility of opposing views is recognised. It is just that the resolution of political disagreements there proceeds by way of the vote of the many, not by appeal to the superiority that was claimed to go with birth, or with wealth, let alone simply with greater force.

Politics in the Greek style, in other words, was in this way confrontational through and through, whatever the political preference, whatever the view as to how that confrontation was to be managed.

Moreover, all states exhibited a fundamental cleavage between citizens and the rest. Greek democracies were participatory, not representative, and they involved every citizen far more than the modern democracies to which we are accustomed in the West (cf. Osborne 1994), a point we have already had occasion to stress in relation to Greek experience of evaluating arguments and rhetorical performance in general. However it was, of course, *only* the citizens, even if *every* citizen, who participated, who voted in person in the Assembly, served on the jury-courts and so on.

The contrasts between citizen and non-citizen, and again between free and slave, and again between Greek and barbarian, and again between male and female, all lie beyond the reach of

17. This contrast provides the articulating framework for Aristotle's six-fold classification of political constitutions, into three good, and three deformed or perverted, types, at *Politics* 1279a22ff.

any egalitarianism actually practised in classical Greek city-states
– indeed beyond most theoretical conceptions of egalitarianism
that were ever expressed there. A female 'citizen' was so called
because she was the daughter of a citizen father (in the strict
sense) and a 'citizen' mother (in the same sense as herself). The
idea of an Assembly of women is an absurdity fit only for comic
exploitation. Again, Greeks and barbarians are both humans, to
be sure: but it took the upheavals of Alexander's conquests, and
the effective crippling of the city-state autonomy, before the notion
that Greeks and non-Greeks alike participated equally as citizens
of the world was adopted as an ideal by some political philosophies, notably Stoicism, founded by the Phoenician Zeno of
Citium.

It is not that Greek democracy was only a charade. The differences between Greek democracies and Greek oligarchies
were real enough, for whether or not political rights should be
restricted by criteria of wealth or birth was a live issue. But at a
level beyond that contrast, all Greek city-states depended on hierarchical structures that distinguished, or rather opposed, those
with and those without political rights at all. While some Chinese
notions of the *inter*dependence of certain categories can, of course,
be paralleled in Greece (for the Greeks appreciated well enough
the interdependence of male and female in reproduction), in
certain key Greek social relations the ideal is of the *in*dependence of the superior from the inferior, of the citizens from the
non-citizens on whom, economically, they nevertheless did most
assuredly depend. That independence is fundamental to the Greek
notion of freedom, *eleutheria*, for what marked out the slave was
the necessity to obey, while the free were, precisely, free to decide
for themselves.

Any claim that these basic political structures have any relevance to, let alone influence on, the general uses of opposites in
Greek philosophy and science that are our *explananda*, will strike
many as extravagant. Slave and free, it will be objected, do not
figure in scientific, nor even in metaphysical, Tables of Opposites, and their only importance is strictly in the domain of Greek
political theory, where indeed the issue of their relationship was
not taken for granted, but the subject of some debate,[18] even if

18. As is recorded by Aristotle at *Politics* 1253b20ff, 1254a17ff, 1255a3ff.

the opposed theoretical positions adopted were no more than *just* theoretical since they had no actual outcome on the institution of slavery.

That objection has some force, for indeed Greek uses of opposites cannot be reduced to those that convey some kind of notion of hierarchy. Yet first, just as we observed that in ancient China we cannot separate out the domain of the political from the scientific or cosmological, so we may remark that, for all the Greeks' interest in the demarcations of inquiries, their cosmology, their metaphysics, their science all remain deeply permeated by *values*. We shall be returning, in later chapters (pp. 182–3, 185, 199), to the explicit justification that many of the writers in question offer for the inquiries they undertook.

Secondly, the interest in determining *what rules* continues, not just in cosmology but elsewhere in physics, wherever the term for principle, *archē*, still carried its original associations with rule (see above, pp. 100, 116). Greek metaphysical principles *govern* the cosmos, but that meant, for the Greeks, a one-way relationship of dependence – of the cosmos on them, but not of them on the cosmos.

The third and most important point is this. The Greeks did not deploy opposites to legitimate a single particular type of political regime. But over and over again their uses of opposites mirror an essential feature of the social structures of Greek society, namely the fundamental division between rulers and ruled. A perceived hierarchical distinction within pairs of opposites that we might have expected to have been totally value-free is a feature that is made to do explanatory work in a variety of scientific contexts.

This claim needs elaborating briefly, though many examples will be familiar from other studies (cf. Lloyd 1966, pp. 48ff, cf. above, pp. 114f). In Aristotle's view, as we have noted, male is held to be 'naturally' superior to female, the latter said to be a 'natural' 'deformity'. Again, the members of each of the pairs right and left, above and below, front and back, are strongly differentiated as to value. Right, above and front are the principles (*archē*), first of the three dimensions (breadth, length and depth respectively), and then also of the three modes of change in living beings, namely locomotion, growth and sensation. Moreover, this doctrine provides him with the basis of his explanation of a range of real or assumed anatomical facts (the relative positions of the windpipe and the oesophagus, those of the two kidneys, the function of the diaphragm and the positions of the vena cava and the aorta)[19] and even further afield it is the principle he invokes in his admittedly tentative discussion of the difficult problem of why the heavens revolve in one direction rather than in the other.[20]

The point can be extended even to what we might have assumed to be the purely neutral mathematical pair, odd and even. They provide the basis for the Greek classification of integers and are thus fundamental to Greek arithmetic. But we also find them associated with good and evil respectively in the Pythagorean Table of Opposites (cf. above, p. 114). Further afield still, in classical Greek medicine, the contrast between odd and even days is the basis of one theory of 'critical days', by which the course and outcome of diseases were supposed to be determined and from which they could be predicted. So here too values, even though, of course, not directly political ones, are in play and are used to structure reality. As we should expect from the disputatious relationships between Greek medical theorists, it was not as if the reality so structured was agreed by all of them, for there were many different theories of 'critical days' employing many different sequences of numbers. But one recurrent Greek feature of the evaluation of odd and even and many other pairs of opposite terms is that there was no room for compromise as to the good or evil character in question, once that had been settled in the theory. There was no room for an idea corresponding to the Chinese perception of the *yin* in *yang* and the *yang* in *yin*.

I began with two opposing and admittedly simplistic views, that laid the emphasis the one on the similarities, the other on the contrasts, between the uses of opposites in classical Greece and China. Both similarities and differences can, indeed, be suggested, though they are not the ones we started with.

In both China and Greece many oppositions are either directly

19. See, for example, *On the Parts of Animals* 665a18ff, 667b34ff, 671b28ff, 672b19ff.
20. See *On the Heavens* 287b22ff. Since movement must be 'from the right' and 'rightwards', he accepts that the 'upper' celestial pole is the invisible southern one, not the visible celestial north pole, *On the Heavens* 285b22ff.

political or carry political, often hierarchical, overtones. Thus far there are some broad similarities.

But first the political messages in the two cases differ, and so too, secondly, do the notions of hierarchy in play. Moreover, thirdly, it is not just that the political situations that obtained in Greece and China in the periods we are concerned with are very different: so too are the positions of intellectuals of different types in the two societies, especially their relationships with political authority and with their own rivals and colleagues.

All three points affect, in differing ways, the styles of argument mounted using opposites. In China, the main points emerge from Sivin's analysis. The reciprocity of heaven and earth, of *yang* and *yin* in all their manifestations, is a key feature of the synthesis that at once legitimated the place of the emperor as mediator between heaven and earth, and secured the role of the literati who acted as his advisers. This synthesis took over many earlier ideas and themes, but it served a distinctive function in its elaborated form in the crises that followed the first grand unification of China.

In Greece, by contrast, dialectical debate, on which the reputations of philosophers and scientists alike so often depended, stimulated, when it did not dictate, confrontation, between theories of opposites as between theories of every kind. So often Greek intellectuals elaborated their own ideas via the negative route, not just of the criticism, but, precisely, the contradiction, of alternative views. The recurrent confrontations between rival masters of truth left little room for the development of a consensus, let alone an orthodoxy, little sense of the need or desirability of a common intellectual programme, let alone of one setting out to legitimate an agreed political regime.

However, below or beyond the level of explicit dialectical debate, the hierarchical structures of Greek society are mirrored in much Greek theorising with opposites, not just in overtly authoritarian philosophers such as Plato and Aristotle, and not just in philosophy, but also in such other fields as medical theory. Thus notions of the inherent superiority of male to female pervade even those medical theorists who disagreed with the Aristotelian view according to which the male alone produces seed. Even when that view was contradicted and the female too was recognised as producing seed, it was not as if male and female seed were deemed equal.[21]

Besides, as we said, hierarchy appears in different guises when we compare Greece and China. The Chinese repeatedly stress the interdependence of ruler and ruled, of emperor or king and ministers, of high and low. *Yin* and *yang* themselves are in constant interaction and can only be defined in terms of one another. The Greek ideal, by contrast, was often one of the independence, the autonomy, of what is superior, the superiority of which is not threatened by the inevitable cyclical exchanges that characterise *yin* and *yang*.

Thus even when Aristotle recognises that male and female have to cooperate in procreation, he claims that it is a mark of the superiority of those species of animals where male and female are distinct that that should be the case. While he defines the male by a capacity, he defines the female not by a complementary capacity, but by an incapacity. The male provides the moving cause and the form in generation, according to many texts, while the female provides merely the matter – and that is a mark of the greater 'divinity' of the male (*On the Generation of Animals* 732a1ff). Again, where ruler and ruled more generally are concerned, the fact that the household has to be there for the head of the household to rule is not allowed to obtrude in the characterisation of the freedom of the latter. The implicit contrasts with the non-citizen (let alone the slave) are not permitted to surface in the definition of the autonomous activities of the citizen. In one instance after another, the converse of the Greek recognition of the potential hostility between pairs of opposites was a desire to separate them, even when their very opposition connects or joins them.

In the perspective I have adopted here, the usefulness of the study of beliefs concerning opposites in different societies, ancient and modern, lies not in any contribution such a study might be supposed to make to the understanding of universal features of human communication, let alone of the structure of the human mind. No: the debate between universalists and relativists on those

---

21. The notion that females too produce seed is developed in such Hippocratic treatises as *On the Seed, On the Nature of the Child* and *On Regimen*, but *On the Seed* especially correlates female-producing and weakness, ch. 6, L VII 478.5ff, on which see, for example, Lloyd 1983, pp. 86ff, 89ff, and Dean-Jones 1994, ch. 3.

questions can hardly be advanced by invoking either the similarities or the differences between the kinds of beliefs we have been discussing, since any argument would presuppose a judgement as to the relative significance of those similarities and differences and so risks being merely circular. Rather, the study of those beliefs provides, if we are careful, an invaluable resource for investigating, first, the styles of communicative exchange cultivated in different societies, and beyond that, secondly, the underlying value systems of the societies in question, as these are exemplified not just in their political ideas, ideals and institutions, but also in their cosmological and scientific beliefs.

CHAPTER 7

Finite and infinite in Greece and China

Are the notions of finite and infinite used in similar or in different ways in ancient Greek and Chinese thought? It is typical of a certain naive approach to the problems of comparing Greek and Chinese science to accept the question posed in such brutally simplistic and vague terms, and then to proceed to answer it by developing either the thesis of a basic similarity, or the antithesis of a fundamental contrast, between the two ancient societies. Indeed this may happen without due consideration being given to how the term 'infinite' itself is to be understood, whether in the loose sense (where it stands merely for the immense or the indefinitely large), or in a strictly defined mathematical one (for example uncountability, where it is a property of infinite sets that they are neither increased by addition nor decreased by subtraction). Further ambiguities in the Greek terms will be examined in due course.

The aim of this chapter is not so much to attempt a comprehensive analysis of what is potentially a vast topic, as to indicate some of the complexities of the issues. The primary task, as I have emphasised before, is to define the problems to be investigated and to clarify how we should go about comparing. Only then can we begin to advance some suggestions that may help to resolve substantive issues. Moreover we should underline, at the outset, that much that is accepted as orthodoxy – and not just on the Greek side – is open to challenge, and that much remains unclear and puzzling, not just because lines of interpretation are disputed and controversial, but also because many of the problems remain largely unexplored, notably with regard to the interconnections between what we should call physics and mathematics. However, one important item on our agenda is the critical examination of a number of sweeping generalisations that are to be found in the literature.

140

To achieve that end it will be necessary first to evaluate some of the simplistic theses I began with, developing an argument in three stages. In the first the focus will be on the imagined contrasts between Greece and China, and in the second the emphasis will shift to points of comparison. This will clear the ground for a return to the topic of contrasts with an attempt to clarify and redefine the *explananda* in my final section. What are the issues that we should be concerned with here, and what light does this topic throw on the content, and on the conduct, of Greek and Chinese inquiries? I shall argue that it is not so much this or that concept or use of the finite or infinite that is important: rather the interest lies in how the ways they are used can illuminate the aims, presuppositions and interactions of Greek, and of Chinese, thinkers, and the nature of the philosophical exchanges cultivated in each society.

Thus the first stage in the argument might begin with a set of common assumptions about contrasts. Some might claim that it is obvious that there is a massive difference in emphasis between ancient China and Greece in that the latter tolerated, and even cultivated, the infinite in a range of contexts where the Chinese either deliberately excluded it or, more often, never even considered it. There were plenty of ancient Greeks who considered the universe to be spatially infinite and quite a few who believed that there was an infinity of worlds. Both ideas come in different forms. Thus for the atomists, both matter (the atoms) and the void (where matter is not) are infinite. Again for the Stoics, who denied void *within* the cosmos, there is infinite space *outside* it.[1]

Again infinite worlds were sometimes conceived by the Greeks as succeeding one another temporally, though others held that at any given time there is an unlimited number of worlds. In quite what form infinite worlds were maintained by some of the earlier Presocratic philosophers, such as Anaximander, is disputed.[2] In the −4th century a pupil of Democritus named Metrodorus is said to have claimed that it is as absurd to believe that one ear of corn would be produced in a great plain as to

1. See, for example, Stobaeus I 161.8ff, 17ff, Sextus Empiricus *M* x 3, Simplicius, *In Cael*, 284.28ff, translated in Long and Sedley 1987, I pp. 294ff. Cf. below, pp. 147f.
2. The issue is discussed at some length by Guthrie 1962, pp. 106ff, who sets out the principal ancient sources. Cf. also the sceptical views expressed by Kirk, Raven and Schofield 1983, pp. 122ff.

hold that just one world would be, in the infinite void (Aetius 1 5 4, DK 70 A 6). That just suggests a very large number of worlds. But our source goes on to make the argument that they are indeed infinite in number, since the principles, *aitia*, from which they are formed (that is, atoms and the void), are infinite.

The topic generated a good deal of speculation about what the other worlds may be like. In the –5th century Anaxagoras, who held that matter is infinitely divisible, believed that the cosmos contained an immense variety of seeds, and in Fragment 4 he describes the formation of humans and other animals in situations other than the one we are familiar with:

And [we must suppose that] men have been formed and all the other animals that have life; and the men have settled cities and cultivated fields as with us, and sun and moon and the rest as with us; and the earth grows all sorts of produce for them, the most useful of which they gather into their houses and use. This is my account of the separating off, that it must have taken place not only where we live, but elsewhere also.[3]

The contrast, here, between 'as with us' and 'elsewhere' is ambiguous: Anaxagoras could be thought to refer not to another world, but just to another part of the earth. But Democritus, as reported by Hippolytus, leaves no doubt that he has other worlds in mind:

There are innumerable worlds of different sizes. In some there is neither sun nor moon, in others they are larger than in ours and others have more than one. These worlds are at irregular distances, more in one direction and less in another, and some are flourishing, others declining. Here they come into being, there they die, and they are destroyed by collision with one another. Some of the worlds have no animal or vegetable life nor any water.[4]

Spatial infinity was sometimes maintained with an argument, versions of which were put forward by both the Stoics and the Epicureans,[5] though the original may go back to pre-Aristotelian

---

3. Translation from Guthrie 1965, p. 314. Anaxagoras was also famous, or rather notorious, among the Greeks, for having proclaimed that the sun and moon themselves are 'incandescent stones' (the ancient evidence is set out by Guthrie 1965, pp. 307ff).
4. Hippolytus, *Refutation of the Heresies* I 13.2–3, in DK 68 A 40. Translation from Guthrie 1965, p. 405.
5. See Simplicius, *In Cael.* 284.28ff, Lucretius I 968ff, Long and Sedley 1987, I pp. 45, 295.

Pythagoreans. Archytas, in the −4th century, is reported to have asked: 'If I were at the extremity, say at the heaven of the fixed stars, could I stretch out my hand or staff or could I not?' It would be absurd to think you could not do so. But that means that there will be either body or place outside the supposed extremity – an argument that can be repeated for whatever extreme point is postulated.[6]

Temporal infinity, in turn, was even more common, in that some who thought the world spatially finite held nevertheless that it is eternal. Here too different positions were adopted. Some held that the universe has neither beginning nor end, others merely that it has no end. Aristotle took the first view and argued that any supposed beginning to the cosmos must itself have a *prior* beginning, leading to an infinite regress of beginnings and so to the denial of any *first* one. Plato presents the second option, in his cosmological dialogue the *Timaeus*, where it is emphatically stated that the cosmos came to be, though it will not be destroyed. Already in antiquity, however, some thought that that statement, that the cosmos came to be, was only introduced for the sake of the narrative exposition in the dialogue, and did not represent Plato's own belief.[7]

So far I have taken cosmological examples. But Greek mathematics provides many more examples – so it could be argued – where the infinite is accepted and used readily enough. This could be said to be the case in arithmetic, with the number series, including such famous arguments as Euclid's proof of the infinity of primes (*Elements* IX 20), and in geometry, where the standard Greek view is that geometrical space is infinitely divisible.

Some of these Greek ideas no doubt find parallels in ancient Chinese thought. But the classical Chinese were evidently less inclined to try to prove a strict spatial infinity and less prone to speculate about an infinite number of worlds separated from ours in either space or time or both. So at a first stage it might seem that the contrasts between Chinese and Greek thought on

6. See Simplicius, *In Ph.* 467.26ff, DK 47 A 24, where Simplicius claims to be drawing on the −4th-century historian Eudemus. Translation from Guthrie 1962, p. 336, who discusses further Pythagorean ideas on time and the unlimited.
7. For Aristotle's own view, see *Physics* VIII chh. 5 and 6, e.g. 258b10ff, *On the Heavens* I chh. 10–12. For Plato's statement, see *Timaeus* 28b, and for the ancient dispute on that, see Aristotle, *On the Heavens* 279b32ff, and the other texts collected and discussed by Taylor 1928, pp. 67ff.

this topic are overwhelming – and to those to whom they do, that no doubt would be the moment when speculative explanations would be invoked to *account* for those differences. But that would be premature.

At a second stage of reflection much of the above picture, both of the Greeks and of the Chinese, has to be modified. Let me deal first with Greek physics, then with Greek mathematics, before turning to some of the Chinese materials.

Both the belief in spatial infinity and that in infinite worlds can, it is true, be found in Greece. But two points need to be made even in this regard. First, there is a lexical point that is relevant to the whole of our analysis of Greek thought on the subject. The Greek word often translated 'infinite' is *apeiron*, which combines a negative alpha with the term *peras* meaning limit. But *apeiron* often carried the weaker sense of *indefinite*. So maintaining *apeiroi kosmoi* sometimes implied no more than a belief in a large number of worlds, an indefinite number in fact. However, it has also to be said that in other contexts, infinite in the strict sense *is* the right translation of *apeiron*, and not just in some of the mathematical work. Archytas' argument, for instance, suggests that the notion of an extreme point is self-contradictory.

Secondly, it might be argued that those who made most use of the notion of the infinite in cosmological and physical speculation were the atomists, Leucippus and Democritus in the –5th century, Epicurus and his followers in the –4th and later centuries. But atomism, it might further be claimed, was never the *dominant* tradition in Greek philosophy and science, which is represented, rather, by Plato and Aristotle in the mid –4th century, and then by the Stoics from the late –4th century onwards. Plato, Aristotle and such Stoics as Zeno of Citium and Chrysippus disagreed on a number of issues, but all were continuum theorists and all teleologists.

The assumption that many of the Greek cosmologists made was that the sphere of the fixed stars marked the limits of the cosmos and this was shared by most of the astronomers. Otherwise why would Archimedes have tried to calculate how many grains of sand it would hold? Of course Archimedes' interest is in developing a mathematical notation to express very large numbers, and it is for that purpose that he conducts his thought experiment with the grains of sand idea. Indeed he sets out by denying both that the grains of sand would be infinite and that they exceed any expressible number (*Sandreckoner*, HS II 216.2–9). But practising astronomers too, down to Ptolemy in the +2nd century and beyond, assumed that the so-called fixed stars bound the cosmos, and while that did not rule out the Stoic view of infinite space outside the cosmos, for some – as for Aristotle – cosmos and universe are alike bounded and coterminous.

The first-stage presentation of Greek thought on the infinite might be criticised as seriously misleading in that many Greek philosophers, including some of the most prominent ones, fought shy of the notion of the infinite in many of its forms. Aristotle might be cited as a prime case in point.[8] True, he allows, as we have noted, that the universe is temporally infinite. But he opts firmly for a *spatially* limited universe. The heavens form a sphere with the heavenly bodies moving with eternal circular motions in the superlunary region. The earth is at the centre of the entire system, and there can, in this picture, be no question of a plurality of worlds. In *On the Heavens* Aristotle first devoted three chapters (I chh. 5–7, 271b1ff) to showing that there can be no infinite body, neither simple nor composite, and then proved (I chh. 8–9, 276a18ff) that there cannot be more than one world. This he does in part on the basis of his analysis of natural motions, which he claims must be either rectilinear – to or from the centre of the universe – or circular. That consideration also provides him with one of his arguments to show that the earth itself is spherical, but in this context he is concerned to establish that there can be only one centre and only one circumference to the world as a whole.[9]

Moreover so far as the infinite in mathematics goes (to which I shall be returning) Aristotle's view is that the mathematicians do not need the number series *actually* to be infinite: all they need – so he believed, wrongly, as has recently been claimed (Hintikka 1973, pp. 118ff on Aristotle, *Physics* 207b27ff) – is the idea that that series can be indefinitely extended. Even when it comes to the geometrical and physical applications of the notion of the continuum, where Aristotle is clear that it *is* a matter of

8. See Evans 1964, and cf. Mondolfo 1956, Hintikka 1973, Knorr 1982, Sorabji 1988.
9. Aristotle, *On the Heavens* 276b7–21, cf. II ch. 14, 297a8ff, on the sphericity of the earth.

infinite divisibility, the infinite in question, there, is, in both cases, potential, never actual. You can cut a line or a stick wherever you like. But Aristotle resists the idea (that he nevertheless records) that it is sensible to think of an actual division everywhere of what can potentially be divided anywhere.

There is a famous argument in *On Coming-to-be and Passing Away*, 316a14ff, that may give an atomist's point of view. Suppose that magnitudes *are* infinitely divisible. Then let them be divided everywhere. What have you left? You cannot be left with *nothing*, nor with what is dimensionless such as a point (since in both cases summing nothings, or what is dimensionless, gives nothing). Nor yet can you say you are left with a magnitude, because *ex hypothesi* you are supposed to have carried out the division *everywhere*. That may have been an argument that led the atomists to the conclusion that magnitudes (of any sort, or at least physical ones) must be constituted from *indivisible* atomic quanta.[10] But Aristotle simply denies that it could ever be the case that a magnitude is divided 'everywhere'. That is just something potential, never actual, even though there is some difficulty in squaring that view with Aristotle's insistence, elsewhere, that what is potential must be thought of as actualisable and that must mean at some point actualised – the idea that has been dubbed the principle of plenitude (Lovejoy 1936, cf. Hintikka 1973, ch. 5).

A similar potentially tricky deployment of the distinction between potential and actual infinities appears also in Aristotle's critique of Zeno. In the so-called Stadium argument,[11] reported by Aristotle at *Physics* 233a21ff and 239b9ff, Zeno had claimed (1) that to cross a stadium a runner must touch infinitely many points in the ordered sequence $\frac{1}{2}, \frac{1}{4}, \frac{1}{8}$ and so on, traversing on each occasion half of the total space remaining to be crossed; (2) that it is impossible to touch infinitely many points in a finite time; therefore (3) the runner cannot reach his goal. But Aristotle replies that the finite time itself, like the space to be

---

10. The answer to the question of how far Leucippus and Democritus had been anticipated by earlier views postulating atomic quanta depends on the interpretation of the evidence for Zeno and for the Pythagoreans: see further below, p. 158 n. 30.
11. This analysis is based on that in Kirk, Raven and Schofield 1983, pp. 269ff. The so-called Achilles argument, reported by Aristotle at *Physics* 239b14ff, similarly depends on the assumption that space is infinitely divisible.

traversed, is infinitely divisible: so (2) can be denied, and the conclusion (3) also. But while he believes that that is a sufficient argument *ad hominem*, to answer a questioner who raises the point at issue in (2), he comes back to the problem in a later passage, *Physics* 263a11ff, that reveals his continuing worries over the distinction between potential and actual infinities:

'So when someone asks the question whether it is possible to traverse infinite things, either in time or in distance, we must reply that in a way it is but in a way it is not. For if they exist actually, it is not possible, but if potentially, it is; for someone in continuous movement has traversed infinite things incidentally, not without qualification; for it is incidental to the line to be infinitely many halves, but its essence and being are different' (*Physics* 263b3ff, translation Kirk, Raven and Schofield 1983, p. 271).

Aristotle's difficulty is as before: the continua of space, time and motion are all infinitely divisible, for that is what it is to be a continuum. Yet they can be infinitely divisible only in potentiality. That move gives Aristotle his reply to those arguments of Zeno, and yet that leaves the relationship between the potential and the actual, in these cases, unclear, given Aristotle's usual insistence that the potential corresponds to what can indeed be actualised.

But as a source of qualifications to the contrasts suggested between China and Greece in my first-stage argument, the Stoics are just as important as Aristotle. Several features of Stoic cosmology, the finite cosmos, *pneuma*, the active and passive principles, seem, at least at first sight, close to Chinese ideas. True, outside the cosmos, as noted, they hold that there is infinite void. But so far as the cosmos itself goes, they (like Aristotle) hold that there is just the one, even though (unlike him) they believe it to be subject to periodic conflagration.[12] Furthermore they are continuum theorists in a strong sense. The cosmos is finite and there is no void within it. Unities come in different forms (the unity represented by a living organism is greater than that of inanimate substances), but everything forms part of a single interconnected whole. That different parts of that whole resonate with

---

12. See, for example, Nemesius 309.5ff, and other evidence collected by Long and Sedley 1987, I sections 46 (pp. 274ff) and 52 (pp. 308ff).

one another is the basis of their doctrine of *sumpatheia*, sympathy, which, as noted (p. 102 at n. 10) is made to do some explanatory work in a number of different contexts, in biology, in medicine and in physics.[13] More remarkably still, from the point of view of those looking for parallels between Greece and China, the Stoics held that *pneuma* permeates the whole cosmos: as such it could be thought to be the nearest the Greeks got to 氣, *qi*.

The very fact that Stoic *pneuma* is so badly *mis*represented by their opponents (Plutarch, Galen, Alexander of Aphrodisias, all the way down to Simplicius and Philoponus in the +6th century) is interesting and indicative. The questions that the opponents keep pressing include how many elements there are, what the relation between fire and the rest is, how breath can pervade everything, and what the relation is between its different modalities or manifestations, in inanimate substances, in plants and in animals ('tenor', *phusis, psuchē*). But it is clear that the Stoics worked rather with a notion of active and passive principles, not with one of four static elements.

At that point a general similarity with *yin* and *yang* might suggest itself, even though the Stoics never developed the systems of correspondences with which those principles eventually came to be associated in China (cf. above, p. 112 at n. 19, p. 123 at n. 8). Long and Sedley remark that, for the Stoics, 'four distinct elements . . . are not, as they are in Aristotle's cosmology, permanent features of the Stoic universe, but the basic qualifications of matter throughout the duration of each temporally limited world-order.'[14] That is correct in general terms, although one may question just how far those elements are indeed 'distinct'. Even so, the more important difference from Chinese *yin yang* is that they, *yin yang*, are, as we have said (p. 121 at n. 6) essentially functional and relational, and as such *not* basic qualifications of matter.

Then there is a further feature of Greek philosophy that can be taken to suggest a resistance to the notion of infinity at least in certain contexts. This is the recurrent idea, found for example

13. See, for example, Alexander, *On Mixture* 223.25ff, and other texts discussed by Long and Sedley 1987, I section 47 (pp. 28off) for the Stoic view.
14. Long and Sedley 1987, I p. 286. The Stoic evidence for elements and unities is collected at pp. 28off.

in Plato, Aristotle and Plotinus, that the infinite is not *intelligible.* Whatever has to be called *apeiron* is, as such, no proper subject of inquiry and understanding. There are texts in Aristotle that say as much in so many words. Thus in the *Physics* 187b7ff he puts it that 'the infinite *qua* infinite is unknowable: what is infinite in multitude or size is unknowable in quantity, and what is infinite in form is unknowable in quality.' He uses a similar argument in the *Metaphysics* 1036a8ff, 1037a27ff, to suggest that matter, as indeterminate, is unknowable in itself, and again at *Physics* 207a14ff, 25ff, he attacks Melissus for having asserted that the whole is infinite, repeating the point that the infinite as such is unknowable.

Plato too equates what can be known with what is limited or determinate. In a late and rather neglected dialogue, the *Philebus,* that draws on Pythagorean ideas, especially in the fundamental contrast it uses between limit and the unlimited, Plato makes it clear that the world as a whole, and its parts, can be understood only insofar as it, or they, manifest limit. True, there is also what is there to be limited, the as-yet-to-be-determined, that of which the limit is the limit. But it is the determinate or what has been determined that is there to be known (*Philebus* 16c–17a, 24a–25b).

Finally the +3rd-century neo-Pythagorean Plotinus was to go so far as to make explicit what had been implicit already in the Pythagorean Table of Opposites reported by Aristotle in the *Metaphysics* 986a22ff, namely that the infinite is evil, *kakon* (*Enneads* VI 6 1).

But it is not just Greek philosophy that provides evidence to suggest that certain important qualifications need to be entered before we accept the idea that Greek thinkers tolerated and used the notion of infinity with equanimity. Reservations also need to be expressed with regard to our earlier, first-stage, characterisation of Greek mathematics.

First it is well known that what is called, most misleadingly, the 'method of exhaustion' *avoids* infinite processes. The method, usually thought to have been developed by Eudoxus in the −4th century, depends on the principle expressed in Euclid *Elements* X 1. 'Two unequal magnitudes being set out, if from the greater there be subtracted a magnitude greater than its half, and from

that which is left a magnitude greater than its half, and if this
process be repeated continually, there will be left some magnitude
which will be less than the lesser magnitude set out.'[15] Used, as
for example in *Elements* XII 2, in the investigation of the ratios of
circles to their diameters, it allows the inscription of regular
polygons in a circle such that their area can be made to approximate *as close as one likes* to the area of the circle. But the area is,
precisely, *never* exhausted. Euclid then shows that of two circles
A and B, the area of A must be to that of B as the square on its
diameter is to the square on the diameter of B, by showing that
it can be neither greater nor less than that ratio. This gives a
proof procedure that is rigorous, but involves no breach in the
continuity axiom. There is no suggestion that the circle can be
identified with the infinite-sided regular polygon inscribed within
it. The Greek preference for the method of exhaustion is thus
evidence *both* of their demand for rigour *and* of their avoidance
of infinite processes wherever possible.

When, as in Archimedes' *Method*, the continuity axiom is
breached at least insofar as a curvilinear area is there treated as
made up of the indivisible line segments it contains, this is recognised as disqualifying the procedure as demonstrative: it can be
no more than heuristic. As we have discussed before (pp. 51ff),
Archimedes is clearly on the defensive, not just because of the
use of indivisibles, but also because he treats plane figures as
having determinate centres of gravity and as balanced around
a fulcrum. Judged by the usual standards of Greek demonstrative rigour, the method falls short. But it is remarkable that, if
not demonstrative, it is at least accorded heuristic status. Since
it was, after all, in conflict with the common Greek assumption
of the infinite divisibility of geometrical magnitudes, it might be
thought surprising that it is allowed in at all, even as a method
of discovery.

Archimedes also provides us with most of our not very extensive evidence for the summing of infinite series in Greek mathematics. The lack of a clear distinction between converging and
diverging series had caused difficulties already in the days of

15. Translation from Heath 1926, III p. 14. See Knorr 1975, pp. 256ff, 271ff, who argues
   that the stipulation 'more than half' may suggest an origin in relation to the anthy-
   phairetic approach to incommensurables, cf. Fowler 1987 and further discussions by
   Knorr 1978, pp. 200ff, 235ff, 1982, pp. 120ff, 1986, pp. 78ff.

Zeno of Elea.[16] Nor perhaps should we be surprised that the examples of Greek mathematicians confidently summing infinite series are rare,[17] when we reflect that, expressed in Greek, the notion of taking the limit (*peras*) of any series that is limitless (*apeiron*) certainly ran the risk of appearing flatly self-contradictory.

So much for some of the reservations that should be expressed with regard to our initial characterisation of Greek thought. But equally on the Chinese side, any thesis that would have it that Chinese thought in general was reluctant, even incapable, of dealing with the infinite, encounters considerable counter-examples.

It is true that the evidence for some uses of infinity in Chinese thought is late or unreliable or both. That applies especially to cosmology, where many invocations of the notion of the infinite, such as, for instance, the idea of infinite worlds, betray clear Buddhist influence (cf. Gernet 1993–4) and so fall outside the period with which we are chiefly concerned. Again, for the so-called 宣夜, *xuan ye*, cosmology,[18] we have an early +4th-century source, 葛洪, Ge Hong, who reports the view that the heavens are empty, immensely high and far away, and without bounds. But the writer does not inspire confidence in that he states that the books that set out this view were all lost, even though he claims to be reporting what a late Han librarian, 郗萌, Qi Meng, said that its earlier masters had taught.[19]

However, in other contexts we are on firmer ground. In a variety of areas of Chinese thought we have good evidence that recurrent procedures of different types were used with some

16. Thus in the arguments (Fragments 1 and 2) attacking the many on the grounds that they must be 'both so small as to have no size and so large as to be unlimited' (Simplicius, *In Ph.* 141.7f), there is an ambiguity in the term 'unlimited'. Most ancient commentators took it to mean 'indefinitely large'. But that had not been shown. Zeno had argued that there is an infinite number of parts: but the sum of a -converging – infinite series may be finite. It is controversial whether Zeno himself is under an illusion on the point, or whether it is rather just his opponents who may be. But either way the conclusion could easily have been resisted by an appeal to the distinction between converging and diverging series.
17. Thus Knorr 1982, p. 125 n. 30, cited Archimedes, *On the Quadrature of the Parabola*, Proposition 23, HS II 310.6–24, as unique: but that is to ignore other cases, cf. Sato 1987, pp. 114ff.
18. Needham 1959, p. 219, refers to the *xuan ye* teaching as a cosmology of 'infinite empty space'. Nakayama 1969, p. 39, cites a Qing scholarly gloss on the term as meaning '[the fruit of] the labour of the night'.
19. Needham 1959, p. 219, cites Ge Hong from the +10th-century encyclopaedia, 太平御覽, *Taiping yulan* 2: 2a and the early +7th-century *Jinshu* 11: 279. I am grateful to Nathan Sivin for stressing to me the difficulties of accepting this report.

confidence. One such text comes in the paradoxes reported towards the end of the *Tian Xia* 'chapter' of *Zhuangzi* (33: 70ff). They begin with a set of ten directly attributed to Hui Shi himself, and several of these evidently challenge conventional notions of space and time. Thus the first states: 'The ultimately great has nothing outside it . . . The ultimately small has nothing inside it', and the second: 'The dimensionless cannot be accumulated, yet its girth is a thousand *li* ("leagues")' (translation after Graham 1989, p. 78).

The contexts of these remarks are not recorded either here or in our other ancient evidence for Hui Shi, and modern scholarly interpretations diverge radically.[20] But Hui Shi's own paradoxes are then followed by others, including: 'if from a stick a foot long, you cut off half every day, it will not be exhausted in ten thousand generations' (*Zhuangzi* 33: 78). Once again we are at a loss for the precise context, but what is beyond doubt, in this instance, is that we have a clear appeal to a recursive bisection principle, similar in that respect at least to those attested for Zeno of Elea.

Our evidence for early Chinese mathematics is both richer and more complete, even though, to be sure, not without its own problems of interpretation. Thus in Liu Hui's commentaries on the *Nine Chapters* recurrent procedures are used both in the investigation of the area of the circle in Chapter 1, and in that of the volume of the pyramid in Chapter 5.[21] In Chapter 1 (103–6), he first establishes that the area of the circle is given by the formula, $A = \frac{1}{2}c$ times $\frac{1}{2}d$, where A is the area, c the circumference and d the diameter. He then proceeds to an evaluation of the ratio between the circumference and the diameter (that is π). In this a hexagon is first inscribed in the circle, then a dodecagon, and the procedure of doubling the sides of the inscribed polygon is then continued to give increasingly accurate approximations to the area of the circle itself. In ch. 5 (167–8) similarly, Liu Hui proceeds by inscribing, in the pyramid to be determined, figures that approximate closer and closer to it.[22]

20. With Needham 1956, pp. 190–1, compare Reding 1985, pp. 350ff, 435ff, and Graham 1989, pp. 78ff.
21. In tackling the problems addressed in this section I have benefited a great deal from an extensive exchange of correspondence with Drs Donald Wagner and Karine Chemla.
22. The problem is to find the formula for the volume of the figure called 陽馬 *yangma*, a pyramid with rectangular base and one lateral edge perpendicular to the base. It

塹堵 *qiandu*   陽馬 *yangma*   鱉臑 *bienao*

Figure 1

Figure 2

Figure 3

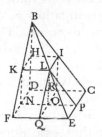

Figure 4

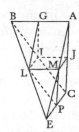

Figure 5

is first stated that a *yangma* plus a 鱉臑 *bienao* (pyramid with right triangular base and one lateral edge perpendicular to the base) form a 塹堵 *qiandu* (right prism with right triangular base) (Figure 1 sets out the shapes, Figures 2 and 3 show the result of adding the *bienao* BACE to the *yangma* BFECD: from Wagner 1979). But the volume of a *qiandu* is given as half length times breadth times height. So Liu Hui has to show that one *yangma* equals two *bienao* in order to give the formula for the volume of the *yangma* (namely one third length times breadth times height). This he does by first dividing the *yangma* and the *bienao*. On one interpretation (Wagner 1979) he does so as in Figures 4 and 5. Thus the *bienao* in Figure 5 (BACE) is divided into two *qiandu* (AGIJML and ILMJCP) and two smaller *bienao* (BGIL and EPML). The *yangma* in Figure 4 (BDFEC) is divided into one box (HILKNDRO), two *qiandu* (ILORCP and KLONFQ) and two smaller *yangma* (BHIIK and LOPEQ). But the sum of the two *qiandu* in the *bienao* (Figure 5) can be seen to equal half that of the box and the two *qiandu* in the *yangma* (Figure 4). So he must now show that the remaining, smaller, *bienao* of the *bienao* are half the remaining, smaller, *yangma* of the *yangma*. But they can be subdivided in exactly the same way as the original *bienao* and *yangma* were. Again part of the components thus distinguished can be seen to fulfil the requirement of the proportion, one *yangma* equals two *bienao*, leaving a remainder that on each iteration is a quarter of the previous remainder. If the process is continued, the series converges on the formula one *yangma* equals two *bienao*. Several points in the detailed interpretation of this text are disputed (with Wagner 1979 compare Chemla 1992b), but, as is agreed on all sides, Liu Hui evidently here uses iterative procedures in order to determine the proportions that hold between *yangma*, *bienao* and *qiandu*.

In ch. 1 he remarks: 'the finer one cuts, the smaller the loss [or error, 失, *shi*]; if one cuts it and further cuts, until one reaches [至, *zhi*] what one can no longer cut, then it coincides with [or fits, 合體 *he ti*] the circle and there is no loss/error'.[23] Here Liu Hui *may* envisage the convergence of the perimeter of the inscribed polygon and the circumference of the circle, though it is clear from the subsequent discussion that it is recognised that the circle is greater than any determinate-sided inscribed polygon: any such polygon is still a polygon, not a circle. Precisely which sections of the ensuing investigation of the value of the circumference-diameter ratio are Liu Hui's own work, and which the work of later commentators, is disputed (Wagner 1978b, pp. 206ff), but their efforts are directed at better and better approximations and never claim an *exact* value.

Moreover in the otherwise similar investigation in ch. 5, Liu Hui uses a rather different expression for his result. 'The smaller they are halved, the finer are the remaining [dimensions]. The extreme [至, *zhi*] of fineness is called "subtle" [微, *wei*]; that which is "subtle" is without form [形, *xing*]. When it is explained in this way, how could one get a remainder?'[24]

Both the similarities with, and the differences from, Greek procedures are alike remarkable. In neither case does Liu Hui proceed, as some Greeks would normally have done, via an indirect proof.[25] Those Greeks would have demonstrated that, for example, the area to be determined cannot be either greater or less than a given area and so must be equal to it.[26] Liu Hui's attack is direct: he does not proceed by disproving inequalities, but seeks to establish the formulae, for the circle and for the pyramid, directly, and as we have seen, his circle discussion continues with an evaluation of the circumference-diameter ratio that aims at securing closer and closer approximations.

Again the Greeks, as we noted, generally thought that the area

---

23. Ch. 1, 103.11–104.1 in Qian's edition of the *Nine Chapters*. Compare Chemla 1992b, p. 41 n. 15. Volkov's recent study (forthcoming) suggests that the explanation for the termination of the procedure of cutting lies in the numerical features of the calculation that follows and the degree of precision there sought.
24. Ch. 5, 168.2–3, translation adapted from Wagner 1979, p. 173, Cf. Chemla 1992b, pp. 38f, who translates the last phrase: 'comment obtiendrait-on un reste?'.
25. The point has been made by Chemla 1992b, pp. 42ff.
26. As in Euclid's investigation of the circle in *Elements* XII 2 (cf. also Archimedes, *Measurement of the Circle*) and the discussion of the pyramid at *Elements* XII 3 (cf. Chemla 1992b, pp. 42ff).

to be determined is, precisely, *not* exhausted, for Eudoxus' principle allows the insertion of a further rectilinear figure between any rectilinear figure and the circumference to which it approximates. True, there is one notable Greek exception, namely Antiphon, who is reported to have claimed that the circle is 'at some point' (*pote*) exhausted by the inscribed polygons.[27] But his suggestion was rejected by philosophers and mathematicians alike as being in conflict with the principles of geometry, that is to say the continuum assumption. Aristotle curtly notes (*Physics* 185a16ff) that whereas other attempts to square the circle need refuting, 'it is not the business of the geometer to refute that of Antiphon'.[28]

Liu Hui, for his part, is clear, we said, that any determinate-sided inscribed polygon is still a polygon, not a circle. Both here and in the pyramid investigation he envisages iterations that can be continued at will. It is interesting, however, that there is a certain variation or hesitation in the strength of the claims made at the end of his two inquiries. In ch. 1 you continue until no further cuts are possible and 'there is no loss/error', while in ch. 5 the conclusion is a question: 'how could one get a remainder?' Moreover the mathematical results obtained in the two cases differ. In ch. 5 the formula for the volume of the pyramid is *exact*. In the circle division, while the formula A = $\frac{1}{2}$c times $\frac{1}{2}$d is also exact, that is no use until c is known – that is, until a value can be assigned to the length of the circumference. Moreover, in fact, in the subsequent discussion, the numerical value for the circumference-diameter ratio is no more than approximate, though it can be made increasingly accurate.

The question then arises as to whether Liu Hui's expressions imply that he has a clear grasp of the notion of taking the limit of an infinite series, and it should be stressed that much of the background we need to answer that is lacking. We simply do not have good contemporary texts that could throw light on the extent to which a technical vocabulary had been developed in Chinese mathematics at this time.

27. As reported in Simplicius, *In Ph.* 54.20ff (note *pote dapanōmenou* at 55.6), on which see Mueller 1982, pp. 154ff, Knorr 1982, pp. 130ff.
28. The contrast is with Hippocrates of Chios, at least according to the ancient commentators, Themistius, *In Ph.* 3.30ff, cf. Simplicius, *In Ph.* 54.12ff, though it is doubtful if Hippocrates was guilty of any fallacy (Lloyd 1987b).

The key question is the expression we rendered 'there is no loss – or error', which can be taken either loosely – there is no appreciable error, the error can be discounted – or strictly – there is no error, since what is envisaged is the strict coincidence of the infinite-sided polygon with the circle. On the one hand, there is no talk of infinite sides, and no clear Greek-style definition of limit. On the other, the term *wei* is clarified in ch. 5 and not just for use in that investigation, since it is applied also elsewhere in the commentary.

Moreover, the term *zhi* is used in both discussions, of the 'extreme', or of 'what one reaches', in ch. 1 of 'reaching' what one can no longer cut, and in ch. 5 of the 'extreme of fineness' that is 'without form'. That last expression, too, can be taken strictly or loosely, but offered as an *explanation* for why there is no remainder, it may suggest Liu Hui's confidence that the formula for the volume of the pyramid (that is, one third length times breadth times height) is exact – as indeed it is. If the variation in the expressions used for the claims made in the two cases is *mere* variation, for stylistic purposes, that would be compatible with the hypothesis that Liu Hui is in complete control of procedures that imply the taking of a limit of a converging infinite series. Yet we have to admit that that is, in the state of our evidence, a mere conjecture.

But if we have to suspend judgement on that point, nevertheless, for our purposes here, the upshot of this rapid survey is clear. It is obvious that Liu Hui is as much at home as any Greek geometer with the deployment of indefinitely recurring procedures, and it is possible that he was a good deal more at home than most with the notion of convergence to a limit.

So at the second stage in our argument, we can say that good grounds have been identified for revising quite drastically a number of the generalisations about Greece and China propounded at the first stage in the discussion. However, a more radical approach to the issues needs to be adopted. What both lines of argument so far developed have in common, and where *both* seem flawed, is in this: they focus on similarities and differences in *concepts* or *theories* (between Chinese and Greeks) and then strive to identify, on the Chinese or on the Greek side, what the majority of thinkers, or the most important ones, maintained in most contexts. They then attempt to use what has been identified as *the* Chinese or Greek view as the basis for an argument insisting either on the contrasts (as in stage one) or on the similarities (stage two). But – quite apart from the risky, even illicit, character of any generalisation as to what *the* Chinese or *the* Greek view is – that may miss the point.

On the Greek side, first, it is easy to see that on this subject, as on so many others, there was no uniformity, let alone orthodoxy. Almost any position, any use of infinity, can be attested, and most theses that were put forward by ancient Greek thinkers were challenged by – other – Greek thinkers themselves. So it is no wonder that both the claim that the Greeks espoused the infinite with equanimity, and the claim that they fought shy of it, have some evidence that can be cited in apparent support. But that does not get us anywhere.

But more importantly, secondly, the Greeks often maintained whatever position they took up on these issues in direct opposition to the alternative. First, they were generally conscious of the alternative, and secondly, and again more importantly, they often generated arguments for their own positions *by way of* refuting those alternatives.

It is not as if Plato and Aristotle simply ignored the opposition: they *used* it. Aristotle, especially, develops atomistic arguments then to put them down – as we have seen in the text from *On Coming-to-be and Passing Away* cited before. The same dialectical confrontations recur in the Hellenistic period, though the quality of the polemic varies. Thus Epicurus sometimes proceeds by simply denying the opposition's case or dismissing it out of hand, though there are also plenty of arguments against rival views in him and in one of our fullest later sources for Epicureanism, the +1st-century Roman poet, Lucretius. Again, I have remarked that neither Galen nor Alexander is exactly fair to the Stoic view of matter when they attack it. However, the point remains, that there continues to be a heavy use of whatever opposition you face, not just for destructive purposes, to show that they are mistaken, but also for constructive ones, to build up your own position. The alternatives, indeed, were often seen as mutually exclusive and exhaustive: that allowed arguments to proceed by exclusion. It cannot be the case that the universe is finite/infinite: *so* it must be infinite/finite. It cannot be the case that matter, space and time are infinitely divisible: so they must be constituted by indivisibles. Or vice versa.[29]

The dialectical confrontations get an added twist with the Hellenistic Sceptics. Dilemmatic arguments presenting antinomies were used already, long before, notably by Zeno of Elea, who aimed to defeat the assumption that motion is possible *whatever* view was taken on how space and time were composed.[30] But the Hellenistic Sceptics held that on every theoretical issue, relating to underlying reality or hidden causes, *both* sides were wrong.[31] One should, as they said, suspend judgement. But the way they proceeded was, precisely, to match every positive ('dogmatic') thesis to its antithesis – to leave not just one of them, but both, undermined. *Isostheneia*, equal strength on either side, is what they called this: but if equally strong, equally weak.

Here then, in stage three of our discussion, we rejoin some familiar topics on the Greek side, at least, namely the antagonistic strands that are such a feature of Greek thought, together with the recurrent concern for foundational questions and the ultimate justification for a position (cf. above, pp. 12f, Chapter 2). In the latter regard, both atomic and continuum theories addressed the issue of the *ultimate* constitution of matter, space and time. It is striking that continuum theorists tend to be continuum theorists *across the board* – and so too were atomists (cf. Furley 1987). That is, when a continuum view was adopted, it was adopted not just for physical matter, but also for space and time and indeed for geometrical magnitudes: all were treated as

29. I explored the use of this and other types of 'polar' arguments in Lloyd 1966, pp. 103ff, 111ff.
30. This remains the case, even though Zeno's presentation of the dilemma was not as crisp as Tannery 1930 thought, when he envisaged Zeno attacking motion first on the assumption that space and time are infinitely divisible, then on the assumption that they consist of strict indivisibles. The second limb of that reconstruction faces two difficulties, (1) that it conflicts with how the ancient commentators took Zeno, (2) the notion of strict quanta of time is otherwise not attested before the late –4th century. But even if Zeno did not use the idea of strict quanta of time, the arguments called the Arrow and Moving Rows attack motion on the basis of some looser notion of the component elements of space and time. See, for example, Furley 1967, pp. 71ff, Owen (1957–8) 1986. The further suggestion, developed by Tannery and others, that Zeno's target was a specific Pythagorean doctrine according to which numbers, points and atoms are identified, is nowadays discounted for lack of reliable primary evidence for what, after all, would be a gross confusion.
31. Cf. above, p. 15, p. 38 at n. 38. Some of the primary texts are collected in Long and Sedley 1987, I sections 68–72, pp. 438ff, and cf. Schofield *et al.* (eds) 1980, Burnyeat ed. 1983.

infinitely divisible. Similarly, the atomists often deny all these modalities of continua, and postulate atomic quanta, physical, spatial,
temporal, geometrical, instead. Mixtures of the two types of position are rare, even if not (as Furley suggested) quite unknown:
one possible exception is Democritus, who *may* have combined
physical atomism with an assumption of a geometrical continuum,
though the point is certainly controversial.[32]

I am tempted to argue, therefore, that the plurality of theoretical positions different Greeks adopted on this set of issues is the
– all too predictable – outcome of their fondness for the dialectical exploration of abstract ideas. That in turn relates (1) to the
rivalry between those who claimed special knowledge which we
have discussed before, and (2) to their sense of how to present
their cases in the best possible light in relation to the audiences
they were hoping to persuade – often general audiences, indeed,
present at open debate between rival views set out by contending parties. *Advocacy*, practised extensively in the Greek law-courts,
comes to be a prominent feature of many Greek intellectual exchanges, when opposing 'masters of truth' set out to challenge
conventional wisdom and each other's replacements for it.

Standard, conventional or 'common-sense' opinions thus get
to be overturned and repudiated, in ancient Greece, across the
board, and on some unlikely issues, by people who claimed to
know better. The sensible assumptions that the earth is flat, the
heavens a dome above it, physical objects are solid, and so on,
are confronted with all sorts of rival theories proposed by speculative thinkers of varying degrees of fame and respectability. As
for the fine structure of time and space, common assumptions
did not really tell people quite what to think. You certainly did
not need to have a view on that to order your life according to
the cycle of the seasons and the passing of the years. But once
Greek speculative thought began in earnest with the Presocratic
philosophers, then just about every thesis – and its contradictory
– are examined, and quite a few are seriously entertained. On
that line of argument, it is not at all surprising that, once Greek
philosophy got going, then sooner or later infinite worlds, atomic
quanta of time, even indivisible lines, would find proposers and

32. The way in which these positions may have been reconciled has been discussed by
    Meakin 1990.

seconders – as well as opponents – in the to and fro of abstract debate.

This argument, on the Greek side, does not, to be sure, resolve the problems, so much as redefine them, setting a new agenda. The chief *explanandum* becomes not why this or that idea of the infinite was promulgated in this or that context, but rather the conditions that allowed such abstract debate to develop. We rejoin, that is to say, the topics we have discussed in previous chapters, the recruitment and interactions of intellectuals, the contexts of their communicative exchanges, the audiences they were trying to win over, the techniques available to them to gain a reputation for themselves. The topic of the finite and the infinite suggests not just a gift for abstract analysis, but also a readiness to take on opponents and to pursue arguments wherever they may lead.

But what about China? Here too it is essential to be clear as to what the focus of the inquiry should be and what it can hope to achieve. Our task here, in my view, should not be to attempt to explain some supposed Chinese readiness, or reluctance, to espouse, or to shun, the infinite as such, but rather to see what light our study of the actual, complex, diverging views on the infinite can throw on the aims and presuppositions of the thinkers concerned, whether in mathematics or in philosophy. What does the material we examined tell us about what their goals, in those inquiries, were?

Two tentative general suggestions, in that regard, may be followed up briefly in conclusion, the first to do with the balance between theoretical interests and practical applications in mathematics, the second to do with the conduct of philosophical exchanges in China more generally.

First, it has often been claimed that Chinese mathematics is essentially pragmatic, if not indeed directly practical, in aim, and this has been a standard way of contrasting Chinese mathematics with the dominant Greek tradition represented by Euclid or Archimedes. However, our analysis of the use of recurrent procedures suggests that qualifications need to be recognised. First, to take one example of many, the exploration of the ratio of circumference to diameter is certainly carried far beyond any possible practical application. For practical purposes, a value of 3 or $3\frac{1}{7}$ is perfectly adequate. But the commentaries on ch. 1 of the

Nine Chapters pursue the analysis to the point where the area of a polygon of 192 sides is being determined and that of polygons up to 3072-sided ones is being contemplated.[33]

It is true that the computation of the circumference–diameter ratio (π) does not envisage a proof, but the best approximation possible. Yet that is not to say that nothing like proofs are ever attempted in Chinese mathematics. We have criticised that thesis before (Chapter 3) and here too our investigation of recurrent procedures throws further light on the issue. Liu Hui's preliminary study of the area of the circle *shows* that the formula he states is correct, namely that the area is equal to half the circumference multiplied by half the diameter. True, the form of the proof differs from the style of axiomatic-deductive demonstration favoured by Greek mathematics in the Euclidean tradition. However, the fact that axiomatic-deductive demonstration does not figure in Liu Hui nor in any other classical Chinese mathematical text should not blind us to the further point, that what we have in Liu Hui, in this context as in others (cf. pp. 61ff), are perfectly proper procedures to verify correct results – proving them, indeed, in just *that* sense.

Moreover on the question of pragmatics, Liu Hui himself notes, at the end of his pyramid investigation, that 'the object [called] *bienao* has no practical use; the shape [called] *yangma* can be long or short, or broad or narrow. Nevertheless without the *bienao* there is no way to investigate the number [that is the volume] of a *yangma*; and without the *yangma* there is no way to know the kinds of 錐, *zhui*, and 亭, *ting* [by which Liu Hui means a variety of shapes connected with the cone and the truncated cone]. These are primary in application' (ch. 5, 168, 3–4, translation adapted from Wagner 1979, p. 182).

Two points are striking about this remark, first that Liu Hui clearly recognises that his study goes beyond what is of direct practical use, but then secondly that he registers a certain defensiveness on the point. It is as if he feels some obligation to *justify* himself here, as if his assumption, or that of other students, is that mathematical investigations *should* prove themselves to be, directly or indirectly, of practical use. In that latter regard, the

33. Ch. 1, 104–6. As already noted, the problem of which parts of this discussion are the work of Liu Hui, which that of later commentators, is disputed: see Wagner 1978b.

contrast can still be remarked between Liu Hui's views and those of those Greeks who rated mathematics the higher the more abstract, the further removed from practice, it was.[34]

My second, final, more general point relates to debate. I have stressed elsewhere the antagonistic characteristics of much Greek speculative thought, and they are certainly in evidence in discussions of infinity. Face to face confrontation, often before a general audience, the public who in some cases adjudicated who had won the contest,[35] is typically Greek and hard indeed to parallel in China, certainly so far as reference to the public for judgement is concerned.

But as has been pointed out before, that is not to say that there is no criticism, sometimes indeed hard-hitting criticism, of rivals in Chinese philosophy and science. Two examples relating to our topic can be used to illustrate this. We noted before that the evidence for the *xuan ye* idea of a boundless heaven is late. In Han times, as we shall be considering in greater detail in the next chapter, two main cosmological ideas were current, in both of which the world is thought of as finite. In the *Gai Tian* system, described in the *Zhoubi suanjing*, the heaven is a circular canopy set over a central earth. In the *Hun Tian* view, the heavens are a complete sphere, with half of this invisible below the earth at any time. Each view was associated with, indeed closely tied to, observational techniques – using the gnomon and the armillary sphere respectively – and they are better considered not so much as cosmological theories, as rather ways of doing astronomy (Nakayama 1969, pp. 24ff, Cullen forthcoming, cf. below, Chapter 8).

Although the two are sometimes combined, the period of the rise of the *Hun Tian* view is characterised by texts that criticise *Gai Tian*. Thus the 太平御覽, *Taiping yulan*, preserves an account of a discussion from the lost work 新論, *Xin Lun*, by 桓譚, Huan Tan (c. −43 to +28). In this the *Gai Tian* view is duly set out and

34. This is a prominent and recurrent theme among those who considered themselves Platonists, such as Proclus, in his commentaries on the *Timaeus* and on Euclid's *Elements* I, especially. But they could and did cite texts from Plato himself as their ancient authority, for example Socrates' remarks on the so-called propaedeutic studies in the *Republic* (525a ff, for instance). Thus it is claimed at *Republic* 530bc that the chief usefulness of astronomical study lies, precisely, in its value in training the soul in abstract thought.

35. This is the case, for example, with what are called sophistic *epideixeis*, or display speeches, examples of which are extant in our Hippocratic Corpus and which are referred to in *On the Nature of Man*, ch. 1, *CMG* I 1, 3, 164.3–166.11.

then criticised from a *Hun Tian* perspective, on the grounds, for example, that it could not account for the equality of day and night at the spring and autumn equinoxes, and with a direct appeal to the actual experience of the movements of the sun's shadow in the White Tiger Hall where the purported discussion took place.[36] While that is still a far cry from Greek debates aiming to establish by argument that the heavens must be finite, or again that they must be infinite, it illustrates an openness to alternatives and a recognition that they are just that, potential competitors.

As a second example we may revert to the way in which the topic of the infinite provided resources for paradox in China, as it also did in Greece. We mentioned the dicta attributed to Hui Shi and others reported in the *Tian Xia* 'chapter' of *Zhuangzi*. However, the reaction that Hui Shi provoked, in that discussion, is interestingly different from the reception that later Greek philosophers accorded to Zeno. Aristotle, at least, as we saw, wanted to defeat Zeno by argument, the effect of which was to claim that Zeno had ignored a distinction that he, Aristotle, maintained to be important.

The reaction to Hui Shi in *Zhuangzi* is milder, if condescending, and it proceeds not by an attempted refutation, but by lamenting the waste of his talents. 'He had many formulae, his writings filled five carts, but his way was eccentric . . .'

Hui Shi day after day used his wits in disputation with others, but it was only in the company of the disputers in the world that he distinguished himself as extraordinary . . . What a pity Hui Shi's talents were wasted and never came to anything, that he would not turn back from chasing the myriad things. He had as much chance of making his voice outlast its echo, his body outrun its shadow. Sad, wasn't it? (*Zhuangzi* 33: 69–87, translation adapted from Graham 1981, pp. 283ff)

We have remarked before that the Greeks lacked the Chinese sense of the need to develop a common language, a characteristic increasingly manifested in China from Han times on. What this text in *Zhuangzi* helps to bring out is a related difference in the manner of dealing with disagreement. The reaction to Hui

---

36. *Taiping yulan* 2: 6b–7a (cf. *Jinshu* 11: 282). This evidence is discussed in Cullen forthcoming, who speaks of an 'age of polemics' when the *Hun Tian* system comes on the scene.

Shi's speculations in this chapter is not to confront, let alone refute him, but rather to pour scorn on his wasted effort. From the earliest Presocratic philosophers, down to the +6th-century Aristotelian commentators Philoponus and Simplicius, the preferred Greek style of reasoning, on the finite and infinite as on most other topics, was rather to attempt to disprove opponents by argument. But that, we can see, had the effect of prolonging dispute, rather than resolving it, and may thus have been one factor militating against the formation of an orthodoxy, whereas the Chinese, from Han times on especially, worked hard to produce one and largely succeeded in securing a common framework for discussion. Our next chapter will follow these last points up in relation to the aims and goals of astronomical cosmology in the two ancient civilisations.

CHAPTER 8

Heavenly harmonies

When the heavens were studied in ancient Greece or China, what were they studied *for*? Historians who attempt general surveys of astronomy still often focus on what they see as developments: who was responsible for the first correct explanation of lunar or solar eclipses? Who first discovered the phenomenon of the precession of the equinoxes? And so on. Indeed a preoccupation with priorities colours much of the comparativist work in the tradition of Needham's *Science and Civilisation in China.* From the point of view of subsequent European astronomical theories, the centre of attention, so far as ancient Greece is concerned, has often been the construction of geometrical models to account for the movements of the planets, sun and moon. It is the sequence of such models, with the varying fortunes of concentric spheres, epicycles and eccentrics – together with the stillborn ancient Greek debate between geocentricity and heliocentricity – that provides the articulating framework of the story. That story is written as if ancient Greek astronomy were just waiting for Copernicus, Kepler and Newton to come along to continue and complete it.

The fundamental flaw in any such approach is obvious. It ignores the question of what the ancients themselves thought they were doing, what their aims were, what they were interested in. Or rather, it assumes that the answers to those questions correspond, more or less, to the way astronomy has been defined since (say) the seventeenth century. It is as if there were nothing at all puzzling or problematic about, for example, why some of the ancient Greeks attempted those geometrical models of planetary motion.

Yet that clearly *is* puzzling, as soon as one reflects on the fact that the issue of devising geometrical models to explain planetary motion just did not figure on the agenda of ancient Babylonian, Egyptian or Chinese astronomy – to go no further afield – and that despite much sophisticated work in many areas, including, in some cases, the construction of numerical tables of periodicities relating to the movements of the planets themselves.

Here, as elsewhere in this study, our starting-point must be the premiss that there is nothing automatic about the way in which the subjects to which we attach our modern labels – in this case astronomy – were studied in the ancient world. We have to assess what the ancients themselves said about the subjects they were engaged in, their aims and interests, their carrying through of their programme. *A priori* assumptions about how they should have defined their task merely prejudice our inquiry – though that is not to suggest that history can be anything other than evaluative, for it can certainly never be value-free.

But if the Chinese and Greek terms used for different branches of the study of the heavens differ – as we shall see in a minute they do – is there any basis for a comparison at all? Sufficient general similarities in aims and subject-matter appear to exist for the answer to that question to be a cautious yes, even though due allowances have to be made for how such aims fitted more general ambitions, the extent to which they constituted popular, or specialised, interests and so on.

To explain both points very briefly at this stage. In China a broad distinction is drawn between 曆法, *li fa*, and 天文, *tian wen*. The first is conventionally translated 'calendar studies', though it comprised more computational work, for example of occultations of Venus or of solar eclipses, than that term suggests. The second consisted in the essentially qualitative study of celestial patterns of any kind, including cosmography and the interpretation of celestial phenomena deemed to be ominous.

The Greeks, by contrast, refer to the study of the stars either as *astronomia* or as *astrologia*. These do *not* correspond to the distinction we draw between astronomy and astrology, even though the Greeks could, and sometimes did, draw an equivalent distinction, namely between predictions of heavenly movements, and predictions of their effects on earth. Ptolemy, for one, does so at the beginning of the *Tetrabiblos* (I 1, 2.16ff). But *astronomia* and *astrologia* are often used interchangeably, as also are their Latin transliterated equivalents (*astronomia*, *astrologia*), even though attempts at systematising the boundaries between them begin to be made in late antiquity (Hübner 1990).

However, while Greek and Chinese terms for different types of celestial study evidently differ, we can identify also appreciable apparent similarities between some of the subjects investigated, even though on close inspection the nature of the interest, in either case, turns out to differ. Three topics that stand out are (1) the regulation of the calendar, (2) cosmography and the description of celestial movements, and (3) the investigation and prediction of omens and portents. My central concern here will be with the second of these topics and in particular with the analysis of the different ideas of celestial harmony and order found in China and in Greece. But briefer comments should also be made on the other two issues, while acknowledging that a comprehensive survey lies well beyond the scope of this chapter.

I

The topic of calendar studies immediately brings to light a difference in the institutional framework within which Chinese and Greek astronomers operated that must be considered fundamental. In China, the whole study of the heavens, both *li fa* and *tian wen*, was of intense importance to rulers even before the unification of China, and especially so, after it, to the emperor. This was because rulers were personally responsible for keeping the order of the heavens and order on earth in harmony with one another.[1] As Sivin has put it (1969, p. 7), 'the Chinese theory' was of 'the natural order and the political order as resonating systems, with the ruler as a sort of vibrating dipole between them'. The regulation of the calendar was not just a matter of practical concern, for instance for agriculture, but one with far-ranging implications for the order of the state. Indeed that Chinese theory, to quote Sivin again, 'imposed on the history of astronomy an insatiable demand for increased precision – far exceeding, in the area of the calendar, any conceivable agricultural, bureaucratic, or economic necessity'.

1. Thus it was often represented as common practice for a new ruler, or a new dynasty, to assert their authority by the introduction of a new calendar taking a new month as its starting-point. This is a prominent theme, in, for example, the 春秋繁露, *Chunqiu fanlu*, of 董仲舒, Dong Zhongshu (c. –179 to c. 104) (23: 174–9), and cf. *Shiji* 26.

The perceived importance of the study of the heavens, in China, was directly reflected in the institutionalisation of the subject. An imperial Astronomical Service was already set up in Han times, with an officer called the 太史令, *Taishi ling*, responsible with his aides for observations of celestial and meteorological phenomena (see Hucker 1985 at pp. 315f and 482), and under various titles, 太史局, *Taishi ju*, 司天監, *Sitian jian*, 欽天監, *Qintian jian*, the Astronomical Bureau continued all the way down to the Qing, the last imperial dynasty, that is for close on 2,000 years.[2]

Monitoring the calendar was one of several on-going tasks and calendar reform was always potentially on the agenda, especially though certainly not exclusively on a change of dynasty, when reforms would have a particular symbolic charge, reflecting and endorsing the legitimacy of the new ruler. It is true that some important ideas for reform originated with outsiders, though if their ideas proved acceptable, their originators often found themselves appointed to posts within the Bureau. That even happened, eventually, to the Jesuit Schall in the seventeenth century.[3] But the existence of the Bureau testified to the political significance of the subject. Calendar regulation, in China, was of direct interest to the emperor and under direct imperial control.

The situation in ancient Greece, and even also in Rome, at least until the mid –1st century, was, by comparison, chaotic. Each Greek city-state had its own luni-solar calendar, with its own names for the months. Each state had its own officials responsible not just for observation of the new moon, to determine the beginning of a new month, but also for deciding on the timing of intercalary months. These were, of course, necessary to keep the cycle of months given by lunar phenomena from becoming hopelessly out of step with the solar year by which farming activities had to be guided. Each month in each state had its own festivals associated with it, a matter of concern, in the first instance, specifically to the state in question. Participation in inter-state festivals, the Olympic, Pythian and other pan-Hellenic games, led to no overall standardisation in the states' own calendars.

Getting the calendar right was, to be sure, as much an interest of Greek as of Chinese astronomers: but the great difference was

2. On the history of the Astronomical Bureau in China, see, for example, Ho 1969, Porter 1980.
3. See Huang 1991, and cf. above, p. 32 at n. 23.

that the reception of their work was quite haphazard. Attempts to arrive at an accurate determination of the lengths of the solar year and the lunar month go back, in Greece, to the work of Meton and Euctemon at Athens around –430. How far they were aware of, and drew on, Babylonian and Egyptian data on this problem, and the extent of their own first-hand observations, are disputed questions,[4] but that does not affect the main point of contrast between Greece and China. This is that the immediate practical impact of their work on the civil calendars in use at Athens and elsewhere was nil. Even in the longer term, attempts to apply the Metonic cycle and its successors, such as the cycle of Callippus, were only ever at best sporadic.[5] Those who undertook the determination of the year and the month, Meton and Callippus and the rest, were not employed by rulers eager to implement the results they obtained. They were entirely *private individuals*, and as we can see from the caricaturing of Meton in Aristophanes' *Birds*, 992ff, he came across as a somewhat eccentric whiz-kid.

Eventually, to be sure, Greek *astronomers* settled on a practical universal calendar for astronomical purposes. They adopted the conventional Egyptian 365 day year, and Ptolemy took the first year of the reign of the Persian king Nabonassar (–747) as epoch. But so far as the calendars in use for civil purposes went, the problems of intercalation continued long after the studies of Meton and Callippus in the –5th and –4th centuries, It took, in fact, the Roman Julius Caesar to *impose* a more orderly calendar across most of the Greco-Roman world, with the reforms he instituted as Pontifex Maximus in –46.

So to sum up on this first topic: the accurate determination of the solar year and the lunar month was of fundamental importance for all Greek theoretical astronomy, and the results arrived at were *potentially* of considerable practical relevance in relation to the regulation of civil calendars. However, the actual implementation of those results, in Greece, was hamstrung by the indifference of the political authorities. The Greek astronomers were ordinary citizens, private researchers, not key advisers to rulers.

4. See especially Aaboe and Price 1964, Neugebauer 1975, II pp. 601ff, 622ff, Goldstein and Bowen 1983, Bowen and Goldstein 1989.
5. On the on-going dispute about the Athenian calendar, and how far it was modified to take into account the work of Meton and of Callippus, see especially Pritchett and Neugebauer 1947, van der Waerden 1960, Meritt 1961.

Moreover Greek astronomy never had an institutional framework of the kind eventually provided by the imperial Astronomical Bureau in China. There the direct responsibility the emperor had for the welfare of 'all under heaven' ensured that what were perceived or accepted as the most accurate determinations of calendrical parameters were bound to be of more than just learned, scholarly, interest.

II

The second field of common interest is cosmography. No detailed astronomical knowledge at all is necessary to have some idea of the general relations between the heavens and the earth. In Greece, Homer already refers to a domed and apparently solid heaven over an earth thought to be surrounded by a circular river of Ocean. Below the earth, there is Hades, the abode of the dead, and below that again is Tartaros 'as far beneath Hades as the sky is from the earth' (*Iliad* VIII. 16). Hesiod, in a fashion that is characteristic of the competitiveness between Greek 'masters of truth', seeks to be even more specific about just how far this invisible region is below the earth. *Theogony* 722ff has it that a bronze anvil, falling from heaven, would reach earth on the tenth day, and Tartaros ten days later.

In China, as we have noted before (p. 162), two main cosmographies are recorded, each with its own observational techniques and instruments. In the *Gai Tian* ('canopy heaven') system, as we have it in the *Zhoubi suanjing*, the heaven is a circular canopy set over a central earth. The earth is imagined as an upturned bowl, but it is essentially square, its shape being given by the four cardinal points – or five, counting the centre itself. In the *Hun Tian* ('enveloping heaven') view, the heavens are a complete sphere, with half of this invisible below the earth at any time. As discussed in Chapter 3 (pp. 59f), the *Zhoubi* establishes a method by which the height and size of the sun can be got by observations of the shadows cast by gnomons and by sighting the sun down a tube. The results obtained are that the sun is at a height of 80,000 *li* ('leagues') and has a diameter of 1,250 *li* (*Zhoubi* 23ff, cf. Cullen forthcoming).

In both China and Greece, the function of cosmographical systems was never purely descriptive. In pre-philosophical Greek accounts the interest shown in what there is under the earth reflects beliefs in underworld gods, in the realm of Hades and the abodes of the Titans, who were defeated in battle by Zeus when he imposed his rule over the heavens and the earth.

In China, there was no such belief in Tartaros. But what was at stake in any description of the heavens was the key notion of the complementarity of the heavens and the earth. Cosmic harmony, in the Chinese view, was not just a matter of the good order secured by the due sequences of events in heaven and on earth, but also one of the sounds produced by the associated notes of the twelve-tone scale.

There are several classical texts that set out the correspondences to be expected between the movements of the sun, seasonal phenomena and the pitch-pipes that give the notes of the scale (cf. Granet 1934, pp. 209ff). One such is *Huainanzi* 3. Since there are twenty-four solar nodes, each of the pitch-pipes figures twice in the complete cycle. From the beginning of spring, for instance, the sequence is rain, the awakening of insects, the spring equinox, 'clear and bright', grain rain and the beginning of summer, with correspondences to the notes called (in Major's translations) Southern Regulator, Tranquil Pattern, Forest Bell, Luxuriant, Median Regulator, Maiden Purity, and Pinched Bell.[6]

Cosmographies may, but need not, incorporate detailed knowledge of the complexities of the movements of the heavenly bodies. The *Zhoubi* describes the circuits of the sun at different seasons. The complexities of the moon's motion were well known. There are references to the retrogradations of the planets at least from the time of Sima Qian onwards (−1st century). One frequent idea, appearing in various forms in China as in Greece, was that of the Great Year, when all the heavenly bodies return to the same position in relation to one another. Thus in the Great Planetary Cycle (of +1st century) the period of return, from one general conjunction of all the planets to the next, is put at 138,240 years.[7]

---

6. *Huainanzi* 3: 12b ff, Major 1993, pp. 88ff, who notes that there is a slightly different account of the sequence in *Lüshi Chunqiu*.

7. See Sivin 1969, pp. 16ff, cf. also p. 8 and pp. 21ff. At p. 24 Sivin remarks 'there was consistent improvement in knowledge of planetary periods'. However, 'only mean values are given for the various planetary cycles, and there is no indication that variations were accounted for'.

Of course accounts of such general conjunctions (with the five planets like 'strung pearls') often owed more to theoretical considerations than to observable data, as Huang 1990 showed. But the notion of the Great Year itself depended on *some* conception of the periodicities of the planets, and in fact increasingly accurate data for these and other phenomena appear in our classical sources, such as the *Lüshi Chunqiu*, the *Wuxingzhan* Mawangdui text, *Huainanzi*, the *Shiji* (27) and the *Hanshu* (26). At the same time, the symbolic associations of the planets certainly remained important, and the possibility of their moving *irregularly* was countenanced and treated as ominous. Mars ('Sparkling Deluder'), for example, was associated in *Huainanzi* 3, with disorder, robbery, sickness, mourning, famine and warfare. Moreover, 'when its leavings and enterings [of lunar lodges] are irregular, there is disputation and change'.[8]

What is not attested, however, in extant classical Chinese texts, is any attempt at the *spatial* representation of the paths of the planets. For that we have to wait until Shen Gua in the +11th century, though even here the representation is merely qualitative and does not attempt quantitative parameters (see Sivin 1969, Appendix C, pp. 7off). *A fortiori*, there is no suggestion, in classical Chinese texts, that the movements of each of the sun, moon and planets can be resolved into a set of components, the combination of which yielded the observed complex motion. This is the feature that is shared by the various Greek geometrical models that were proposed, beginning with Eudoxus in the late −4th century, whether these were based on concentric spheres, on epicycles, on eccentrics, or on some combination of the last two.

Quite why the Greeks should have embarked on that enterprise is the simple-minded, difficult, question that I now want to consider in some detail. To be sure, the question of why Eudoxus did the work he did is sometimes answered straightforwardly on the basis of a report in Simplicius (*In Cael.* 488.18ff) who cites Sosigenes who may in turn be drawing on the history of astronomy of Aristotle's pupil Eudemus. According to this, it was Plato who set contemporary astronomers the task of accounting for the apparent irregular movements of the planets in terms of

8. *Huainanzi* 3: 7a, Major 1993, p. 74: cf. Nakayama 1966, pp. 446ff.

combinations of uniform and orderly motions.[9] If this is accepted, the reason Eudoxus set to work might be thought to be simple: Plato told him to do so.

But quite apart from the question of the historical reliability of the Simplicius report, it does not, of itself, suggest any particular reason why Plato should have set that task and set it in the terms he did. The problem does not go away, and *our* first task must be to investigate the antecedents of Eudoxus' theory to see what light they can throw on the question.

It should be stressed, at the outset, first that not all Greek astronomical theories took the form of quantitatively precise geometrical models, and in particular the earliest Presocratic ones did not. We said that Eudoxus was the first to *attempt* this, and even there, although his theory incorporated certain concrete parameters, it is well known that it failed to provide a fully comprehensive quantitative account.[10] Moreover, secondly, we know of a quite different solution to the representation of the order in

9. At *In Cael.* 492.31ff Simplicius further specifies that the uniform and orderly motions should be circular. To understand this, it is not necessary to appeal to any supposed Greek obsession with the perfection of circularity, for the reason may be much simpler, namely that in resolving complex motions into simpler ones, circular movements have distinct advantages in the ease with which the relevant calculations may be made.

10. The reliable ancient evidence on Eudoxus is very incomplete and it is impossible to rule out a wide variety of diverging interpretations: see, for example, Maula 1974. Reconstructions based on the work of Schiaparelli have tended to proceed on the methodologically quite unjustified hypothesis that Eudoxus had available to him accurate data on a broad range of topics, including, for instance, the maximum lengths of the retrograde arcs of each of the planets. But if we confine ourselves to the definite information conveyed by Aristotle and Simplicius, the following points emerge. For each of the sun, moon and planets, the complex apparent path was represented as the product of a combination of the simple circular movements of a certain number of concentric spheres, three each for the sun and moon, four each for each of the planets. The outermost sphere, in each case, moves with the movement of the fixed stars – and corresponds therefore to the daily rotation of the heavens as a whole. The second sphere, again in each case, produces the apparent motion of the body along the ecliptic. Moreover the two extra spheres for each of the planets were designed to account for their stations and retrogradations. These two spheres, we are told, rotate at equal speeds and in opposite directions, their combined movement producing the figure of eight curve known as the 'hippopede'. In *qualitative* terms this provided an excellent basis for an account of their movements. Moreover Simplicius gives *some* definite values, namely for the speeds of revolutions of the first two spheres in each case, and that suggests the *beginnings* of an attempt at a *quantitative* account. Yet we do *not* have equivalent data for the speeds and angles of inclination of the spheres responsible for the hippopedes. Moreover on *any* interpretation of their values, the theory breaks down both for Mars and for Venus, where the data we already have do not permit retrogradation at all. See Neugebauer 1975, II, IV C 1, pp. 675ff.

the heavens before Plato, namely the notion of the harmony of the spheres. If we are to understand the power of the attraction of geometrical models – to the Greeks, that is – we have to assess this other evidence carefully first.

The first point can be illustrated most easily by reference to Anaximander's cosmography insofar as that can be reconstructed.[11] The earth is a flat-topped cylinder at the centre of the universe and our sources report that it is three times as broad as it is deep. Round it, there are three circles of fire, through apertures in which the heavenly bodies appear, the outermost the circle of the sun, the middle that of the moon, while the lowest is that of the stars. These are arranged symmetrically, at 27, 18 and 9 earth-diameters from the earth, but those figures are not motivated by any attempt to explain astronomical data, but purely out of considerations of symbolic appropriateness. No explicit provision for the planets as such is made at all. This is a geometrical representation, certainly, but not a quantitative model from which positions and paths could be deduced.

The evidence for pre-Platonic Pythagoreanism is richer but also more confused. According to Aristotle (*Metaphysics* 986a8ff, cf. *On the Heavens* 293a20ff), one Pythagorean view was that there are ten moving heavenly bodies. First there are the fixed stars (they count as one), then the five visible planets, and the sun and moon. But in addition they postulated a Central Fire and a Counter-Earth, introducing the latter – so Aristotle protests – purely to bring the number up to the sacred number ten. Whatever the rights and wrongs of that criticism,[12] on the view in question the earth itself was treated as one of the planets, circling, like them, round the Central Fire.

In this theory each of the planets is located on a separate circle or sphere. Indirect evidence that their speeds were distinguished comes from a further text in Aristotle that discusses the harmony of the spheres. In *On the Heavens* II ch. 9 he reports that certain theorists, among whom he again numbers Pythagoreans (291a7ff),

11. See, for example, Kahn 1960, Guthrie 1962, pp. 89ff. The question of Anaximander's possible debts to Iranian ideas is disputed (see, for example, Burkert 1963, West 1971), but that is not relevant to our present concerns.

12. However, at *On the Heavens* 293b23ff Aristotle implies that the counter-earth was used to account for the greater frequency of lunar eclipses than solar ones – that is those visible from any particular point on the earth's surface.

held that each of the heavenly bodies is responsible for a note. These notes are concordant, but we do not hear them because we have been used to them from birth – a fantasy that Aristotle dismisses with contempt.[13]

The details of this theory are not recorded, and just how far it was indeed worked out in *detail* is doubtful. The chief musical concords are, of course, expressible in terms of the ratios 2:1, 3:2 and 4:3. The notes made by the heavenly bodies correspond, we are told, to their speeds (and it is independently attested that the Pythagorean Archytas held that pitch varies with speed[14]), and the speeds in turn vary, it seems, with their distances (*On the Heavens* 290b21ff).

It might look as if we could supplement Aristotle's report with some of the material in the astronomical passages in Plato, to give a moderately comprehensive account of the planets. Thus Plato certainly picks up the notion of the harmony of the spheres, in the *Republic* 617b, though there he has a Siren responsible for each of the eight notes made by the heavenly bodies. In the account of the construction of the world-soul, in the *Timaeus*, 34b ff, 36d, the inner circle, the circle of the Other, is cut in six places, giving a complete sequence of 1, 2, 3, 4, 8, 9, 27 – numbers that represent two series, one in arithmetical, the other in geometrical, proportion. They certainly provide the basis for obtaining the ratios of the principal concords, 2:1, 3:2 and 4:3, though the series as a whole yields other, non-concordant, ratios (such as 9:8 or 9:4) as well.

All of that might seem rather promising. One might conjecture that in the Pythagorean view mentioned by Aristotle, the planets move with speeds and at distances that correspond to the *Timaeus* sequence and that the notes they each make can be arranged to yield a series of ratios corresponding to the principal concords. That would be pure conjecture, but would provide a possible interpretation for *a* notion of the harmony of the spheres. However, the strain the doctrine is under, in the version

---

13. Given the size and the speeds of the objects in question, the noise they would make – if they made any noise at all – would be tremendous. But the reason we do not hear any noise is that they make none: their movement is effortless, through a non-resistant medium, Aristotle's postulated fifth element, *aithēr*.

14. Archytas Fr. 1, which also refers, in an earlier context, to the speeds of the stars. See Huffman 1985, Barker 1989, pp. 39ff.

reported by Aristotle, becomes apparent when we consider first just what is supposed to be harmonious and secondly how the harmonies in question are thought to fit the astronomical data.

Since the two types of difficulties are not generally pointed out, it is worth spending some time on them. First the theory reported by Aristotle has notes that correspond to speeds which correspond in turn to distances. But for the notes to correspond to speeds, we must have a way of determining the mean or aggregate speed. We need one figure for each speed, to which the note corresponds: for there is no suggestion that each note changes, and indeed if it did, that would make keeping them harmonious intolerably complicated.

On the most promising suggestion, the speeds might correspond to the periods of the sidereal or zodiacal revolution – the time taken for a planet to return to the same position in relation to the same fixed star. But that would mean that the actual apparent accelerations, decelerations, stations and retrogradations of the planets are – for the purposes of their harmonies, at least – discounted. The sole figure that would count is that of the sidereal revolution.

However, that does not get round all the difficulties. One considerable one is the following. The sidereal periods of what were eventually called the inferior planets, that is Venus and Mercury, are identical to that of the sun, namely one (sidereal) year. That would give them, on the view so far presented, the same speed and so the same note. Plato certainly was aware of this datum, since he refers to it directly in the *Timaeus* (36d5). But then in his version of the harmony of the spheres, in the *Republic*, it is not said that the notes correspond directly to speeds, but rather that they are produced by the Sirens stationed on each sphere.[15]

Now this difficulty might be met as follows. Granted that the sidereal periods of the sun, Venus and Mercury are identical, their angular speeds as measured from the earth will be the same in aggregate. But their actual *linear* speeds differ, since, precisely,

15. In the *Timaeus*, the soul is said to partake in reason and *harmonia* at 36e6f, for instance, but there the claim is made in purely general terms: cf. also 47d2, and again the general claim concerning the harmony or attunement of the whole, 90d3f. Cf. also below (p. 178) on the assertion that the movements of the three outer planets are commensurate with one another, 36d6f.

they are not at the same distance from the earth. That would allow for different actual speeds and so different notes. However the problem that would then arise is that of how the distances of these and indeed the other planets could be determined. Eventually lunar parallax was one method used to get the distance of the moon, and some attempts were made to determine the sun's distance by a similar technique. But otherwise the distances of the planets were generally derived from their speeds[16] – the assumption being that the longer the period of sidereal revolution, the greater the distance.

But that just takes us back to the fundamental question of how the original doctrine of the harmony of the spheres was supposed to fit the astronomical data known at the time. It is true that we do not have definite information about precisely what data were available to the Pythagoreans to whom Aristotle refers in *On the Heavens* II ch 9. It cannot be ruled out that the whole system was largely symbolic, like Anaximander's, that is, that the harmonies were just postulated as the type of relationship that the heavenly movements *should* embody. But if that was not the case, *if* an attempt was made to accommodate the data likely to be available in the late –5th, let alone the early –4th, century, the difficulties it faced are formidable.

Thus we have already mentioned the work of Meton and Euctemon, in the –430s, on the determination of the solar year and the lunar month. Meton's result (and it does not matter, for our purposes, how it was arrived at) was that 235 lunations correspond to 19 solar years. Where was the harmony there? Moreover other evidence confirms that it was well known, in the late –5th century, that the ratio between the solar year and the lunar month is a highly complex one. The author of the Hippocratic treatise, *On Prognosis*, ch. 20 (L II 168.16ff), clearly states that neither can be expressed exactly in terms of whole numbers of days.

That is the first major difficulty, but a second relates to the planets themselves. We have noted that the sidereal periods of the sun, Venus and Mercury are the same. All well and good. But those of the outer planets can hardly be got to fit into a neat

16. That is rather to reverse the direction of inference implied by Aristotle when, at *On the Heavens* 290b21ff, he reports that the speeds were obtained from the distances.

sequence. Take the rather rough figures Eudoxus is reported to have used, where Saturn has a sidereal period of 30 years, Jupiter 12, and Mars 2.[17] Once again, once some such figures were available, the speeds, judged by the periods, fail to tally with the *simple ratios*, 2:1, 3:2 and 4:3, that express the chief musical concords.

Yet interestingly enough, the securing of tolerably accurate data for planetary periods did not by any means spell the end of the belief in the harmony of the spheres, which continued, in one form or another, right down to Kepler and even beyond. However, the ancient Greeks needed all the ingenuity they could muster to find some kind of simple harmonic relations in the heavens. As we have seen, Plato fudges the issue, in the *Republic*, by having Sirens produce the notes: they could be counted on to be tuneful, whatever sphere they had responsibility for. In the *Timaeus*, where the speeds of the sun, Venus and Mercury are recognised to be the same, the *claim* is made that the ratios of the other speeds are also expressible *en logōi*, 36d6, that is that they are all commensurate with one another. But that is not further explained, and it sounds like nothing more than a pious hope.[18]

As for later Greek theorists, a bewildering variety of options is on offer, all purporting to secure celestial harmonies. The planets could be associated with certain qualities, of beneficence or maleficence, of masculinity and femininity and so on, as frequently in astrological theory. These qualities could then be given numerical interpretation, in terms of odd and even numbers, and so the concordances between different pairs of heavenly bodies were thereby assured. That is one idea alluded to in the mutilated final section of Ptolemy's *Harmonics* (III ch. 16). Another, found in Aristides Quintilianus, was to associate the simple bodies of which the universe is composed with simple numbers (4 for fire, 6 for water, 8 for air, 12 for water) and to find the harmonies between them.[19] A third was to proceed via the subdivision of the ecliptic circle into twelve parts, where it was not

17. See Simplicius, *In Cael.* 495.26ff. The figures correspond to Babylonian values and may well have been derived from them. See Dicks 1970, p. 167, cf. Neugebauer 1975, II pp. 681f.
18. In the *Republic* 530ab, however, Plato had rather insisted that the movements of the heavenly bodies do not conform to exact proportions.
19. Aristides Quintilianus III ch. 19. Other ideas are further developed in III ch. 12 and III chh. 20–23. See Barker 1989, pp. 513ff.

difficult to suggest ratios of 2:1, 3:2 and 4:3 between different chords, an idea developed by Ptolemy himself.[20] Yet among those who adopted the idea in a form closer to Plato's, it was not as if there was agreement even about whether the further away the planet was, the higher its note (that was the usual view, but it was denied by Nicomachus, *Harmonicum Enchiridium* ch. 3, Barker 1989, pp. 250ff, 251 n, 20), nor even about the correct order of the planets themselves. While Plato had put the sun next after the moon, many adopted the order: moon, Mercury, Venus, sun, Mars, Jupiter, Saturn.[21]

My survey of the fortunes of the doctrines of the harmony of the spheres shows how enthusiastic many Greek theorists were about *discovering* celestial order, but also how problematic the application of music theory to that end was. Of course celestial order and cosmic harmony were as deeply rooted in Chinese thought as in Greek. In both, these ideas were firmly linked first to the idea of the moral governance of heaven and earth, and further to moral recommendations concerning the need for ordinary humans to behave with due circumspection.[22] Yet so far as harmonies went, the Chinese found these principally between heaven and earth: some of the Greeks thought the movements of the planets themselves could also be deemed concordant. That bare contrast needs qualifying, to be sure: for the Greeks too had their cosmic 'sympathies' (as we have seen, p. 102 at n. 10, p. 148 at n. 13), except that there the emphasis was not so much on resonance between the cosmic and the political, as between different aspects of the physical.

20. *Harmonics* III chh. 9, 14 and 15, cf. Aristides Quintilianus III ch. 23. See Barker 1989, pp. 381ff, 524ff.
21. Some Greek and Latin commentators betray a certain impatience with what they consider the excessive subtlety of some attempts to elaborate the doctrine of the harmony of the spheres. Thus in chh. 31f of *On the Creation of the Soul in the Timaeus*, 1028a ff, 1029a ff, Plutarch mentions various versions of this, but remarks that some go beyond what is useful in geometrical demonstrations. Again in the *Natural History* II ch. 84, Pliny implicitly criticises as over-subtle a Pythagorean view according to which the distances between the heavenly bodies correspond to intervals of semitones, tones or one and a half tones.
22. In Greece, Plato suggests that the revolutions in your head should be regulated to correspond to the harmonious revolutions of the cosmos, *Timaeus* 47bc, 90d, and Ptolemy too holds that astronomy should help people become morally better individuals, see below at n. 36. In China, the chief responsibility for keeping the order of the heavens and the order on earth in harmony rested – as explained – with the emperor, but any breach of good order in the one domain had dire repercussions in the other.

But concordant planetary motions were not the only manifestation of the Greek expectation of celestial order, for there were also those geometrical models – which eventually won out as the preferred basis for astronomical theorising. From one point of view, once the periodicities of planetary motion had been determined within sufficiently close limits, that *in itself* (one might have thought) showed well enough that those movements are orderly in the sense of regular. But some Greek theorists demanded much more. Why? If numerical tables are perfectly adequate to enable *predictions* to be made of the planets' movements, geometrical models enable them in addition to be *deduced* and so explained and even *demonstrated.*

To be sure, the accuracy of geometrical models can never exceed that of the quantitative parameters they incorporate. But the characteristic that geometrical models possess that purely numerical ones lack is the possibilities they afford for would-be demonstrative explanations. The array of concentric spheres, or of epicycles and eccentrics, allows the resultant movements to be derived from the geometrical structure of the model. That model has, indeed, to be interpreted with specific values for its various components, such as the radii and speeds of rotation of the circles in the epicycle model. But once interpreted, the model permits the movements of each of the planets, sun and moon not merely to be predicted (as they could also be, by being read off periodic tables or by applying suitable algorithms) but also to be explained.

True, the nature of the explanation on offer will reflect the views adopted on the underlying physical correlate to the geometrical figures used. It has sometimes been argued that Greek astronomers treated their models as no more than calculating devices and were indifferent to the question of the underlying physical realities. That does not, in my view, tally with the position of the major Greek astronomical theorists where we have positive evidence on the point.[23] But that controversy should not distract attention from the main point at issue here. What *all* the geometrical models we know about do is to derive apparently irregular motions from combinations of regular ones, and so in that sense explain the former in terms of the latter: indeed

23. This evidence is analysed and discussed in Lloyd 1991a, ch. 11.

all have the potential for physical application. That potential is already evident in references, in Plato onwards, to the possibility of constructing physical scale models of the motions of the heavenly bodies (*Timaeus* 38de, 40cd). Meanwhile the fully fledged physical systems (such as Ptolemy set out in the *Planetary Hypotheses*) fulfil the further requirement of an Aristotelian demonstration, that of specifying the physical causes of the effects in question.[24]

The consequence of the application of geometry is that the apparent irregularities in the observed movements can be treated as evidence not of disorder, but of order itself, not as conflicting with, but as confirming, that order. So far from being a possible source of embarrassment, those irregularities thereby become the occasion for astronomy's claims for demonstrative power.

So the conjecture would be that it was the possibility of such geometrical demonstrations that proved the principal attraction – to the Greeks – of the styles of astronomical theory that we find from Eudoxus down to Ptolemy and beyond, and the absence of such theories in China is not so puzzling when we reflect on a general absence of that type of Euclidean geometrical demonstration.

Indeed this is not just pure conjecture, on the Greek side, since two pieces of evidence (at least) can be cited in its support. First, there is Plato's own reaction to the discovery that the sun, moon and planets do not, as their Greek name seemed to imply, 'wander'. In the *Timaeus* the complexities of their movements, even their wanderings (*planē*) are still emphasised.[25] But in the *Laws* his spokesman, the Athenian Stranger, expresses shock at the ignorance of his fellow Greeks who believe this, even though he says that he only learned the truth of the matter 'not long ago' (821e). In fact, however, he claims, each of these bodies 'moves in the same track, not many, but one, circular, path always, though they appear to be borne on many' (822a). The difficulties of this text are notorious, but it is the continuation that concerns

24. Indeed in the *Planetary Hypotheses* Ptolemy not only gives a physical interpretation of the system of epicycles and eccentrics, but also attempts a dynamical account, explaining the movements of the heavenly bodies in vitalist terms.
25. Concerning the planets, Timaeus says at 39c, only a few human beings have understood their revolutions. What are called their 'wanderings', which constitute time, are of 'extraordinary number' (*plēthei amēchanōi*) and 'wonderfully complexified' (*pepoikilmenas thaumastōs*), 39d1–2. He speaks of their 'wandering' again at 40b6 when referring to their 'turnings'.

us here, since the Stranger goes on to say that the true role of
astronomy is to *show* that this is so, and if these matters cannot
be *shown*, then the study should not be engaged in at all (822c).
The term is *deiknumi*, show, prove, in both cases, but this is clearly
not a matter of showing by pointing – either at the heavenly
bodies or at models of them[26] – but, precisely, *showing by argument*, that is, in this case, giving a geometrical demonstration of
the movements.

So for Plato, at least in this text, astronomy is worthwhile precisely insofar as it is demonstrative.[27] If we just had Plato to go
on, maybe the argument would not be very impressive.[28] But
my second piece of evidence comes from Ptolemy, no less, who,
as one of the foremost Greek astronomers, speaks with some
authority. In the Proem to the *Syntaxis* he expresses his view as
to where the great strength of mathematical astronomy lies. It
is superior, he says, both to 'physics' (the study of nature) and
to theology. But why? Physics deals with the unstable qualities
of changing material objects, and theology is concerned with
what is utterly obscure. Mathematics (including astronomy), by
contrast, holds out the promise of firm and unshakeable knowledge, since its proofs proceed by indisputable methods, namely
those of arithmetic and geometry.[29] What this study yields is not

26. In the *Timaeus* 40d2f, as already remarked, any attempt to explain the motions of
the planets without reference to a visible model is said to be a waste of time – one
of the reasons why Timaeus cries off a detailed account in that dialogue. According to the *Laws*, however, it would seem that *just* referring to a model would not
be enough. Already in the *Republic*, 529d, 530bc, the usefulness of astronomy in the
education of the Guardians is as a training in abstract thought – to study what can
be grasped 'by argument and intelligence, but not by sight'.
27. We cannot, of course, determine the extent to which Eudoxus himself may have
shared such a view, since we have only indirect evidence for his theories and no
explicit testimony as to his views on their aims or status. However, so far as his work
in geometry goes, it is remarkable that one of his best attested contributions is the
introduction of the so-called (but misnamed) 'method of exhaustion' and this aimed,
precisely, to preserve strict demonstrative rigour: see above, p. 150 at n. 15.
28. Aristotle, too, can be cited as another philosopher who insisted on the necessity of
the subject-matter of astronomy. This is, for him, a matter, in the first instance, of the
eternal, unchanging nature of heavenly movements, but this in turn has implications
for the account of these that should be offered, for the astronomers should be able
to state the necessity of their explanations, even though Aristotle professes himself to
be no astronomer, *Metaphysics* 1073b10ff, 1074a14ff, *On the Parts of Animals* 639b21ff,
On Coming-to-be and Passing Away 337b9ff.
29. Ptolemy, *Syntaxis* I 1, Proem H I 6.17–21: μόνον δὲ τὸ μαθηματικόν, εἴ τις ἐξετασ-
τικῶς αὐτῷ προσέρχοιτο, βεβαίαν καὶ ἀμετάπιστον τοῖς μεταχειριζομένοις τὴν
εἴδησιν παράσχοι ὡς ἂν τῆς ἀποδείξεως δι' ἀναμφισβητήτων ὁδῶν γιγνομένης,

merely a matter of the demonstration of a number of abstract mathematical theorems, but – as Ptolemy claims – an understanding of 'what is divine and heavenly', the heavenly bodies and their movements.

If our conjecture has some validity, we rejoin a theme familiar from earlier chapters, the determination of many Greek scientists, whatever their field, to pursue demonstration *more geometrico*, that is in the Euclidean axiomatic-deductive mode. To get this into perspective in the present context, three points need to be stressed. First, it is not the case that there are *no* proofs in Chinese mathematics. We have stressed before (pp. 61ff) that there are many occasions when, for example, an algorithm is checked and shown to be correct. These are perfectly adequate proofs, provided we do not stipulate that proof has to be cast in the axiomatic-deductive mode. Where the classical Chinese exhibit a total indifference is, precisely, to the search for axioms – to the bid to deduce mathematical or any other kind of theorems from a small set of supposedly self-evident indemonstrable starting-points.

Secondly, it is not as if that Greek determination was always and everywhere an unmixed blessing. On the contrary, some Greek scientists were obsessed with demonstration well beyond the point where it might be considered appropriate or even plausible. We shall be considering some further instances from Greek medicine in Chapter 9, where Galen, for example, seeks to apply Euclidean style demonstration to physiology and pathology.

Thirdly and most fundamentally, the Greek preoccupation with demonstration was not just a reflection of a laudable desire for high standards of intellectual rigour. That is no doubt part of the story. But axiomatic-deductive demonstration also has a crucial role to play, so I argued, in the context of the kind of intellectual rivalry we discussed in Chapters 3 and 4. Strict proof is the key notion some of the philosophers invoked to distinguish and contrast their styles of argument with the merely persuasive reasoning that they represent as all too common in other fields of inquiry. Plato and Aristotle in particular were both concerned to emphasise the differences between their styles of high philosophy

ἀριθμητικῆς τε καὶ γεωμετρίας. ('Only mathematics, if one attacks it critically, provides for those who practise it sure and unswerving knowledge, since the demonstration comes about through incontrovertible means, by arithmetic and geometry.')

on the one hand, and rhetoric, sophistic and eristic on the other.

Demonstration was thus something of a trump card, enabling you to defeat the opposition, not just from the likes of the sophists, but also from philosophical and scientific colleagues. What it did, indeed alone could do, was to justify your claim to yield certain, even incontrovertible, results – whereas the best the opposition could offer was generally represented as merely plausible arguments. Even though the claim actually to have delivered such results often seems extravagant, or just plain wishful thinking, not least in astronomy itself,[30] nevertheless to succeed against all comers that had to be your aim.

On this line of interpretation, the types of astronomical model developed in Greece and China reflect the influence of the styles of intellectual exchange cultivated in each society. The modes of rivalry among astronomers differed, in that, in Greece, the stakes were those of strict proof. The Chinese demand, as we have seen, was for accuracy in prediction: there was plenty of competitiveness in delivering that. But deductive certainty, incontrovertibility, were a red herring. The enterprise of demonstrating the movements of the planets by way of geometrical models, if it had been attempted – which it was not – would have been considered irrelevant.

III

This major divergence in the aims of astronomical theory in China and in Greece has repercussions also on the third principal branch of the study of the heavens that I identified, namely the investigation of portents and the prediction of events on earth. The preferred mode of astrological prediction in Greece, from the Hellenistic period on, is genethlialogy, that is, the casting of horoscopes, geometrical and deductive in character, though recognised by Ptolemy as far from demonstrative. This is because its starting-points were matters of opinion. The interpretation of

30. This applies to Ptolemy himself, who nevertheless, as we have seen above, n. 29, sets such store by the ability of astronomy to demonstrate its results. Yet in the body of the *Syntaxis* he recognises, often enough, that doubts and difficulties remain. He does so particularly forcefully in referring to the problems posed by the latitudinal movements of the planets, for example, *Syntaxis* XIII 2, H II 532.12ff, 534.1–6.

the characters of each of the planets, for instance, was given by ancient tradition, though he would have claimed that that tradition was generally reliable and had stood the test of time.

Compared with the study of the movements of the heavenly bodies themselves, the attempt to derive predictions from them for events on earth is, in Ptolemy's view, secondary, uncertain and conjectural (*Tetrabiblos* I 1, 3.5ff, I 2, 8.1ff, III 2, 109.1ff). However, against those who attacked astrology – for it was, like so much else in Greece, controversial[31] – he defended it, again in typically Greek fashion, with argument. The *Tetrabiblos* maintains that it is both possible and useful, claiming, indeed, its potential utility for all sorts of practical questions concerning the lives of individual human beings. While he attempts no specific horoscopes himself, but confines himself to generalities, the types of subject on which astrology can be brought to bear include the mental and physical capacities of individuals, the diseases they will be liable to, and the external goods they can expect, 'property', 'marriage', 'honour' and 'dignities'. Astrology will not only enable one to grasp what is appropriate for the 'temperament' of the body, but above all will be conducive to calm, well-being and joy.[32]

In China, by contrast (where horoscopes as such are, in any event, a relatively late import: see Nakayama 1966, p. 442), the chief astrological concern was not with the fortunes of private individuals, but overwhelmingly with that of a single person, the ruler himself, and thus with the welfare of the empire as a whole. Portents, on this view, are expressions of the will of heaven, communicated to the ruler to encourage or admonish him (Nakayama 1966, p. 443, Yabuuti 1973, p. 93).

Chinese astronomers certainly shared with Greek ones ambitions to extend the domain of what can confidently be predicted, to limit the sphere of the truly portentous in the sense of the totally unpredictable. In China, this was a major stimulus to the concerted attack on eclipse predictions, first those of lunar eclipses,

---

31. One of the most comprehensive texts setting out the arguments *pro* and *contra* astrology from Greco-Roman antiquity is Cicero, *On Divination*. See, for example, Long 1982, Ioppolo 1984, Denyer 1985, Fazzo 1991.
32. Ptolemy, *Tetrabiblos* I 3, 10.14–17.10. In the case of what is inevitable, foreknowledge enables one to view this with peace and steadiness (12.4f). But not everything is inevitable, and influences that might lead to one outcome can, if they are anticipated, be countered, so that on this score, too, astrology is useful and beneficial.

then the far more difficult problem of solar eclipses, where, as Sivin 1969, pp. 24ff, has shown, one cycle, theory or technique after another was developed over the many centuries of the functioning of the Astronomical Bureau. However, the goals and expectations, in China and in Greece, were different in one crucial respect. The chief aim of the Chinese predictions, in this context, was *not to miss* an eclipse.[33] But if they predicted one that did *not* occur, that was of no astrological significance. Indeed in Tang times the non-occurrence of a predicted solar eclipse was sometimes put down to the great virtue of the emperor. Such was his virtue, the thought was, that an eclipse that would have occurred but for it, did not. So the non-occurrence of a predicted event did not then count *against* the astronomer, but *for* the emperor.

The order of the heavens was a major preoccupation in both classical China and Greece, and in both ancient civilisations a matter with grave consequences for politics and morality. But the order came in different guises, both as between China and Greece, and indeed also as between different Greek theorists, and so too did the moral and political implications.

Thus Greek teleologists[34] insisted that in their motions the heavens manifest the intelligence, rationality, even providentiality, that are at work in the cosmos as a whole. The anti-teleologists[35] denied the inference to that intelligence, but did not deny that those movements display intelligible causal relations. Again, as we have seen, many Greek theorists tried to find harmonies in the heavens – not the harmony the Chinese had in mind when they spoke of the resonance between heaven and earth – but harmonies, so these Greeks thought, produced by the various heavenly bodies themselves, though quite how they did this was very far from agreed.

33. See Sivin 1969, p. 25, cf. Nakayama 1966, p. 446: at pp. 53f Sivin mentions the further problem of selective reporting in the Chinese sources.
34. What unites such thinkers as Plato, Aristotle, the Stoics and Ptolemy is a belief in the intelligence at work in the cosmos, even though their interpretations of that idea differ in important respects.
35. Both the pre- and the post-Aristotelian atomists rejected final causation, but accepted, nevertheless, the importance of causal explanations. The Epicureans insisted, however, that where various accounts of an obscure phenomenon are possible, none should be ruled out.

As for morality, those Greeks who believed, as Ptolemy did, that the heavens exhibit 'sameness, good order, proportion and freedom from arrogance', claimed that the study of those features in heaven would help to produce the same qualities in ourselves.[36] That at any rate was the hope – and indeed the basis of one of his claims for the usefulness of astronomy itself.[37]

But we may note how individualistic that is, and how forlorn, by Chinese standards, that claim is. If we contrast the Chinese imperial astronomers, no one was in any doubt about their importance, since the interpretation of the heavens was of crucial concern for the welfare of the empire. But while the emperor was intent on what could be learnt about his rule, it was not to be expected that the heavens would have much to reveal about the fate of ordinary folk, even though, of course, they had better behave themselves and would be subject to dire sanctions for disrupting order if they did not. As for people becoming better by studying astronomy, that was not to be achieved, in China, by imitating god doing geometry, but (if at all) in a spirit of the self-cultivation that hopefully led to sagehood.

The Greek preoccupation with geometrical models produced something of a double bind. On the one hand, it enabled what had seemed to threaten the order of the heavens, namely the

---

36. Ptolemy, *Syntaxis* I 1, Proem, H 1 7.17–24: πρός γε μὴν τὴν κατὰ τὰς πράξεις καὶ τὸ ἦθος καλοκαγαθίαν πάντων ἂν αὕτη μάλιστα διορατικὴς κατασκευάσειεν ἀπὸ τῆς περὶ τὰ θεῖα θεωρουμένης ὁμοιότητος καὶ εὐταξίας καὶ συμμετρίας καὶ ἀτυφίας ἐραστὰς μὲν ποιοῦσα τοὺς παρακολουθοῦντας τοῦ θείου τούτου κάλλους, ἐνεθίζουσα δὲ καὶ ὥσπερ φυσιοῦσα πρὸς τὴν ὁμοίαν τῆς ψυχῆς κατάστασιν.

('Of all studies this one especially would prepare men to be perceptive of nobility both of action and of character: when the sameness, good order, proportion and freedom from arrogance of divine things are being contemplated, this study makes those who follow it lovers of this divine beauty and instils, and as it were makes natural, the same condition in their soul'.)

37. In the Proem to *Syntaxis* 1, Ptolemy offers four distinct but overlapping arguments for the worthwhileness of astronomy. First, there is the ability of mathematical astronomy to provide unshakeable knowledge (see above at n. 29). Secondly, astronomy can make a contribution to the other two theoretical studies, of physics and theology. Thirdly, there is an argument from the personal comfort or satisfaction that the study affords the astronomer himself (at 7.25ff Ptolemy speaks of his love – *erōs* – of the contemplation of what is eternal and unchanging). In addition, there is the argument in question in my text. The heavenly bodies are unchanging, well-ordered and not 'puffed up': by studying such objects, the claim is, you acquire orderliness and rationality yourself. The argument echoes Platonic themes (see above n. 22), but is here expressed not by a philosopher commenting from the outside on astronomy, but by a practising astronomer himself.

irregularities of planetary motion, to be explained. Indeed they could then be cited as evidence, not of irregularity, but of *regularity*. What might have proved a source of some embarrassment was thereby turned into the occasion for astronomy's foremost demonstrative triumphs: or so it was claimed.

But there was a price to pay for this. The geometrical models were supposed to yield sure and certain proofs: those were the high stakes the astronomical theorists played for. But just as certainly, they ruled out anything that suggested change, anything that looked exceptional.

But in China, the order was subject to exceptions that Greek geometrical models could not, in principle, admit. It is well known that the Chinese paid a lot of attention to such phenomena as sun-spots and supernovae that were all but totally ignored in the Greco-Roman record.[38] Comets, too, were a possible source of embarrassment for those who maintained the unchanging heavens: Aristotle's solution there, in the *Meteorologica* I ch. 7, was to associate them, so far as possible, with the hot, dry exhalation, viz. of the *sublunary* region. The idea that the heavens could not be subject to exceptions or to change persists right down to the +6th century, where Philoponus had an uphill task arguing *against* it. By then, however, the battleground had shifted, from the disputes between one pagan cosmology and another, to the confrontation between paganism and Christianity.

The paradox is that while the Greeks could never agree on human political ideals (not even when they had been conquered by the Romans), their astronomical models of celestial order were absolutely uncompromising. There was an authority in the sky that belied not just the chaos of actual political arrangements on earth, but even also human disputes about how best they should be arranged.

By contrast, the Chinese had an agreed, indeed an apparently unquestioned, political ideal, that of the benevolent monarchical rule of the wise emperor. But while they saw the heavens

38. This has been the subject of important studies by Xi Zezong (Xi Zezong and Po Shujen 1966, Xi Zezong 1981, cf. Clark and Stephenson 1977, Stephenson and Clark 1978) and by Huang (Huang and Moriarty-Schieven 1987, Huang 1990). While many reports are indeterminate, and the individual phenomena – and even their types – to which they refer are disputed, the general point, namely that strange and striking celestial phenomena were observed with care and interest, remains.

as inherently orderly, their astronomical ideas imposed far less rigid patterns on the order they expected. These did not preclude exceptions, which were of particular interest, indeed, as the source of possible messages for the welfare and good conduct of the empire.

But while the basic regularity of heavenly movements was not in question, the Chinese would certainly have been puzzled at the Greek attempts to demonstrate it: while to some of the Greeks, the Chinese inability to prove it, or rather their indifference towards attempting to do so, would simply have made them seem – to those Greeks – no better than number-crunchers.

At issue, indeed, in the final analysis, are competing models of what science is – models that do not just reflect the considerable intellectual efforts of their creators, but also relate to the institutions, values and ideologies of the societies in which they worked.

CHAPTER 9

The politics of the body

Every society has some more or less clear, more or less determinate, set of conceptions and preconceptions about the human
body, and most no doubt use that set not just to think about
the body itself but to think about a lot of other things as well.
How the body is imagined to function, how it is believed to be
arranged internally, how its well-being or illness are conceived
and how these are to be controlled, may tell us indirectly about
the ideas entertained on a wealth of other subjects too, how the
individual relates to his or her environment, how the unity of the
person is construed, what good social relations consist in, even
about the well-being of the cosmos itself. Ideas about the human
body may mirror, and themselves be mirrored in, ideas about the
body politic: the macrocosm, in turn, is often thought to tally
with the microcosms of the body and the state.

In both ancient China and ancient Greece there is widespread
use of analogies between the macrocosm and those two microcosms. These are the subject of one of the extended investigations in Lloyd and Sivin (forthcoming) to which the reader may
be referred for discussion of the detail of the texts mentioned
here. The object of this chapter is more limited, to review Chinese and Greek ideas about the body from the point of view of
what we can learn from them about the aims and presuppositions of Chinese and Greek investigators, and the modalities of
their interactions and modes of operation in either society. Who
claimed special knowledge of the body and on what basis, and
how did they use that knowledge?

Two key classical Chinese texts that have been the subject of
detailed examination by Sivin will illustrate the importance of
the topic in Chinese thought. The first is a chapter of the *Lüshi
Chunqiu* (20, 5: 1373), one of the first texts systematically to

190

develop macrocosm-microcosm analogies. In Sivin's translation
(1995b):

Human beings have 360 joints, nine body openings, and five *yin* and six
yang systems of function. In the flesh tightness is desirable; in the blood
vessels free flow is desirable; in the sinews and bones solidity is desirable; in the operations of the heart and mind harmony is desirable; in
the essential *qi* regular motion is desirable. When [these desiderata] are
realised, illness has nowhere to abide, and there is nothing from which
pathology can develop. When illness lasts and pathology develops, it is
because the essential *qi* has become static.

This account of the desirable state of the body is then applied
first to natural phenomena (as we might call them) and then to
the body politic:

Analogously, water when stagnant becomes foul; a tree when [the circulation of its *qi* is] stagnant becomes worm-eaten; grasses when [the circulation of their *qi* is] stagnant become withered. States too have their
stases [[that is, stoppages, stagnant states]].[1] When the ruler's virtue
does not flow freely, and the wishes of his people do not reach him, this
is the stasis of a state. When the stasis of a state abides for a long time,
a hundred pathologies arise in concert, and a myriad catastrophes swarm
in. The cruelty of those above and those below toward each other arises
from this. The reason that the sage kings valued heroic retainers and
faithful ministers is that they dared to speak directly, breaking through
such stases.

Here is analogical reasoning applied to remarkable effect. Three
points stand out. First, in the account of the body each of its several parts has its desirable state, tightness in one case, solidity in
a second, harmony in a third. The message is that not all the constituent elements of an organic whole have the same role or the
same 'virtue': each has a different contribution to make to the
overall well-being of the whole.

Secondly, particular emphasis is laid on 'free flow' and 'regular motion': what is static or stagnant is everywhere undesirable,
in the body a cause of illness, in water of foulness, in the state
of catastrophe. What 'free flow' in the last means is explained

1. I add this gloss to Sivin's translation here, in view of the application of the term 'stasis'
   not in the sense of stoppage, or stagnant state, but as a transliteration of the Greek
   term *stasis* used of political turbulence or factionalism. The ambiguities of the Greek
   word, which can *also* mean 'rest' 'standing' 'situation', have been explored by Loraux
   1987.

by Sivin: the ruler's virtue does not flow freely if he does not appoint good officials to keep him and his subjects in touch.

Thirdly, the strategic message of the entire text relates to that final point. Throughout the work, the *Lüshi Chunqiu* is concerned to make recommendations for good government. The person responsible for organising the compilation of the work, 呂不韋, Lü Buwei, was himself an adviser to the man who was to become the first Qin emperor, Qin Shi Huang Di, although Lü died before the Qin conquests and the unification of the empire were complete. There is, of course, particular point in the stress laid on the value that the sage kings placed on faithful ministers who dared to speak out. But it is not just that the *Lüshi Chunqiu* directly emphasises the importance of advisers: it does so also indirectly by invoking the macrocosm in support. 'Free flow' impeded in the body politic leads to disaster: just as it does everywhere else, in water, trees and grasses, and in the human body when the *qi* has become static.

The *Lüshi Chunqiu* was not written by practising physicians: but the authors claim to know all about the 360 joints of the body. The second key classical text comes from the medical classic, the *Huangdi neijing suwen*, 8.1–2, 28 (in Sivin's translation). The Yellow Emperor asks Qi Bo 'about the relative authority of the twelve systems of functions associated with the internal organs, about which is higher in rank and which lower'. As Sivin comments (1995b): 'a key to medicine, in other words, is the social hierarchy of the visceral systems.'

Qi Bo thereupon replies:

The cardiac system is the office of the monarch; consciousness issues from it. The pulmonary system is the office of the minister-mentors; oversight and supervision issue from it. The hepatic system is the office of the General; planning issues from it. The gall bladder system is the office of the rectifiers; decisions issue from it. The *shanzhong* is the office of the envoys; joyous [tidings] issue from it. The splenetic and stomach systems are the office of the granaries; victuals issue from it. The large intestine system is the office of transmission; transformation issues from it. The small intestine system is the office of reception; transformed stuff issues from it. The renal system is the office that exerts great strength (?); skill issues from it. The *san jiao* is the office for clearing channels; waterways issue from it. The urinary bladder system is the office of the regions; the body fluids are stored in it, enabling transformation by *qi* to issue from it. It will not do for these twelve offices to lose their coordination. If the ruler is enlightened, all below him are secure. If one nourishes one's vital forces in accordance with this, one will live long and pass his life without peril. If one governs all under Heaven in accordance with this, it will be greatly prosperous. If the ruler is unenlightened, the twelve offices will be endangered, so that the thoroughfares will be closed off and movement will not be free. The body (形, *xing*) will be greatly injured. If one nourishes one's vital forces in accordance with this, the result will be calamity. One who governs all under Heaven in accordance with this will imperil his patrimony. Take care, take care.[2]

Here too great learning is displayed. Yet there is this difference. The agenda of the *Lüshi Chunqiu* is political through and through. The authors of the *Huangdi neijing* recensions were producing medical treatises, texts that provided the basis for medical education, compendia of medical lore. They were directed at actual, or would-be, doctors, learned ones, to be sure, but people who were liable to encounter sick patients. Not all the knowledge the doctor would need in practice can be spelled out in texts, as we have noted before (p. 65) in connection with Chunyu Yi's pulse lore and the same point could be exemplified in plenty of other connections. But conversely this text in the *suwen* illustrates that ideally the doctor should not *just* know about what we might be tempted to consider strictly medical matters. Indeed he should know about due order, not just in the body, but in the state and in the cosmos as a whole.

Both the similarities and the differences between the *Lüshi Chunqiu* and *Huangdi neijing* texts are alike significant. Both emphasise the importance, medically, politically, cosmically, of everything being in its place and fulfilling its given function. The image in both texts is one of free flow and coordination. The ideal is not a static one; indeed being static, with the 'thoroughfares closed off' and no free movement, are descriptions of the counter-ideal, what has to be avoided at all costs. Well-being in every domain depends on *inter*action.

But apart from the importance of order, thus conceived as due

2. Two of the systems identified are especially problematic. 膻中, *shanzhong*, is apparently named after the corresponding acupuncture point which is often identified – arbitrarily as Sivin 1987, p. 126 n. 14 notes – with the Cardiac Envelope Junction. The 三焦, *sanjiao*, is a *yang* visceral system, conventionally translated 'triple heater' or 'triple burner', though that derives from what Sivin calls (1987, p. 125 n. 13) fanciful extrapolations from the common but obviously irrelevant sense 'to scorch' for *jiao*.

process, a second message both texts convey, but in subtly different modes, is the need for advisers. The difference, in this case,
lies in the actual positions of Lü Buwei on the one hand, and the
authors of the *Huangdi neijing* recensions on the other. The latter would not have owed whatever political influence they may
have had to their being doctors. Indeed the position of doctors
differed from that of some other Chinese intellectuals: they never
had the key political role that the imperial astronomers did, given
the perceived importance of the latter's work for the welfare of
the state.

Yet Qi Bo figures as just as important an adviser to the Yellow
Emperor as Lü Buwei aimed to be to his prince. Qi Bo's advice
is given for all the world as if it were to do with ruling as much
as with health, though the correspondences the medical texts
insist on were, of course, made to do specifically medical work
independent of their possible political implications. However the
power of the suggestions Qi Bo has to make about health owes a
great deal to their being cast in the mode of advice about ruling.

True, the political advice in the *Lüshi Chunqiu* also owes something to *its* parade of learning about the body. But when we
consider the actual status, of doctors on the one hand, and of
statesmen on the other, we can see that the former have, in a
sense, more to gain from the acceptance of one to one correspondences between the body, the body politic and the cosmos as
a whole.

When we turn, now, to Greek views about the human body,
we are confronted with a cacophony of opinions. Whatever was
popularly believed about the body, several of our Hippocratic
authors claim to know a good deal better. One quite common
Greek idea was that the body is a vessel, but the elaboration of
that model in the treatise *On Diseases* IV is breathtaking. That
author maintains that there is a set of five reservoirs in the body
(stomach, heart, head, spleen and liver) between which the four
humours (in his view: blood, bile, phlegm and water) travel. But
to show how this works, he then describes an analogy with an
arrangement of bronze cauldrons, which have first to be set up
on a perfectly level surface and joined together 'as neatly as possible' by pipes. The system as a whole, he points out, can be filled
or emptied by filling or emptying one vessel. So too, he says,

with the body (*On Diseases* IV 39, L VII 556.17ff, cf. Lonie 1981, pp. 296ff).

A second example comes from the treatise *On Regimen*, where the author makes explicit claims for the importance of what he calls his 'discovery', said to be 'a fine thing for me the discoverer and useful for those who have learnt it: and none of my predecessors attempted to understand it though I judge it to be in every respect of great importance' (III 69, *CMG* I 2, 4, 200.25ff, 28ff). This relates primarily to the theory that health depends on a proper balance between the two fundamental elements in the body, fire and water. But he also offers a detailed and very obscure picture of how fire and water are arranged in a system of circuits in the body. The stomach in the middle is said to correspond to the sea. Round it, there is an obscure structure of cold and wet water, and a passage for cold and hot breath, which is said to correspond to the earth. Outside this, in turn, in the body, there are three circuits, composed of water and fire, which are the equivalent of the circuits of the heavenly bodies, first the circle of the moon, then the 'middle circles' (unspecified, but presumably those of the sun and planets) and then the outermost circle of the stars (I 10, 134.5–16).

That is vague enough as an astronomical theory. But trying to make sense of it in *anatomical* terms is even worse. The two accounts are supposed to fit together very nicely, with the microcosm of the body corresponding to the macrocosm. But both halves of the comparison proposed are largely imaginary. However, from the point of view of this author – and of that of *On Diseases* IV – the purpose of their exercises lies elsewhere, namely in the impression they create that these writers are privy to special, esoteric, learning.

To be sure, Chinese theories about the insides of the body were learned too. But certainly by Greek standards they display greater agreement on what they are talking about. That is true of the roles of the main viscera, for example, both of their association with either *yin* or *yang* functions, and of the correlations that eventually came to be proposed between viscera and the five phases. In Greece, by contrast, the topic of the insides of the body is one of intensely idiosyncratic speculation, where one writer after another set himself up as a special authority in the field. Making a name for yourself, as a doctor or any other kind of learned person, in Greece, was, as we have said before, as much a matter of successful self-publicity as of anything else. Having strange and wonderful theories about the insides of the body and the way it worked was certainly one way of attracting attention.

Eventually, to be sure, some questions came to be settled, at least to some theorists' satisfaction, by appeal to a technique of investigation that was ignored by both the Hippocratic treatises so far cited, namely dissection. Aristotle refers to some earlier uses of this in connection with the blood-vascular system especially, though he was himself the first to employ the technique at all extensively: we shall be considering his reasons for doing so in a minute. Meanwhile he criticises his predecessors for their unsystematic and flawed investigations (*History of Animals* III chh. 2f).

So far as our extant evidence goes, it is clear that it suggests that dissection was developed earlier, and used more extensively, in Greece than in China. While the *Huangdi neijing lingshu* 12.2, for instance, suggests the possibility of dissection, the sole apparent record of an actual dissection carried out in Han times is that ordered by Wang Mang reported in his biography in the *Hanshu* 99B: 4145–6 (see Yamada Keiji 1991, p. 39, cf. Kuriyama 1995). In this, Wang Sunqing, a follower of Wang Mang's defeated rival, the rebel Zhai Yi, is opened up. This was done, we are told, by a doctor accompanied by a 尚方 (*shang fang*: 'master of recipes')[3] and a butcher. The text goes on to say that this was for the sake of the knowledge that could then contribute to securing cures, but it may be that the intent was, in the first instance, punitive. Moreover the whole episode may have been recorded, in the *Hanshu*, partly to illustrate Wang Mang's cruelty.

But if we ask why the history of dissection took such different courses in China and in Greece, some parts of the answer can be reconstructed, and some, on the Greek side, are surprising. What we learn from this example is that just focussing on whether or not dissection was used is liable to miss the point, in that it may distract attention from the more fundamental issues of how dissection itself was viewed and what it was good for.

One of the chief contexts in which it eventually came to be

3. The gloss on this term in Hucker 1985, p. 407, suggests that it applies to what he calls, rather more grandiloquently, the 'Directorate for Imperial Manufactories'.

deployed, in China, was post-mortem forensic dissection to establish the cause of death. There was less appeal to dissection to resolve disputes over anatomical points – but then, as we noticed, there were fewer such disputes. That *was* the chief context of its use in Greece, where, conversely, the purely practical, forensic, application does not figure so prominently. Besides, the interest in dissection was sustained, in Greece, in part because it was, as we shall see, itself controversial.

Moreover secondly, we saw that the Chinese model for the body was one of a dynamic, interacting system, rather than a static set of structures. When the Greeks looked at, or into, the body, what they looked *for* was, precisely, stable structures. It is true that dissection was also used to investigate functions, for example the digestive processes. But when Galen, for instance, studied the nervous system by dissection and vivisection, the task he set himself was primarily to establish which structures are responsible for which functions.

We might suppose that, once the idea of dissection had been proposed, no particular reasons would need to be given to justify its use in anatomical research. But the record shows otherwise, and the method remained controversial throughout Greco-Roman antiquity.

First, as to the aims and motivations of Aristotle, a key figure in that he was the first to apply the technique extensively, though only to animals, not to humans. He is clear that the purpose of the study of the parts of animals is to investigate their *causes.* He disclaims being interested in the *material* components of animals (or of anything else) just for their own sake. But forms and final causes are worthy of study everywhere, and it is with them primarily in mind that the dissection of animals is undertaken. Since they are part of the analysis of *any* animal – 'however humble' – *all* animals are worth studying in this way. So the programme, in principle at least, should be comprehensive. So although he explicitly recognises that the parts of animals – blood, flesh and so on – are disgusting in themselves, the inquiry is worth pursuing for the forms and final causes it reveals, that is, for the good and the beautiful that are to be found throughout the animal kingdom. The revolting insides of animals are thereby turned into testimony to the beauty and craftsmanship of nature (*On the Parts of Animals* I ch. 1, 639b5ff, ch. 5, 644b24ff, 645a15ff, 28ff).

Initially, therefore, one of the primary Greek motivations
for dissection was teleology. But not only was teleology controversial (see above, p. 99, p. 186), dissection as such also was.
Although the method was extended to cover the dissection of
humans, and probably also their vivisection, by the early –3rd-
century Alexandrian biologists Herophilus and Erasistratus, it was
rejected by other Hellenistic medical writers on a number of
scores.[4]

Human vivisection, to start with, is cruel. But it is not as if
human dissection serves any valid purpose either, so some said.
One argument was that the body itself is affected by the very process of investigation. What the dissector or vivisector discovers
does not relate to the normally functioning human body, but to
a dead one or to one that has suffered traumatic lesion at the
hand of the vivisector himself. Some argued that knowledge of
anatomical structures is irrelevant to the practice of medicine –
which has no business investigating hidden causes and should concentrate on the primary task of treating the sick. Others took the
more moderate line that such anatomical knowledge as is needed
by the doctor will be revealed to him in the course of his own
medical practice. Both arguments were objections to animal dissection too.

But while human dissection was only carried on for a short
period at Alexandria, animal dissection at least continued. As for
the reasons for discontinuing human dissection, we have first to
note that its practice had depended crucially on the approval of
the first two Ptolemies. Herophilus and Erasistratus, we are told,
had as their subjects 'criminals obtained out of prison from the
kings'.[5] We may conjecture that the lack of equivalent support
from later rulers in Alexandria, or elsewhere, was likely to have
been a more powerful factors in its being discontinued than
either the moral or the methodological arguments that some
doctors mounted, though to them we have also to add general
inhibitions against tampering with the human corpse. That last
factor, it should be noted, did not totally preclude the desecra-
tion of the dead bodies of those considered enemies or outcasts.

4. The principal evidence and arguments on either side of this dispute are set out in
   Lloyd 1987a, pp. 163ff.
5. Celsus, *On Medicine*, I Proem 23f, *CML* I 21.15ff. Miyasita 1967 remarks that criminals were also used when human dissection came to be practised in China under the
   Sung.

The most important later Greek practitioner of animal dissection was Galen in the +2nd century. He defends the practice with
a battery of arguments in *On Anatomical Procedures* – and to those
he explicitly cites, we can add a further consideration that emerges
from the account of some of his most successful, indeed dra-
matic, public performances.

'Anatomical study,' he begins, 'has one use (1) for the "physicist" who loves knowledge for its own sake, another (2) for him
who values it not for its own sake, but rather to demonstrate that
nature does nothing without an aim, a third (3) for one who provides himself from anatomy with premises for the knowledge of
a function, physical or mental, and yet another (4) for the practitioner who has to remove splinters and missiles efficiently, to
excise parts properly, or to treat ulcers, fistulae and abscesses'
(*On Anatomical Procedures* II ch. 2, K II 286.3ff).

Of these four arguments, Galen eventually goes on to privil-
ege the fourth, the practical usefulness of anatomical knowledge
to the surgeon. Yet though he says that that is more important
than knowing the answers to such questions as the number of the
valves of the heart, or the routes of the nerves, he certainly makes
ample use of the findings of dissection in the latter, theoretical,
contexts as well. In part, the theoretical justification depends
on the teleological argument (2) familiar already from Aristotle.
Indeed Galen devotes the whole of his massive seventeen-book
treatise *On the Use of Parts* to showing not just that nature generally does nothing in vain, but the far stronger thesis that *every*
part of the body, without exception, has a purpose and that
nature is perfect (Lloyd 1987a, pp. 324ff).

But to the practical and teleological purposes, Galen now adds
a new consideration, the usefulness of anatomical knowledge in
giving *demonstrations*. I have remarked before on Galen's notion
that the ideal, in medicine, is demonstration in the *geometrical*
manner, *more geometrico*. Why he should have set that as the ideal
can be understood in terms not just of the general prestige of
geometry, but of the unassailability of arguments in the axiomatic-
deductive mode. In any dispute with opponents, they clearly provided 'knock-down' arguments *if* they could be given. But the
question then is: how did Galen think they *could* be given in
medicine?[6]

6. For what follows, see Lloyd forthcoming, and cf. Barnes 1991, Hankinson 1991b.

The general problem is easily stated. Demonstration, as Aristotle defines it in the strictest sense, depends on self-evident, indemonstrable primary premisses, axioms, definitions and so on. But how are such premisses to be secured in pathology or physiology? One of Galen's examples is the principle that 'opposites are cures for opposites'. The problem there is what is to count as an 'opposite'. Even such simple qualities as hot, cold, wet and dry, were, as Aristotle had long ago pointed out, hard to define and controversial. But if the opposites are stipulated to be what produces a cure, that makes the principle true, for sure, but vacuous.

However, Galen also claims to demonstrate (using the same terms, *apodeiknumi, apodeixis* and their cognates) in other contexts where he does not invoke ultimate primary premisses. Thus in his investigations of the seats of various vital functions he claims that he can demonstrate both that the brain is the source of the nervous system and that the heart is of the arterial. In both cases the chief consideration he relies on is the result of interventions in which he ligates the nerves or arteries and observes the consequent effects, that is, the cessation of the functions in question. The conclusions can indeed then be stated in the form of sequences of arguments in which the conclusions are validly inferred from the premisses. But if that certainly secures their claim to be *deductive*, the flaw in the claim that these are geometrical-style demonstrations remains that the premisses can undoubtedly not be thought of as on a par with the axioms of geometry.

Yet that does not make these investigations any less impressive as *proofs* of the very points that Galen seeks to show. The paradox is that Galen provides many excellent *empirical demonstrations* of anatomical and physiological functions: yet he was himself often not satisfied with anything but proof in the Euclidean manner. To seek to recast empirical investigations such as he undertook to have them conform to the geometrical style, with the deductions stemming from starting-points for which axiomatic indemonstrable status is claimed, was at least distracting (since it ignored their actual empirical basis) and at worst misleading (since it gave the whole a spurious air of incontrovertibility).

Once again we find a Greek scientist – and one of the foremost – playing for the highest possible stakes in argumentative disputes with his opponents: one might think, indeed, impossibly high stakes, given the nature of the subject-matter under dispute, in anatomy, physiology, pathology and therapeutics. But if dissection thus serves Galen's demonstrative ambitions in a variety of ways, there is yet another role that it plays, even though this does not figure explicitly among the four types of justification Galen adduces in *On Anatomical Procedures*.

On a number of occasions, including in *On Anatomical Procedures* itself, Galen refers to competitive public dissections, where animals, sometimes exotic ones, were cut up and rival experts attempted to predict the outcome. On one such occasion, at Rome, the animal was an elephant, and the audience placed bets on who would turn out to have predicted the structure of its heart correctly. Not surprisingly, Galen reports that he himself did so (*On Anatomical Procedures* VII ch. 10). On another occasion, a group of Erasistrateans was challenged to demonstrate their theory that the aorta contained no blood, but air alone (*On Anatomical Procedures* VII ch. 16). Galen's own supporters put down a stake of 1,000 drachmae for the opposition to pocket should their view turn out to be correct. Galen records with some relish the mess the dissector made of his task, but he evidently does less than justice to the explanations the Erasistrateans would have given of the blood that most of them knew very well would be found in the arterial system under dissection: for their story would have been that that blood was a result of the dissection itself, being drawn into the arteries from the veins under the action of the principle of *horror vacui*.

But that last point aside, such reports make clear that there was sometimes more to ancient Greek dissections than mere disinterested research or even pedagogy – to train the next generation of doctors. As Vegetti and others have stressed (Manuli and Vegetti 1977, Vegetti 1979, 1983, von Staden 1995), some occasions have a certain theatricality about them. Some performances were for display, and competitive display at that. They were about rivalry, about making a reputation by winning disputes, about impressing as wide an audience as you could attract. They had more in common with the techniques of persuasion we discussed in Chapter 4, than with the axiomatic-deductive style of demonstration that was Galen's expressed ideal.

Greek theorists found plenty to disagree about, concerning the structures of the human body, its functioning, its health and the

causes and cures of disease. Yet that certainly did not inhibit
the Greeks from using the body as a source of ideas in tackling
other subjects as well. It is now time to turn to the Greek equivalents to two of the ideas we found in the Chinese texts we cited,
namely (1), the analogy between the body and the body politic,
and (2) the roles of advisers.

The former idea comes in a variety of forms, as we should
expect from the variety of political ideals, democratic, oligarchic,
monarchic, that different Greek theorists favoured. Sometimes the
main need, in the body politic, was viewed as a matter of the due
balance between interest groups thought of as equal but opposed.[7]
More often, the emphasis was on the need for control or rule,
often indeed oligarchic or monarchic rule in the authoritarian,
anti-democratic, authors who predominate in what has survived
of ancient Greek political theory.

Control was not just a matter of rule being exercised by the
right elements – the analogue, in the body politic, of what was
called the *hēgēmonikon* in the body, that is, the seat of vital activities, located by some (as by Aristotle) in the heart, though by
others (from Alcmaeon onwards) in the brain. The crucial extra
idea the analogy was used to promote is that of the need, and the
justification, for *cures* to secure the *health* of the body politic.

Plato is just the most outspoken representative of such a view.
First of all he argues that injustice in the soul of the individual
is like disease (for example *Republic* 444b ff). Once it is recognised as such, no one would prefer to continue to act unjustly.
This provides him with one of his main arguments for the paradoxical conclusion that no one does wrong willingly.

But similarly injustice in the state also calls, in his view, for
what may have to be drastic measures of cure. Undesirables are
to be purged, and the best purges, we are told (*Laws* 735c ff) are
painful. Such criminals as are classed as totally incurable have to
be got rid of completely. It is true that the legislator envisaged
in Plato's *Laws* is supposed first to use persuasion in order to
obtain agreement to what is proposed, just as the best doctors
should also reason with their patients to get them to take their
medicine. But the crucial difference lies in this, that, if persuasion

---

7. The ideal for *health* is expressed as one of 'equal rights', *isonomia*, by Alcmaeon in the
   –5th century (Fr. 4, cf. above, p. 131).

fails, Plato's legislator can and does then invoke sanctions, if necessary force, to get his way. He, after all, is the expert who knows
what has to be done.

The strategy of many appeals to the medical analogy is, of
course, to represent the particular proposals being advocated
as what alone will secure the *health* of the body politic. But it
certainly raises the stakes of political debate very dramatically, if
those who disagree are represented, as Plato represents them, as
pathogenic elements who have to be removed by purgings, puri-
fications, cauterisations, the knife – or their political equivalents.
Since we all agree that health is a good thing, we should all be
expected to agree also that the health of the body politic is too.
However, the difficulty is obvious. Whatever agreement might be
held to exist about what bodily health consists in, there was certainly no consensus at all, in Greece, in Plato's day or at any other
time, about what the well-being of the state consisted in or depended on.

This takes me finally to the theme of the adviser, or rather,
to recast him in his Platonic mould, the expert. We saw that
the powers of persuasion that Chinese advisers exercised were
increased by their drawing on a comprehensive learning, encompassing body, state and cosmos. So too in Greece, those who knew
about the body – or rather those who could be represented as
knowing about it – were used as models for those for whom the
claim was made that they knew about the body politic, its needs
and the provisions that would secure them.

Yet beyond that point, the differences between the Chinese
and the Greek uses are striking. First Chinese advisers are generally *ministers*. While ministers had many responsibilities, and
especially, precisely, for giving the ruler, the prince or emperor,
good advice, it was not their role, but that of the ruler himself, to rule. In Greece, Plato's ideal is that of philosopher-kings
who are themselves responsible for implementing the whole political programme, not just ensuring that the state enjoyed the best
possible constitution, but also overseeing the political, legal, educational measures that were supposed to secure its complete
well-being. The difference is that the philosopher-kings combine
the roles of arriving at the truth and carrying out the measures
it suggested, the first in their capacity as philosophers, the second
in their function as kings.

Secondly, the learning that Chinese advisers displayed, whether about the body or about the state, was not claimed to be based on *certain knowledge*. Here is the most surprising feature of the Greek medical analogy of all. Plato, for one, repeatedly takes the physician as model to express and justify his claim that there can be, and should be, equivalent experts in the political domain as well. That, to be sure, is not his only way of recommending that idea, but it is a very prominent one.

Yet if we reflect on the *actual* state of Greek medicine in his day, we can see how extraordinary Plato's move was. Reading Plato, one could imagine a confident, united, group of medical practitioners, who knew what they were doing, who agreed about the main principles of therapy, who had a clear enough idea about the principal causes of diseases, and who moved from confident diagnoses to confident treatments with well-based expectations of success. Yet as we have seen, *that* was not what ancient Greek medicine was like in the least. If we turn to the Hippocratic writers (to go no further afield), one sees that every single one of the features of that characterisation is well wide of the mark. Even before we take into account other styles of medicine, such as those practised in the temples of Asclepius, or by the itinerant purifiers, the Hippocratic authors disagreed fundamentally among themselves, not just about the causes of disease, but about what a cause is (cf. Chapter 5), not just about the actual treatments to be used in particular cases, but on the principles that should underlie treatment, as well as on a whole range of questions to do with the basic anatomy and physiology of the body.

We can see the *attraction* of the *idea* of the medical expert to Plato. Such a doctor can, on the basis of his knowledge, and often must, contradict the lay person on matters of importance to lay people themselves. They may think they are perfectly well, perfectly healthy. But the trained medical man knows better. Analogously, that provides Plato with a powerful set of arguments for *setting aside* most ordinary people's views both as to the ends of government and as to the appropriate means to those ends. They may believe that the state is well-run. But the philosopher-king will be able to diagnose its hidden ailments and move in to cure the body politic with the right treatment, not shrinking, as we have seen, even from the most drastic measures.

Yet not only is the idea of the kind of certainty that Plato requires in political science illusory: it was based in part on a concept of a science of medicine that may or may not be attainable, in certain areas, in principle, but that in practice had certainly not actually been attained by the Greek doctors of his day. So powerful was the attraction, to Plato at least, of the notion of the doctor as the possessor of specialist knowledge of the hidden condition of the body, as the person with the right, with the duty, not just to diagnose but also to treat his patients, however painful his prescriptions – so attractive was that set of ideas to Plato that he entirely *brackets* the actual, contemporary lack of anything that could be described as secure knowledge in most areas of anatomy, physiology, pathology, therapeutics. He brackets also the actual *failures* of most ancient Greek therapies – even though these are recorded in some detail, and with great honesty, in many of our Hippocratic texts.[8] Nor can we argue that Plato was simply unaware of those disagreements among Greek doctors on the fundamental issues in medical theory and practice, since, so far as theories of diseases go, Plato himself offers one in the *Timaeus*, and whatever we may think of the contribution it makes to that on-going debate, it certainly shows that Plato was well-informed on many common Greek medical views and practices.

Yet if Plato's picture of the expert doctor does not exactly tally with the realities of Greek medical practice, what it is far more strongly reminiscent of is the type of confident, indeed dogmatic, claims to special knowledge that, as we saw earlier on in this chapter, punctuate several of our Hippocratic texts. And as we also pointed out, Galen was eventually to set his sights higher still, not just on knowledge, but on the certainty secured by strict demonstration. What many Greek medical writes, from the –5th century onwards, needed and sought, were ways and means of winning out over their rivals. Plato's expert doctor is for use as a model for political expertise, and indeed in the political domain such a claim for expertise plays a precisely similar role. Where the abilities of ordinary statesmen – and even of a Pericles – could be downgraded on the grounds that they were based on no more than true opinion, the philosopher-kings

8. Twenty-five of the forty-two individual case histories contained in *Epidemics* I and III end in death: figures for the cases in the other books of *Epidemics* are set out in Lloyd 1983, pp. 67f. Other Greek medical texts that record failures or mistakes in treatment are discussed in Lloyd 1987a, pp. 124ff.

could easily outbid the opposition with the assertion that their policies and practices were based on certain knowledge. Or so at least the claim was.

One might suppose that, given the similarities between human bodies across space and time, their study, too, would not exhibit significant differences, that anatomy (the investigation, that is) would be the same everywhere. But as with astronomy, or what passes as the study of the heavens, we find important divergences, as between ancient Greece and ancient China, and these can tell us a good deal both about the aims of scientists and about their modes of operation.

It is true that we find some remarkable similarities. Three of the most noticeable are: (1) analogies between the body and the state and between both and the cosmos as a whole are highly developed both in Greece and even more especially in China; (2) the body is used, in both, to convey notions of orderly relations and an idea of the value of order; (3) knowing about the body is an important way of knowing, paradigmatic of at least one prized kind of learning.

Yet, in each case, generic similarities, when examined, reveal underlying differences. (1) In Greece, there were radical disagreements in all three areas, cosmology, politics, anatomy, and these are the topic of intense rivalry and dispute between competing would-be experts. To be sure, it was not as if there was complete unanimity, in China, on *all* these subjects, though there was, substantially, on political *ideals*. However, on the body, as on most other topics, the bid to arrive at something of a consensus among the learned is marked, and the idea of claiming to outdo everyone else's theories with your own would rightly have been considered extravagant.

(2) The chief notion of order that the body is assumed to convey and is used to express is different in the two cases. For the Chinese, the ideal is one of 'free flow', interaction, intercommunication between parts, with each fulfilling its due and proper function. That applies to the bureaucracy of the state, and the interrelation of parts of the living organism is conceived similarly bureaucratically. Even while the Greeks studied processes, to be sure, they looked for stable structures. Anatomical research was directed at disclosing such structures, each with its own distinct

form. The emphasis was not, or not so much, on their interdependence or interconnectedness, as on their own several essences. The notion of the good that the body was used to convey was, at least in one prominent – teleological – strand of thought, that of the beauty and intelligibility of nature as a whole.

(3) Finally, so far as knowing about the body goes, the Greeks' frequent ambition to deliver certainty is apparent both in Galen's picture of the biological scientist as master of demonstration *more geometrico*, and in the construction of the idea of the medical expert as model for the statesman. That style of demonstration was never contemplated in China. Rather, what knowledge about the body was useful for, there, was to express that sense of the grasp of the whole that went with the Chinese conception of the man of learning.

True, Chinese doctors did not have the status that astronomers came to have, or rather the official positions open to them did not command the same political significance. So there may be a sense in which the doctors had more to gain than others from their rehearsal of the *summa* of knowledge. Yet what was not thought either necessary or desirable was to make individualistic claims to expertise.

Besides, in its application to statesmanship, this aspect of the medical analogy is bound to differ, in China and in Greece, since the question of whose knowledge, whose credibility is at stake, has to be answered differently. In China, the appeal to command of knowledge of the body helps to bolster the role of the *adviser*. But there is no question of any need to legitimate the right of *rulers* to rule, that is, of rulers *as such* to do so, though of course any given ruler might well have a question mark over *his* right, and if he appeared to lack the necessary virtue would be disqualified from doing so. Ideally, Heaven would see to that on its own, when its Mandate was withdrawn: but that did not rule out its receiving help from human aides or human intervention.

But in Greece, by contrast, where what political regime was best, and who was best fitted to rule, were intensely debated, the doctor as expert served to bolster the *rulers'* position (rather than that of advisers). Every time a Greek orator used the vocabulary of sickness, disease, plague, with regard to the body politic, he was by implication setting himself up as political diagnostician – and analyses of ailments were often swiftly followed by recommendations as to cures. More potently still, in Plato's hands especially, the invocation of the doctor–statesman analogy legitimated the claim that only those with *knowledge* should rule, and, in his strong sense of knowledge, that in theory put the philosopher-kings beyond the reach of challenge from those with mere opinion.

Unchallengeability, of the imperial function as such, was a *given* in China. But in Greece political unchallengeability was no more than the *ideal* that some authoritarian political theorists set up, with the best arguments they could muster – yet an unattainable ideal nevertheless. If, among those arguments, a prominent role was given to the analogy that appealed to the knowledge the doctor could lay claim to, as his justification for his professed ability to diagnose and treat his patients, that may be said to present a flattering view of the actual basis of most ancient Greek medical practice – though it was one to which plenty of the doctors themselves would have been only too happy to subscribe.

CHAPTER 10

Science in antiquity: the Greek and Chinese cases and their relevance to the problems of culture and cognition

The preceding studies have tackled just a few of the important issues in the comparative analysis of ancient Greek and Chinese science. I must underline, yet again, in the strongest possible terms, the difficulties and dangers of generalisation, across subject-areas and across periods, that we identified at the outset. There is, of course, far more to the complexity and variety of both Greek and Chinese science than can conceivably be indicated here.

However, the task of this final investigation will be to reflect on the conclusions that these studies thus far suggest. The three fundamental topics with which this book has been concerned may be expressed, bluntly if naively, in the form of three questions. First, did science develop differently in ancient Greece and in ancient China? If so, secondly, can we say why? Third, what can we learn from such an investigation about more general issues to do with the relationships between culture and cognition?

The answer to the first question that our analyses suggest is clearly yes. Our initial expectation might be just the opposite, namely that science in general, and astronomy, mathematics, medicine, anatomy and so on in particular, must be invariant at all times and across the world. That expectation would be driven by two powerful considerations. First, the truths revealed are universal truths. Two and two make four in whatever language or notation that is expressed and at whatever time and place. The square on the hypotenuse of a right-angled triangle is equal to the sum of the squares on the other two sides, whether this is known as Pythagoras' theorem, or as 句股, *gou gu*. Secondly, it would be impossible for us to compare and contrast astronomy (say) in different times and places unless what we compare and contrast deals broadly with what can be recognised as the same subject-matter.

Both points must be given some weight. Indeed the element-ary truths of mathematics are invariant. Indeed we could not com-pare ancient Greek and Chinese astronomy unless both were, in some sense, studies of the heavens.

But that should not distract attention from the more import-ant respects in which we should acknowledge that science did indeed develop differently in ancient Greece and in ancient China. Even though it is legitimate to talk of both Greek and Chinese *astronomy* precisely for the reason that both are, in some sense, studies of the heavens, nevertheless *why* the heavens were studied, what they were studied for, the aims and preoccupations of the investigators in the two cases, differ – as we saw in Chapter 8 – profoundly, as also do their methods and styles of reasoning. So too our exploration of the study of the human body, in Chapter 9, revealed just some of the radical differences, not only in how the body itself was viewed, and the manner in which it was invest-igated, but also in the ways in which those investigations were brought to bear on other domains, including both politics and cosmology.

Of course there are important similarities too, first at the level of particular concepts and methods, then at the level of aims and goals, and thirdly in the styles of interaction cultivated by those who engaged in different branches of study in the two ancient civilisations in question. It is true that some of the similarities that might be appealed to at the first level are similarities with a difference. It is not much use merely adducing the fact that the pulse is developed as a sophisticated diagnostic and prognostic aid both in China and (eventually) in Greece, if we do not also take into account the very different concepts of the body that underlie the studies in question. The same may also be said of dissection.

Again, we found many examples where the aims of Greek and Chinese scientists of different types can be described, very broadly, as being to reveal the underlying order in the phenomena, in part to illustrate, if not also to promote, a notion of the importance of order more generally. Yet we also found major differences in the way order was understood, both in the scientific and in the political domains. We may certainly say that both ancient Greek and ancient Chinese science – like science everywhere and at all times – were put to the service of the expression of certain values:

but that should not mask the further point, that the values so expressed differed very markedly. As I argued in Chapter 6, even when the hierarchies identified in the phenomena were held to mirror the hierarchies of society in both China and Greece, the emphasis placed on the interdependence of paired opposites, in the one case, contrasts with an ideal of their independence in the other.

Similarly 'harmony' is prized by Greeks and Chinese alike, in social relations and in heaven. But on closer examination the harmony in question differs. The Chinese emphasised the harmonious resonance between heaven and earth and the responsibility of the ruler or emperor to ensure this. But the Greeks tried out a variety of ideas suggesting that the heavenly bodies themselves produce a harmony. However if that were the case, they could do so, for sure, irrespective of terrestrial order or disorder. So one mode of harmony, in Greece, was a purely celestial affair, even if other modes expressed the ideal of a general, cosmic, order.

At a more abstract level still, there is no shortage of common features in the styles of reasoning that can be exemplified in medical writers, mathematicians, astronomers, philosophers, in both Greece and China. Chapter 4 explored some of the interests, including the self-conscious interests, in the techniques of persuasion, and the concern – once again often made explicit – with regard to proper methods. Chapter 2 argued that both criticism of rivals, and respect for authority and tradition, exist, even though they are found in different measures, in both Greece and China, and suggested further that there are, in both cases, significant differences in those measures as between different periods.

Yet to our first – blunt and naive – question, 'did science develop differently in ancient Greece and in ancient China?', the answer must still be that it did, whether we look at mathematics, at astronomy or at medicine. In each of these three important fields, the way the subject was conceived differs in crucial respects: so too do the aims and preoccupations of the investigators, and so too do some at least of their styles of inquiry.

One recurrent difference, between some of the Greek work in those three areas and all of the Chinese, centres round the three interrelated concepts of axiomatisation, certainty and foundations. The distinctive mark of the Euclidean tradition of mathematics – which sets it apart from all other ancient traditions and not just the Chinese – is its insistence not just on deduction, but on axiomatic-deductive demonstration. Similarly, the Greek search for geometrical models for the movements of the heavenly bodies can be related to a concern to be able to demonstrate that the apparent irregularities of the movements of the planets are the product of combinations of regular circular motions. In this case Ptolemy explicitly claims as the great strength of his style of astronomical inquiry that, based on mathematics, it can yield incontrovertible results. Even in medicine, thirdly, Galen pursues proof 'in the geometrical manner' as his ideal, despite the considerable difficulties there are in identifying self-evident starting-points to serve as the axioms of medical reasoning. Further afield still, the recurrent Greek concern with principles, *archai*, and with elements, *stoicheia*, is a concern to establish secure foundations on which the whole of the inquiry, in cosmology, in physics, in physiology, can be based.

Two reservations must now be entered. The first relates to the problem that was emphasised at the outset, namely that of generalising across the whole of Greek science. Euclid is not the whole of Greek mathematics: there are other Greek traditions of mathematical inquiry, such as that exemplified in Hero's studies of problems of mensuration, where no attempt is made to found the entire inquiry on a set of indemonstrable principles. Ptolemy and Galen, equally, certainly do not encapsulate the whole of Greek astronomy, the whole of Greek medicine. The pluralism of Greek science, which we have mentioned so often and to which we shall need to return yet again below, must be given due weight. The concern with axioms, with certainty, with foundations, is a recurrent, but not a universal, one, in Greek science.

Then our second reservation relates to the Chinese side and to the need to be quite precise about the terms in which the contrast we have suggested is expressed. Deductive reasoning is to be found in a wide variety of contexts in Chinese thought, not least in Chinese mathematics. Chinese arithmetic and geometry, we noted, verify results, including carrying out the verification of the algorithms by which the results were obtained. It is not that there are no proofs in Chinese mathematics. Quite the contrary. But the proofs certainly take a different form from those in Euclid. It is the combination of deduction with axiomatisation that principally marks out demonstration in the Euclidean manner. The primary Chinese concerns, as evidenced in Liu Hui, are rather with validating the procedures employed and with identifying the fundamental elements that unify the procedures used in divergent mathematical contexts.

Again, so far as certainty goes, we cited a text from Han Fei (above, pp. 26f at n. 12) that criticises those who make assertions where they cannot be sure of their ground. But here and in many other contexts where similar doubts are expressed in Chinese philosophy and science, the point is a negative and critical one. Han Fei expresses disapproval of those who claim to know what they do not: but it is not that he himself asserts that he can speak with certainty on the subject. It is the readiness of the Greeks – of some Greeks, that is – positively to claim to have secured that, indeed to have established the whole of an inquiry on indubitable foundations, that is exceptional.

Plenty of other contrasts between aspects of Greek, and aspects of Chinese, science at different periods can, of course, be suggested. Our discussion here can broach only a very small area of those vast and complex fields, and other topics will be the subject of more detailed examination in subsequent investigations (Lloyd and Sivin forthcoming). Yet the features thus far identified certainly pose problems enough. The second of my three initial questions was: if science developed differently in ancient Greece and in ancient China, can we say why?

Here too it is essential first to examine the basis on which the question may be posed, the types of explanatory factor demanded, indeed the limits of the explanation possible. Clearly when we attempt to investigate why this or that particular idea or theory was put forward by this or that particular thinker, whether it be Aristotle or Euclid or Hui Shi or Zhuangzi, the range of factors that can and should be taken into account is enormous. They must include, in every case, as detailed an analysis as our evidence permits of the internal dialectic of the problem-situation each thinker faced. At a more general level, if we ask why groups of philosophers, mathematicians, astronomers, doctors, Greek or Chinese, held what they held, the appearance that it may be easier to generalise about the factors to which they were responding may be deceptive, since in every case the validity of the generalisation will depend on the validity of the particular claims on which it is based.

Nor are those by any means the only complications. There are, of course, no agreed limits to the degree of complexity with which we choose to analyse the possible influences at work on the end-products of intellectual activity in any society. Geographical, economic, political, social, cultural factors all have a potential relevance. Nor should it be forgotten that factors invoked at one point, as part of the explanation of certain features of intellectual activity, may, from another point of view, themselves be *explananda* and stand in need of further elucidation. We may, as I noted, ask not just how Greek and Chinese intellectuals may have been affected by factors in the political situation within which they operated, but also why Greek and Chinese society developed and maintained the particular political institutions they did – where, indeed, the development and maintenance may, and in certain respects did, owe something to the political philosophies of some of those intellectuals.

Not only are there going to be no final explanations of the complex phenomena we refer to under the rubrics of Greek and Chinese philosophy and science: there are not even going to be any hard-edged explanations that are at all comparable to those we would demand in other contexts, for example in explaining physical interactions or even clearly motivated intentional acts in terms of those intentions. The best we can hope for is to identify possible influences, possible correlations or conjunctions, that may enable us to understand how the philosophy and science produced relate to the circumstances of their production. It is precisely here that comparative studies can prove so useful, both by highlighting points that might otherwise be missed, and by checking hypotheses as to the interaction of particular factors. Certainly any proposals as to the one-way or mutual influences of some factors on others can be tested by examining whether or not similar combinations of factors cluster elsewhere.

With these caveats duly entered, we may now address our second question, as to *why* ancient Greek and Chinese science took the distinctive forms they did. The argument developed in earlier chapters proceeds in several stages, some features of which, at least, can be directly supported by textual evidence.

First as to axiomatics – so important in Greece: the first extant comprehensive exposition of an inquiry in the axiomatic-deductive mode is in Euclid's *Elements* from around −300. But

the first explicit definition of demonstration in that mode comes
not in mathematics but in philosophy, in Aristotle, who was responsible also for an argument to the effect that such demonstration must depend on ultimate indemonstrable, but self-evident,
starting-points. Both Euclid's mathematics and Aristotle's philosophy of science owe much to earlier work, though we have emphasised that pre-Euclidean mathematics, poorly represented in
our sources, is particularly hard to evaluate. So far as philosophy
goes, a concern for principles, *archai*, goes back to the very early
stages of Presocratic speculation and it is mirrored also in early
Greek medicine. However, the more important influence, on Aristotle's philosophy of science, comes, undoubtedly, from Plato, for
although he did not give a formal definition of demonstration,
he certainly emphasised, in the strongest possible terms, the contrast between proof and persuasion, between the certain and the
merely probable.

In some cases, at least, we can identify some of the major aims
and concerns of the key Greek thinkers who were instrumental
in these developments. They tell us about those aims and concerns themselves, and this constitutes our best direct evidence as
to both the overt reasons, and the underlying factors at work.
Both Plato and Aristotle especially develop the contrasts between
proof and persuasion in part in order to drive a wedge between,
on the one hand, true philosophy of the kind (or rather kinds)
they practise, and, on the other, the inferior styles of reasoning
they associate with sophists, politicians, orators.

These juxtapositions and contrasts enable us to see that there
is more to the development of axiomatisation, and the idea of
the need for certainty and for foundations, in ancient Greece,
than just a laudable desire for the highest possible standards of
intellectual rigour. In the background, first, there is the intense
rivalry for intellectual leadership and prestige. What counted as
true philosophy, true medicine, even true mathematics, were matters of considerable dispute, and those who claimed to be the
genuine representatives were fertile in the invention of categories to describe base imitations, deviations, perversions.

The morality and motivations of those thus criticised were often
challenged, as in the attacks on charlatans, quacks, 'magicians',
in some of the medical writers, such as the author of *On the
Sacred Disease* (Lloyd 1979, ch. 1). But styles of reasoning were

also impugned. In Aristotle himself, demonstrative arguments (where the premisses must be necessary as well as true) are contrasted first with dialectical ones (based on generally accepted opinions or on the admissions of interlocutors) and then with a whole sequence of other, lower, modes of reasoning. These include peirastic (examination arguments), eristic (where the aim is just victory in the argument itself), sophistic (which he thinks of as directed at enhancing reputation, that is showing off) as well as the three main branches of rhetoric, forensic, deliberative and epideictic.

But the second, more fundamental, element in the background is more directly political. Both Plato and Aristotle make no secret of their disapproval of many aspects of contemporary Greek political life. For Plato, the political assemblies and the law-courts of Athens provide paradigm cases of how philosophical debate should *not* be conducted. The problem with those democratic institutions, as he saw it, was that the decisions were taken not by experts, but by the ignorant and gullible masses of ordinary citizens, who evaluated the issues not in the light of reason but as the fancy took them, a gullibility open to exploitation by all the techniques of rhetorical persuasion.

I have stressed just how intense direct political experience was, not just in the democracies, though especially there, and not just in the classical period down to the end of the −4th century, but again especially then. Active participation, in the political assemblies and councils, in the law-courts, whether as litigants or as dicasts, was, by the standards of most other historical societies, extraordinarily widespread and, we may believe, a formative experience for the participants.

Yet for us to assess the impact of this on a variety of aspects of Greek intellectual life, we have, of course, to go beyond the largely hostile reactions of such as Plato and Aristotle. That impact has at least three contrasting features. It is relevant, first, directly, to what I have called radical revisability, secondly, and again directly, to adversariality, and thirdly, though this time indirectly, to the generation of a demand for objectivity.

I remarked that, in principle, in the democracies, the people in assembly were sovereign in all matters. They decided not just issues of tactics, of how to implement policy, of means to ends, but also those of strategy, policy, the ends themselves. In −5th-century Athens they were sovereign over the constitution itself, though later attempts were made to curb the power to modify the very constitutional framework of the state (Hansen 1991, ch. 13). Aristotle, in the –4th century, continues to issue warnings about the dangers inherent in any attempt to change existing traditions, customs, laws:[1] but that just draws attention to the point that they could be so changed.

The Greek lack of agreement as to political ideals was not just a matter of the theoretical debates of the philosophers. It is duly reflected in the repeated major and minor constitutional upheavals and revolutions that many Greek states experienced. It is true that many such changes stemmed simply from the opportunism of self-interested groups: but that did not inhibit them from claiming superiority, as well as legitimacy, for the regimes they put in place, in the name, often, of specific political programmes.

This radical revisability in the political field is repeatedly echoed in the capacity we have observed in Greek thinkers in other domains to challenge and overthrow traditional or accepted views, introducing not just new, but also often highly counter-intuitive ideas and practices. By that I do not just mean what may seem counter-intuitive to us, but what was judged so by other ancient Greeks themselves. We can see this, for example, in Aristotle's dismissive reaction to Parmenides' denial that change exists, and indeed in his labelling as paradoxical many of his predecessors' suggestions, not least the position he attributes to Heraclitus to the effect that change is constant.[2]

We cannot claim that radical revisability in politics directly produced radical revisability in philosophy and science: that would be too simple. But the challenge to traditional assumptions in any one of these domains may be thought to have facilitated the possibility of similar challenges in others. Once again that

1. See Aristotle's critical comments, *Politics* 1269a13ff, on the proposals he attributes to Hippodamus, 1267b22ff, 1268b22ff. Cf. Brunschwig 1980.
2. Thus to attempt to demonstrate that change occurs to someone who denies that it did would be to ignore the distinction between what can, and what cannot, be proved within natural science, *Physics* 184b25ff, 185a12ff, 17ff. Similarly, one cannot demonstrate such an axiom as the Law of Non-Contradiction – for there is no more fundamental principle from which it could be deduced. But if someone were inclined to deny that Law, he could be refuted *ad hominem* as soon as he signified something, for that would imply the truth of the Law: *Metaphysics* 1005a19ff, 1006a5ff, 15ff.

parallelism was not lost on the ancient Greeks themselves, for
Aristotle explicitly draws attention to it in the very passage in
which he warns against the dangers of subverting tradition. In his
view, however, those dangers are appreciably more serious in
the political sphere, than in such a domain as medicine (*Politics*
1268b34ff with 1269a19ff).

The second strand to the impact of Greek political and legal
experience that I suggested relates to adversariality, which I discussed at length in Chapter 2. In Greek philosophy, medicine,
even mathematics, the framework of discussion often takes the
form of a confrontation between opposed views. But the extent
to which this occurs is less surprising, when we reflect on the
models for just such confrontations provided by the widespread
experience of forensic and political debate, where the advocacy
of one's own case often, indeed maybe generally, proceeded by
way of a critical examination and refutation of the theses proposed by the opposition. Even when Greek philosophers and
scientists *deplored* this feature of philosophical or scientific discussion, they recognised its existence.

In philosophy, annihilating the opposition's case was sometimes
undertaken in the name of constructive defence of an alternative
view. But skill in arguing *both* sides of an issue was not just a technique associated with those who – to the scandalised reactions of
Aristophanes and Plato – were said to have taught people how
to make the worse cause appear to be the better. It was also the
cornerstone of the scepticism developed both in philosophy and
in medicine, though there the discovery of equal and opposite
arguments on either side of each question concerning underlying
reality was supposed to lead to the suspension of belief. Further
afield still, the influence of advocacy in the forensic situation can
be detected, so I argued (Chapter 5), in common Greek assumptions to do with both evidence and causation more generally. For
evidence is a matter of the witnesses that can be mustered in support, and causation one of investigating responsibilities.

The *deploring* of the influence of patterns of political and legal
reasoning is a more prominent feature of the ancient Greek reaction to the third item I mentioned, where we come to the nub
of the issues to do with the demand for certainty. It is this characteristic especially, as I argued, that marks out major areas of
Greek mathematics, astronomy, medicine and philosophy itself.

Mere opinion or belief will not do: nor will merely plausible or persuasive arguments. Certainty is the aim, and not just a subjective feeling of being sure, but a matter of the objective, incontrovertible truth. To secure this, what was needed was demonstration, but not in the manner of an orator or a politician seeking to prove a point beyond reasonable doubt, but using rigorous deductive argument from necessary and self-evident premisses.

If it was obvious – and not just to Plato and Aristotle – that what persuaded the dicasts or an assembly might or might not be true, here, by contrast, was a way of presenting a model of the highest styles of reasoning that would defend them from precisely the same charge. Yet it was not as if those styles were thereby *removed* from the competition. Rather, as Aristotle put it (see above, p. 91 on *Rhetoric* 1355a20ff), what is *most* persuasive is the truth. That, the further claim was, could be *guaranteed* only by the combination of valid deductive argument and self-evident primary premisses.

The strictest style of demonstration was thereby an ideal elaborated, in part, to put those who practised it in an unassailable position with regard to their rivals. It is not just Plato and Aristotle who hoped to secure the contrast between the highest style of philosophising and the inferior modes of reasoning of sophists, orators, or worse. Ptolemy and Galen too continue to insist on the ideal as a way of establishing boundaries, in Ptolemy's case between mathematical astronomy and physics, in Galen's between the highest mode of medical theorising and inferior brands. But while there was no difficulty, to be sure, in securing the validity of deductive arguments, the further problem of identifying propositions that would serve as self-evident axioms outside the field of mathematics itself was acute, and the very fact that so many Greek theorists persisted in the search testifies not so much to their confidence that success was near, as to their sense that this was what they needed to secure ultimate victory.

The argument is, then, that Greek intellectuals sought and claimed incontrovertibility chiefly in a bid to outdo their rivals and downgrade their merely plausible arguments. That must be recognised, to be sure, to be no more than a conjecture, indeed a highly speculative one at that. Yet the hypothesis may be said to withstand one negative test rather well. If the demand for certainty, in Greece, owes something to an adverse reaction to the

merely persuasive arguments used in the law-courts and assemblies, we can check whether or not an equivalent stimulus existed
in China by examining their traditions of legal and political argument. Evidently the hypothesis suggested would be seriously
undermined, if there were such a stimulus, and yet no corresponding preoccupation with securing certainty.

The first fundamental point has been made already (p. 90)
and it relates to Chinese attitudes towards the legal experience,
whether in civil or in criminal cases, and to litigiousness in general. Civil law as such was almost unheard of. More generally, so
far from positively delighting in litigation, as many Greeks seem
to have done, so far from developing a taste for confrontational
argument in that context and becoming quite expert in its evaluation, the Chinese avoided any brush with the law as far as they
possibly could. Disputes that could not be resolved by arbitration
were felt to be a breakdown of due order and as such reflected
unfavourably on *both* parties, whoever was in the right.

So forensic advocacy of the adversarial type developed in the
Greek law-courts can hardly be found in China, but that is not
surprising, given that the contexts of its use were lacking. Yet
there were, as we saw in Chapter 4, plenty of other occasions for
the development and practice of the techniques of persuasion.
However, we found that both the theory and the practice differ,
in certain respects, from those of Greek deliberative oratory. First,
the primary contexts for its deployment have nothing to do with
the citizen body in Assembly or even its representatives in Coun-
cil: they relate, rather, in the first instance to the persuasion of
the prince or ruler.

More important, secondly, it seems significant that in Han Fei
the focus of attention is on the psychological aspects of persuasion, rather than on the analysis of the styles of argument as
such. Advice is offered on how to please, and more especially on
how to avoid offending, the prince. Of course analogous considerations are addressed also in Greek manuals of the art of rhetoric. Aristotle, for one, discusses the need to take into account the
emotions and prejudices of the audience and advises on how to
present yourself as a person who can be trusted. But what he also
does, is to give an analysis of the modes of argument available to
the orator, the enthymeme and the paradigm, the equivalent, in
rhetoric, of the syllogism and induction. It is that extra step that

brings to the fore the contrasts between the merely plausible and the certain – the topic we are chiefly interested in as the background to the development of the notion of axiomatic-deductive demonstration.

Several prominent features of Greek philosophy and science thus seem to owe something – whether directly or indirectly – to the distinctive political and social experience of Greek city-states: the features we have identified as radical revisability, as adversarial argumentativeness, and (by reaction, or indirectly) the concern with certainty, with foundations, with axioms.

How far, we may now ask, do the recurrent or characteristic features of Chinese philosophy and science relate, in turn, to the very different political, social and institutional circumstances in which they were produced? Such discussion as we can venture here must be understood as appreciably more tentative even than the hypotheses we have proposed on the Greek side.

We must first go back to one of the points of general similarity between Greece and China that we examined before. Chinese thought, like Greek, is permeated by values, but the values expressed, implicitly or explicitly, in either case, certainly differed. The extant evidence exhibits a remarkable Chinese consensus on the political ideal, and this seems a key point. This is not just a matter of the Chinese not being tempted to engage in speculative forays in political philosophy. The importance of the ideal of the benevolent and wise ruler may be threefold. First, consensus on the political ideal may act as a model for consensus in other domains. The ruler, secondly, is the proper recipient of advice well beyond the political field. Thirdly, the ruler directly or indirectly takes responsibility for the work of his officials – again well beyond the narrowly political domain – indeed responsibility for the welfare of the state in its entirety.

All three points require elaboration and qualification. Consensus on the political ideal does not, of course, rule out substantial disagreements on every matter on which the ruler might be advised. Indeed Chinese princes and emperors were surrounded by advisers competing for their attention and favour on every conceivable issue, including on matters to do with philosophy and science. Yet compared, at least, with those Greeks who adopted a stance of aggressive egotism in debate, the tactics of Chinese advisers was rather to build on what could be taken as common ground, certainly on what could be represented as sanctioned by tradition. The ideal of past wisdom was commonly invoked and, from Han times on, especially, the desire for an orthodoxy, indeed one that legitimated political authority, was strong.

When the target of persuasion was the ruler, that may be thought to have imposed certain constraints not just on the style of presentation, but also on the matter of what was presented. Here the contrast would be with the free-for-all of Greek exhibition lectures or debates held in front of a general audience. Besides, politics, cosmology, science, formed, I said, in China, a seamless whole. It is not too fanciful, therefore, to see a possible connection between the stress so often laid on the interdependence of rulers and ministers in the political domain, and the emphasis elsewhere on a similar interdependence, whether it be of heaven and earth, or of *yin* and *yang*, or of the macrocosm and the two microcosms of the state and the body.

Moreover the ruler was directly concerned, in ways that again have no classical Greek parallel, with the work of scientists who served as his officials. The founding and maintaining of the imperial Astronomical Service is the most striking example. But this was not set up just in a spirit of the desirability of fostering research. Rather the work done there was directly relevant to the emperor in his capacity as the key mediator between heaven and earth. That was not just a matter of the calendar being kept in tune with the seasons, but one of the good order in all the relations of 'all under heaven'.

No similarly prestigious institution existed in other areas of inquiry, even though there were imperial appointments also in such areas as medicine. But as remarked, the elaboration of complex systems of correspondences, covering phases, seasons, cardinal points, colours, tastes, animals, parts of the body and so much else, served in part to produce a comprehensive cosmology to legitimate imperial rule. That is not to suggest that the political application was the *sole* driving force in such elaborations, for they were clearly undertaken in part also for their own sake, in order to provide a framework for understanding widely disparate phenomena. Yet if there is certainly more to Chinese cosmological correspondences than just their political dimension, the latter helps to explain some of their distinctive ambitions for comprehensiveness.

While we might start with some bland generalisation to the effect that the importance of analogies between the macrocosm and the microcosm can be attested in both China and Greece, that statement by itself conceals, or at least does not reveal, the very great differences in the ways in which those analogies were deployed. On the Chinese side, they were the means by which a unified picture, encompassing and making sense of most areas of experience, was achieved, never totally unified, to be sure, but providing, nevertheless, a substantially agreed framework of discourse. On the Greek side, by contrast, what is so striking is the extent of the explicit disagreements, (1) on the nature of the macrocosm itself, (2) on that of the microcosm of the human body, (3) on the political images used to describe both, and (4) on the actual political ideals that those images in turn reflect.

While there are, for sure, many aspects of both Chinese and Greek philosophy and science at different periods that fall outside the range of our discussion here, the points at which an influence from broadly political and social factors can be detected are considerable. These are not the *only* factors that need to be taken into account in the background of the complex ideas, theories and modes of reasoning in question, even in *those* cases. But they are factors that surely have to be included to help to throw light on the divergent early histories of philosophy and science in those two ancient civilisations that are our chief *explanandum*.

The final question I posed, for this concluding discussion, related to the more general lessons that might be learned, from these studies, on issues to do with the problems of the relations between culture and cognition.

Those who investigate problems of cognitive development in children or young adults tend to adopt as their working assumption that there are basic uniformities in all humans. An infant aged one year or a child aged three or six will perform very similarly, in experimental situations, to others of the same age, whatever their background – findings that may, no doubt, be taken to corroborate that working assumption at least up to a point. Some historians and philosophers of science, whether or not taking their lead from cognitive scientists, argue similarly that basic human conceptions of space, time, causality, number, even natural kinds, are cross-culturally invariant.

Yet such a view is obviously under considerable strain from the apparent diversities in the *explicit* theories and concepts *actually* developed in cultures world-wide, including ancient cultures. Wherever ancient Greeks and Chinese may have started, as infants, they certainly seem to have *ended* with quite different sets of beliefs (and not just a single set on either side) about the stars, the human body, health and disease, indeed, as we have seen, on causality and nature themselves – and I would add (though this cannot be justified here) on space, time and number as well.[3]

To that difficulty, two types of retort are possible. The first would argue that whatever views may be expressed by the actors themselves, at a deeper level there are implicit cross-cultural universals, that can be elicited by questioning, provided always that you ask the right questions.[4] That remains, of course, a pure conjecture, where the members of ancient societies are concerned, since we cannot question them. But the more important point is that, if we are studying early attempts to *explain* the world, we have no option but to take the *explicit* theories and concepts actually used, in all their diversity, as the chief, indeed the sole direct, evidence. So there may be a sense in which at points (if not across the board) universalists and comparativists may be arguing past one another, in that the subject-matter they are wrestling with is, in the one case, the postulated implicit assumptions, in the other the explicit theories the actors themselves propose.

But then the second type of retort would have it that the kinds of theories I have been discussing do not count as real science at all. The argument would pick up the point I mentioned at the beginning of this chapter, namely that science, to be science, *has to be* universal. So if there are divergences in the theories in question, that just shows their inadequacies as science.

But that equally *a priori* view is also deeply unsatisfactory. Inadequacies, even failures, cannot be taken to show that an inquiry is *not* science. Even physics in the twentieth century is not adequate through and through: it certainly has not delivered

3. For discussion of the topics of space and time, see Sivin 1986 and Gernet 1993–4, and of number, the articles collected in *Extrême-Orient Extrême-Occident* 16 (Volkov, ed. 1994). For broader, comparativist, discussion of the notion of space, see Levinson forthcoming a and b.
4. See Atran 1990, and 1995.

complete explanations of all the subjects in its purview. Rather, it would be more plausible to argue that the history of science is a history of repeated failures – though that is not totally satisfactory either, in that there are failures and failures, and one should acknowledge the difference between straight failures and failures that are accepted as temporary successes.

What our studies illustrate is that there is nothing inevitable about the way in which astronomy, mathematics and medicine developed, and their international modern character should not mask their very divergent early manifestations (and not just in China and in Greece). Of course, in one sense the subject-matter of both Greek and Chinese inquiries was the same, in that both studied numbers and geometrical figures, the stars and the human body and so on. But as we have seen, the differences in the theories and concepts they developed relate not just to matters of presentation, but also to the questions they focussed on and, correspondingly, to the answers they chose to make central to their understanding.[5]

However, if on the one hand one postulates influences *from* the society in which the science was produced *to* the scientific end-product itself, does that not run the risk of appearing determinist – as if the science could not fail to have taken the form it did? And if on the other hand the science is deemed to vary from one culture to the next, and not just in superficial details, does that not reduce to stark cultural relativism?

Certainly, both types of charge, of determinism and of relativism, have been levelled at the kinds of hypotheses proposed here. But the theses I have put forward, and the programme of further research they suggest, are, I trust, more modulated, more tentative and more modest than the objections based on the use of such sweeping but vague labels as determinism and relativism allow to emerge.

First as to 'determinism'. The lines of attack that our studies suggest relate the differences in the inquiries pursued to differences in the values of the societies in question, to their social

5. Mathematical truths, as we said, are invariant, but what they are thought to be truths *about*, and their status *as* truths, are topics on which differing views can be, and have been, held, as can be seen not just by comparing Chinese mathematics with Greek, but within Greek philosophy of mathematics itself, for example by contrasting Plato's views on those topics with Aristotle's: see Lear 1982, Graeser (ed.) 1987.

and political institutions and to the institutions within which
the ancient investigators themselves worked. But there is no
suggestion that the influences we can point to constrained the
work of every individual operating in those two societies, let
alone that they determined the entire intellectual products of
all that passes as ancient Greek and Chinese science. The very
variety of those products, as I have insisted many times, defeats
simple single causal explanations. Even if we can (I hope) point
to certain widespread influences, we have always to allow that in
both ancient societies there were also highly idiosyncratic individuals who stood outside the main groups and traditions and
who diverged from the commoner patterns – a Heraclitus or a
Wang Chong – even though this was always at the risk of being
marginalised, misunderstood and quickly forgotten.

Then as to 'relativism', where disambiguation is always badly
needed. In one sense, to be sure, the claim that astronomy, mathematics and medicine developed very differently in China and in
Greece is a claim that the different forms they took have to be
related to the varying circumstances of their development. So far
then a relativist position. Yet not at all so in other, more important,
respects. Thus I have been assuming, all through these studies,
that comparison is possible, indeed that judgement and evaluation are inevitable. The factors at work in the developments
we have been studying – and indeed in *our* study of them – do
not solely consist of the influences that come from the values of
society and the institutions of the investigators, but partly also
from the subject-matter of the investigations themselves, even if
there is no such thing as an *unmediated* access to that subject-
matter, whether in science or in the history of science.

It is precisely here that the study of science in ancient civilisations may have some general lessons to offer. The stars that
were there to be observed have not changed – not substantially
at least. We can identify Vega whether as 織女 (*Zhi nü*, Weaving
Girl) or as Lyra (its Greek name) or as alpha Lyrae (even though
in both the Chinese and the Greek cases, constellations were also
named by this star, and they, the constellations, certainly differ).
Nor has the human body changed, for all that some of the diseases that affect it may have. It is the conceptual framework
within which those observations were conducted that has varied
and that continues to do so. To be sure, reality is always socially

constructed in a sense: but that construction reflects the investigators' claims (varied ones, for sure) that it was indeed reality
that they were investigating, and that *sometimes* acts as a check
on the investigations, even if sometimes a reality claim is just a
persuasive device, and even if no one can step completely outside the conceptual framework within which they operate.

What are the limits to which criticism of one's own conceptual
framework is possible? If criticism is possible, does it not presuppose a wider framework? Yes, of course. However, as to explicit
criticisms, and modifications of explicit parts of existing belief systems, we can see this happen, before our very eyes, when we study
both Greece and China, even while the modes of expression of
those criticisms vary. Similar processes were at work in later developments that led eventually to modern science, with *its* distinctive values and institutions. But the history of early investigations
in ancient civilisations is the history of the acquisition of a potential for cognitive development, not just with respect to what was
believed, but also with regard to the ways of getting to believe it.

Where Greece and China are concerned, to go no further
afield, that history shows both that the ways of acquiring that
potential differed, and indeed that the potential acquired did,
for both were deeply influenced by the values of the society and
by the institutions within which the investigators worked. The
Chinese, as we have seen, produced sophisticated mathematics,
astronomy, medicine, cosmology, without an obsession with certainty, with foundations, with axiomatisation, without the models
of confrontational debate that were provided by the Greek political assemblies and law-courts, and without the fondness for a
further notion reflected in, and maybe stimulated by, Greek
political practice, namely that of the radical revisability of basic
assumptions. But the Greeks, for their part, developed their –
different – styles of inquiry without a deep sense of political
cohesion such as is exemplified in China, without a clear perception of what science could contribute to such a cohesion, and
without the guiding idea that what counted was not the ability to
give an account, let alone to win an argument, but the ideal of
the sage as the living embodiment of wisdom, not *logos*, but the
Dao. But *both logos* and *Dao* offered prospects, and – as I hope to
have indicated – interestingly different ones, for the transformation of cognitive capabilities.

Glossary of Chinese and Greek terms

I list below some of the more important or problematic Chinese and Greek terms, the translations used for these, and the main passages where the meanings are explained or exemplified. The terms are listed in the alphabetical order of the transliterations used (Pinyin in the case of Chinese terms).

Chinese

本 *ben*, root: 108–9.

辯 *bian*, dispute: 34 and n. 27.

辨 *bian*, distinguish: 34 and n. 27.

鱉臑 *bienao*: pyramid with right triangular base and one lateral edge perpendicular to the base: 152–3 n. 22 and Figure 1.

道 *dao*, way: 6, 8, 10, 25, 31, 59, 63.

法 *fa*, law, standard, model, principle: 27, 59 and 71 n. 38.

法家 *fa jia*, 'legalists': 25.

分 *fen*, degree, part: 111 n. 18.

蓋天 *gai tian*, 'canopy heaven': 28, 162–3, 170.

綱紀 *gangji*, guiding principles: 61.

句股 *gou gu*: horizontal and vertical lines enclosing the right angle of a right-angled triangle: 209.

故 *gu*, reason, cause: 108–9, 111.

合體 *he ti*, coincide, fit: 154.

渾天 *hun tian*, 'enveloping heaven': 28, 162–3, 170.

家 *jia*, family, lineage: 21, 25, 31–5, 44–5.

經 *jing*, warp, canon, circulation tract: 32–3, 65.

理 *li*, pattern: 6.

里 *li*, 'league' (measure of distance): 60, 170.

曆法 *li fa*, 'calendar studies': 166.

論 *lun*, discussion: 34.

名家 *ming jia*, lineage or family of names: 25, 27, 113.

氣 *qi*: on the problems of translating this, whether as 'breath', 'pneuma' or 'energy', see 65 n. 25, 110 n. 15. The term is normally transliterated as *qi*, see for example 8, 112, 122, 148, 191–2.

齊 *qi*, homogenize: 61.

塹堵 *qiandu*: right prism with right triangular base: 153 n. 22 and Figure 1.

儒 *ru*, 'Confucian', but see 31.

尚方 *shang fang*, master of recipes, director of imperial manufactories: 196 and n. 2.

使 *shi*, send, command, cause: 108–9.

失 *shi*, loss, error: 154–6.

術 *shu*, art, method, working: 59–60, 63.

數 *shu*, number: 63 and n. 23.

說 *shuo*, persuasion, explanation: 41, 113.

算數 *suan shu*, the art or method of numbers: 59.

太史令 *taishi ling*, astronomical official: 168.

太醫 *taiyi*, and 太醫令 *taiyi ling*, palace/imperial physician: 40.

天 *tian*, heaven: 6, 8.

天文 *tianwen*, (the study of) celestial patterns: 166.

同 *tong*, equalize: 61.

微 *wei*, subtle: 154, 156.

物 *wu*, things: 6.

五德 *wu de*, five virtues or powers: 123–4.

五行 *wu xing*, five phases: 9, 122 and n. 7, 123.

邪 *xie*, heteropathy: 8.

性 *xing*, character: 6.

形 *xing*, form, body: 154, 193.

宣夜 *xuan ye*, (the fruit of) the labour of the night, 'infinite empty space' cosmology: 151 and n. 18.

陽馬 *yangma*, pyramid with rectangular base and one lateral edge perpendicular to the base: 152–3 and n. 22 and Figure 1.

業 *ye*, patrimony: 33.

因 *yin*, rely on, because, cause: 108–9.

陰陽 *yin yang*, the shady/sunny side, negative/positive principles: 8, 25, 63, 119, 121–5, 127, 136–8, 148, 191, 195, 222.

由 *you*, proceed from, source: 108–9.

有為, 無為 *you wei, wu wei*, ado/no ado: 7.

原 *yuan*, spring, source, origin: 108–9.

至 *zhi*, reach, extreme: 154, 156.

織女 *zhi nü*, weaving girl (Chinese name for the star Vega): 226.

自然 *zi ran*, spontaneous, 'self so': 6–7.

Greek

aitia (αἰτία), *aition* (αἴτιον), *aitios* (αἴτιος), cause, what is responsible or to blame: 94–6, 98–100, 103–4.

anamphisbētēton (ἀναμφισβήτητον), indisputable: 181.

anelegktos (ἀνέλεγκτος), irrefutable: 53.

apeiron (ἄπειρον), infinite, indefinite, limitless: 144, 149, 151.

apodeiknumi (ἀποδείκνυμι), *apodeixis* (ἀπόδειξις), demonstrate, prove, demonstration, proof: 56–8 and nn. 10, 11 and 14, 84–5, 200.

archē (ἀρχή), beginning, starting-point, principle, seat of authority, magistracy: 14, 55, 66, 100, 116, 135, 212, 215.

autotelēs (αὐτοτελής), complete (of causes): 97.

basanizein (βασανίζειν), *basanos* (βάσανος), torture, test, touch-stone: 107.

deiknumi (δείκνυμι), show: 56, 182.

dikastēs (δικαστής), *dikastērion* (δικαστήριον), judge/juror, law-court: 79, 86, 106, 109.

dikē (δίκη), justice, penalty: 22 n. 4, 121.

dokimazein (δοκιμάζειν), test, evaluate (of candidate's eligibility for office, for example): 107.

eikos (εἰκός), likely, probable: 86.

elegchos (ἔλεγχος), examination, refutation: 107.

endoxa (ἔνδοξα), generally accepted or reputable opinions: 57 n. 13, 85.

enthumēma (ἐνθύμημα), 'enthymeme', rhetorical syllogism: 85–6.

epideiktikē (ἐπιδεικτική), 'epideictic', rhetoric of praise and blame: 82.

epideixis (ἐπίδειξις), proof, display speech: 56, 162 n. 35.

hairesis (αἵρεσις), sect, choice: 21, 35, 37 n. 36, 45.

harmonia (ἁρμονία), harmony, attunement, concord: 174–6 and n. 15.

hodos (ὁδός), way, method: 8, 66.

isonomia (ἰσονομία), equality of rights: 131, 202 n. 7.

isostheneia (ἰσοσθένεια), arguments of equal strength: 38 n. 38, 158.

isotēs (ἰσότης), equality: 131.

koinotētes (κοινότητες), common conditions: 70.

logos (λόγος), word, speech, account, argument, ratio: 8, 56 n. 10, 57, 67, 82–3.

marturion (μαρτύριον), witnessing, evidence: 107.

methodos (μέθοδος), method: 50.

nomos (νόμος), contrasted with *psēphismata* (ψηφίσματα), laws versus decrees: 80.

parabolai (παραβολαί), illustrations: 87.

paradeigma (παράδειγμα), 'paradigm', rhetorical induction: 85.

peras (πέρας), limit: 151.

philotimia (φιλοτιμία), ambition: 29 and n. 20.

phusikoi (φυσικοί), *phusis* (φύσις), natural philosophers, nature: 6–7, 103, 105, 117.

planē (πλάνη), wanderings (of heavenly bodies): 181 and n. 25.

pneuma (πνεῦμα), 'pneuma', breath: 147–8.

proēgoumenon (προηγούμενον), antecedent (of causes): 98.

prokatarktikon (προκαταρκτικόν), 'procatarctic', preliminary (of causes): 97–8.

prophasis (πρόφασις), cause, pretext: 94, 105.

rhizōmata (ῥιζώματα), roots: 115.

sēmeion (σημεῖον), sign: 94.

sophia (σοφία), *sophistēs* (σοφιστής), *sophos* (σοφός), wisdom, 'sophist', wise man: 16, 22 n. 2, 45, 83.

stasis (στάσις), faction, rest, standing: 191 n. 1.

stoicheion(στοιχεῖον), element: 9, 11–14, 50–1 and n. 3, 212.

sumpatheia (συμπάθεια), 'sympathy', resonance: 102 and n. 10, 148, 179.

sunaition (συναίτιον), joint (of causes): 97–8.

sunektikon (συνεκτικόν), 'synectic', sustaining (of causes): 97–8.

sunergon (συνεργόν), auxiliary (of causes): 97–8.

sustoichia (συστοιχία), table of opposites: 114, 119.

technē (τέχνη), art, craft: 66, 81, 103, 117.

tekmērion (τεκμήριον), witnessing, evidence: 107.

Bibliography

Aaboe, A. and Price, D. J. de S. (1964) 'Qualitative measurement in antiquity', in *L'Aventure de la science*, Mélanges A. Koyré (Paris) vol. I, pp. 1–20.

Allen, J. (1993) 'Pyrrhonism and medical empiricism: Sextus Empiricus on evidence and inference', in *Aufstieg und Niedergang der römischen Welt* Teil II, 37.1 (Berlin) pp. 646–90.

Atran, S. (1990) *Cognitive Foundations of Natural History* (Cambridge).
  (1995) 'Causal constraints on categories and categorical constraints on biological reasoning across cultures', in *Causal Cognition*, ed. D. Sperber, D. Premack, A. J. Premack (Oxford) pp. 205–33.

Barker, A. (1989) *Greek Musical Writings*, vol. II: *Harmonic and Acoustic Theory* (Cambridge).
  (forthcoming) *Ptolemy's Harmonics* (Cambridge).

Barnes, J. (1981) 'Proof and the syllogism', in *Aristotle on Science: The Posterior Analytics*, ed. E. Berti (Padua) pp. 17–59.
  (1982) 'Medicine, experience and logic', in *Science and Speculation*, ed. J. Barnes, J. Brunschwig, M. Burnyeat, M. Schofield (Cambridge) pp. 24–68.
  (1983) 'Ancient Skepticism and causation', in *The Skeptical Tradition*, ed. M. Burnyeat (Berkeley) pp. 149–203.
  (1991) 'Galen on logic and therapy', in *Galen's Method of Healing*, ed. F. Kudlien and R. J. Durling (Leiden) pp. 50–102.

Bates, D. (ed.) (1995) *Knowledge and the Scholarly Medical Traditions* (Cambridge).

Bielenstein, H. (1980) *The Bureaucracy of Han Times* (Cambridge).

Bloom, A. H. (1981) *The Linguistic Shaping of Thought* (Hillsdale, NJ).

Bodde, D. (1981) 'Harmony and conflict in Chinese philosophy', in *Essays in Chinese Civilization*, ed. C. LeBlanc and D. V. Borei (Princeton) pp. 237–98.
  (1991) *Chinese Thought, Society, and Science* (Honolulu).

Bowen, A. C. and Goldstein, B. R. (1989) 'Meton of Athens and astronomy in the late fifth century B.C.', in *A Scientific Humanist: Studies in Honor of Abraham Sachs*, ed. E. Leichty, M. de J. Ellis, P. Gerardi (Philadelphia) pp. 39–81.

Bray, F. (1995) 'A deathly disorder: understanding women's health in late imperial China', in Bates, ed. (1995), pp. 235–50.

Bridgman, R. F. (1955) 'La Médecine dans la Chine antique', *Mélanges chinois et bouddhiques* 10: 1–213.

Brunschwig, J. (1980) 'Du mouvement et de l'immobilité de la loi', *Revue Internationale de Philosophie* 133–4: 512–40.

Brunt, P. A. (1994) 'The bubble of the Second Sophistic', *Bulletin of the Institute of Classical Studies* 39: 25–52.

Burkert, W. (1959) 'ΣΤΟΙΧΕΙΟΝ. Eine semasiologische Studie', *Philologus*, 103: 167–97.
  (1963) 'Iranisches bei Anaximandros', *Rheinisches Museum* NF 106: 97–134.
  (1972) *Lore and Science in Ancient Pythagoreanism* (revised trans. E. L. Minar of *Weisheit und Wissenschaft*, Nuremberg, 1962) (Cambridge, MA).

Burnyeat, M. (1994) 'Enthymeme: Aristotle on the logic of persuasion', in *Aristotle's Rhetoric*, ed. D. J. Furley and A. Nehamas (Princeton) pp. 3–55.

Burnyeat, M. (ed.) (1983) *The Skeptical Tradition* (Berkeley).

Caveing, M. (1982) *Zénon d'Elée. Prolégomènes aux doctrines du continu* (Paris).

Chemla, K. (1988) 'La pertinence du concept de classification pour l'analyse de textes mathématiques chinois', *Extrême-Orient Extrême-Occident* 10: 61–87.
  (1990a) 'Du parallélisme entre énoncés mathématiques', *Revue d'histoire des sciences* 43: 57–80.
  (1990b) 'De l'algorithme comme liste d'opérations', *Extrême-Orient Extrême-Occident* 12: 79–94.
  (1991) 'Theoretical aspects of the Chinese algorithmic tradition (first to third century)', *Historia Scientiarum* 42: 75–98.
  (1992a) 'Résonances entre démonstration et procédure', *Extrême-Orient Extrême-Occident* 14: 91–129.
  (1992b) 'Méthodes infinitésimales en Chine et en Grèce anciennes: les limites d'un parallèle', in *Le Labyrinthe du continu*, ed. J. M. Salanskis, H. Sinaceur (Berlin) pp. 31–46.
  (1994) 'Nombre et opération, chaîne et trame du réel mathématique', *Extrême-Orient Extrême-Occident* 16: 43–70.

Chemla, K. and Guo Shuchun (forthcoming) *Les neuf chapitres sur les procédures mathématiques* (Paris).

Clark, D. H. and Stephenson, F. R. (1977) *The Historical Supernovae* (Oxford).

Cornford, F. M. (1932/1965) 'Mathematics and dialectic in the *Republic* VI–VII' (*Mind* NS 41, 1932: 37–52 and 173–90), in *Studies in Plato's Metaphysics*, ed. R. E. Allen (London) 1965, pp. 61–95.

Crump, J. I. (1964) *Intrigues: Studies of the Chan-kuo Ts'e* (Ann Arbor).
  (1970) *Chan-Kuo Ts'e* (Oxford).

Cullen, C. (1976) 'A Chinese Eratosthenes of the flat earth: a study of a fragment of cosmology in Huai Nan-Tzu', *Bulletin of the School of Oriental and African Studies* 39: 106–27.
(1993) 'Motivations for scientific change in ancient China: Emperor Wu and the Grand Inception Astronomical Reforms of 104 B.C.', *Journal for the History of Astronomy* 24: 185–203.
(forthcoming) *Astronomy and Mathematics in Ancient China: the Zhou Bi Suan Jing* (Cambridge).
Cuomo, S. (1995) *The Ghost of Mathematicians Past: Tradition and Innovation in Pappus of Alexandria's Collectio Mathematica* Ph.D. dissertation (Cambridge).
De Lacy, P. H. (1991) 'Galen's response to skepticism', *Illinois Classical Studies* 16: 283–306.
Dean-Jones, L. A. (1994) *Women's Bodies in Classical Greek Science* (Oxford).
Denyer, N. (1985) 'The case against divination: an examination of Cicero's *De Divinatione*', *Proceedings of the Cambridge Philological Society* NS 31: 1–10.
Desideri, P. (1978) *Dione di Prusa: un intellettuale greco nell'impero romano* (Florence).
(1991a) 'Intellettuali e potere a Roma', in *Civiltà dei Romani. Il potere e l'esercito*, ed. S. Settis (Milan) pp. 235–40.
(1991b) 'Tipologia e varietà di funzione comunicativa degli scritti dionei', in *Aufstieg und Niedergang der römischen Welt*, Teil II, 33.5 (Berlin) pp. 3903–59.
Detienne, M. (1967), *Les Maîtres de vérité dans la Grèce archaïque* (Paris).
DeWoskin, K. J. (1983) *Doctors, Diviners, and Magicians of Ancient China* (New York).
Dicks, D. R. (1970) *Early Greek Astronomy to Aristotle* (London).
Dillon, J. M. (1988) ' "Orthodoxy" and "Eclecticism": Middle Platonists and Neo-Pythagoreans', in *The Question of 'Eclecticism'*, ed. J. M. Dillon and A. A. Long (Berkeley) pp. 103–25.
Eberhard, W. (1957) 'The political function of astronomy and astronomers in Han China', in *Chinese Thought and Institutions*, ed. J. K. Fairbank (Chicago) pp. 33–70.
Evans, M. G. (1964) *The Physical Philosophy of Aristotle* (Albuquerque).
Fazzo, S. (1991) 'Un' arte inconfutabile: la difesa dell' astrologia nella *Tetrabiblos* di Tolomeo', *Rivista di storia della filosofia* 46: 213–44.
Fowler, D. H. (1987) *The Mathematics of Plato's Academy* (Oxford).
Fraser, P. M. (1972) *Ptolemaic Alexandria*, 3 vols (Oxford).
Frede, M. (1980) 'The original notion of cause', in *Doubt and Dogmatism*, ed. M. Schofield, M. Burnyeat, J. Barnes (Oxford) pp. 217–49.
(1985) *Galen: Three Treatises on the Nature of Science* (Indianapolis).
(1987) *Essays in Ancient Philosophy* (Minnesota).
Furley, D. J. (1967) *Two Studies in the Greek Atomists* (Princeton).
(1987) *The Greek Cosmologists*, vol. I (Cambridge).

Gagarin, M. (1990) 'The nature of proofs in Antiphon', *Classical Philology* 85: 22–32.

Gernet, J. (1993–4) 'Space and time, science and religion in the encounter between China and Europe', *Chinese Science* 11: 93–102.

Goldstein, B. R. and Bowen, A. C. (1983) 'A new view of early Greek astronomy', *Isis* 74: 330–40.

Goody, J. (1977) *The Domestication of the Savage Mind* (Cambridge).

Gourevitch, D. (1992) 'Comment parlent d'elles-mêmes les sectes médicales dans le monde romain? Comment en parle-t-on?', *Revue de Philologie* 66: 29–35.

Graeser, A. (ed.) (1987) *Mathematics and Metaphysics in Aristotle* (Bern).

Graham, A. C. (1978) *Later Mohist Logic, Ethics and Science* (London).

(1981) *Chuang-tzu: the Seven Inner Chapters* (London).

(1986) *Yin Yang and the Nature of Correlative Thinking* (Singapore).

(1989) *Disputers of the Tao* (La Salle, IL.).

Granet, M. (1934) *La Pensée chinoise* (Paris).

Griffin, M. T. (1976) *Seneca. A Philosopher in Politics* (Oxford).

Griffith, M. (1990) 'Contest and contradiction in early Greek poetry', in *Cabinet of the Muses*, ed. M. Griffith and D. J. Mastronarde (London) pp. 185–207.

Gulley, N. (1958) 'Greek geometrical analysis', *Phronesis* 3: 1–14.

Guthrie, W. K. C. (1962) *A History of Greek Philosophy*, vol. I (Cambridge).

(1965) *A History of Greek Philosophy*, vol. II (Cambridge).

Hadot, P. (1979) 'La division des parties de la philosophie dans l'antiquité', *Museum Helveticum* 36: 201–23.

(1990) 'Forms of life and forms of discourse in ancient philosophy', *Critical Inquiry* 16, 3: 483–505.

Hall, D. L. and Ames, R. T. (1987) *Thinking Through Confucius* (Albany, NY).

Hankinson, R. J. (1987) 'Causes and Empiricism', *Phronesis* 32: 329–48.

(1991a) *Galen on the Therapeutic Method Books I and II* (Oxford).

(1991b) 'Galen on the foundations of science', in *Galeno: Obra, Pensamiento e Influencia*, ed. J. A. López Férez (Madrid) pp. 15–29.

(1992) 'Doing without hypotheses: the nature of *Ancient Medicine*' in *Tratados Hipocráticos*, ed. J. A. López Férez (Madrid) pp. 55–67.

(forthcoming) *Galen on Antecedent Causes* (Cambridge).

Hansen, C. (1983) *Language and Logic in Ancient China* (Ann Arbor).

Hansen, M. H. (1991) *The Athenian Democracy in the Age of Demosthenes* (Oxford).

Harbsmeier, C. (1981) *Aspects of Classical Chinese Syntax* (London).

(forthcoming) *Science and Civilisation in China*, vol. VII, part 1 (Cambridge).

Hartog, F. (1988) *The Mirror of Herodotus* (trans. J. Lloyd of *Le Miroir d'Hérodote*, Paris, 1980) (Berkeley).

Heath, T. E. (1912) *The Works of Archimedes with the Method of Archimedes* (Cambridge).

(1926) *The Thirteen Books of Euclid's Elements*, 3 vols, 2nd ed. (Cambridge).

Henderson, J. B. (1984) *The Development and Decline of Chinese Cosmology* (New York).

(1991) *Scripture, Canon, and Commentary* (Princeton).

Hintikka, J. (1973) *Time and Necessity* (Oxford).

Hintikka, J. and Remes, U. (1974) *The Method of Analysis* (Dordrecht).

Ho Peng Yoke (1962) 'Ancient and mediaeval observations of comets and novae in Chinese sources', *Vistas in Astronomy* 5: 127–225.

(1966) *The Astronomical Chapters of the Chin Shu* (Paris).

(1969) 'The astronomical bureau in Ming China', *Journal of Asian History* 3: 137–57.

(1991) 'Chinese science: the traditional Chinese view', *Bulletin of the School of Oriental and African Studies* 54: 506–19.

Hsü, E. (1987) *Lexical Semantics and Chinese Medical Terms*, M.Phil. dissertation (Cambridge).

(forthcoming) *Canggongzhuan*.

Huang Yi-Long (1990) 'A study of five-planet conjunctions in Chinese history', *Early China* 15: 97–112.

(1991) 'Court divination and Christianity in the K'ang Hsi era', *Chinese Science* 10: 1–20.

Huang Yi-Long and Moriarty-Schieven, G. H. (1987) 'A revisit to the guest star of A.D. 185', *Science* 235: 59–60.

Hucker, C. O. (1985) *A Dictionary of Official Titles in Imperial China* (Stanford).

Hübner, W. (1990) 'Der Titel zum achten Buch des Martianus Capella', in *Vorträge des ersten Symposions des Bamberger Arbeitskreises 'Antike Naturwissenschaft und ihre Rezeption'*, ed. K. Döring and G. Wöhrle (Wiesbaden) pp. 65–86.

Huffman, C. A. (1985) 'The authenticity of Archytas fr. 1', *Classical Quarterly* 35: 344–8.

(1993) *Philolaus of Croton* (Cambridge).

Hulsewé, A. F. P. (1955) *Remnants of Han Law*, vol. 1: *Introductory Studies* (Leiden).

(1986) 'Ch'in and Han law', in *The Cambridge History of China*, ed. D. Twitchett and M. A. N. Loewe, vol. 1, ch. 9, pp. 520–44.

Ioppolo, A. M. (1980) *Aristone di Chio e lo stoicismo antico* (Naples).

(1984) 'L'astrologia nello stoicismo antico', in *La Scienza Ellenistica*, ed. G. Giannantoni and M. Vegetti (Naples) pp. 73–91.

Jaeger, W. (1948) *Aristotle: Fundamentals of the History of his Development* (trans. R. Robinson), 2nd ed. (1st ed. 1934) (Oxford).

Joly, R. and Byl, S. (1984) *Hippocrate: Du Régime* (*Corpus Medicorum Graecorum I 2,4*) (Berlin).
Jullien, F. (1995) *Le Détour et l'accès: stratégies du sens en Chine, en Grèce* (Paris).
Kahn, C. H. (1960) *Anaximander and the Origins of Greek Cosmology* (New York).
Keegan, D. J. (1988) *The 'Huang-ti nei-ching': the Structure of the Compilation; the Significance of the Structure*, Ph.D. dissertation, University of California, Berkeley.
Kirk, G. S., Raven, J. E. and Schofield, M. (1983) *The Presocratic Philosophers*, 2nd ed. (Cambridge).
Knechtges, D. R. (1976) *The Han Rhapsody* (Cambridge).
Knorr, W. R. (1975) *The Evolution of the Euclidean Elements* (Dordrecht).
   (1978) 'Archimedes and the pre-Euclidean proportion theory', *Archives Internationales d'Histoire des Sciences* 28: 183–244.
   (1981) 'On the early history of axiomatics: the interaction of mathematics and philosophy in Greek antiquity', in *Theory Change, Ancient Axiomatics and Galileo's Methodology*, ed. J. Hintikka, D. Gruender, E. Agazzi, vol. 1 (Dordrecht) pp. 145–86.
   (1982) 'Infinity and continuity: the interaction of mathematics and philosophy in antiquity', in *Infinity and Continuity in Ancient and Medieval Thought*, ed N. Kretzmann (Ithaca, NY) pp. 112–45.
   (1986) *The Ancient Tradition of Geometric Problems* (Boston).
   (1990) 'Plato and Eudoxus on the planetary motions', *Journal for the History of Astronomy* 21: 313–29.
Kroll, J. L. (1985–7) 'Disputation in ancient Chinese culture', *Early China* 11–12: 118–45.
Kuriyama, S. (1995) 'Visual knowledge in classical Chinese medicine', in Bates, ed. (1995), pp. 205–34.
Laks, A. (1983) *Diogène d'Apollonie* (Lille).
Lear, J. (1982) 'Aristotle's philosophy of mathematics', *Philosophical Review* 91: 161–92.
LeBlanc, C. (1985) *Huai-nan Tzu. Philosophical Synthesis in Early Han Thought* (Hong Kong).
Levi, J. (1992) 'L'Art de la persuasion à l'époque des Royaumes Combattants (ve–iiie siècles avant J.C.)', *Extrême-Orient Extrême-Occident* 14: 49–89.
Levinson, S. (forthcoming a) 'Frames of reference and Molyneux's question: cross-linguistic evidence', in *Language and Space*, ed. P. Bloom, M. Peterson, L. Nadel, M. Garrett (Cambridge, MA).
   (forthcoming b) 'Relativity in spatial conception and description', in *Rethinking Linguistic Relativity*, ed. J. Gumperz and S. Levinson (Cambridge).
Li Yan and Du Shiran (1987) *Chinese Mathematics: a Concise History* (trans. J. N. Crossley and A. W.-C. Lun) (Oxford).

Lloyd, G. E. R. (1966) *Polarity and Analogy* (Cambridge).
  (1979) *Magic, Reason and Experience* (Cambridge).
  (1983) *Science, Folklore and Ideology* (Cambridge).
  (1987a) *The Revolutions of Wisdom* (Berkeley).
  (1987b) 'The alleged fallacy of Hippocrates of Chios', *Apeiron* 20: 103–28.
  (1988) 'Scholarship, authority and argument in Galen's *Quod animi mores*', in *Le Opere psicologiche di Galeno*, ed. P. Manuli and M. Vegetti (Naples) pp. 11–42.
  (1990) *Demystifying Mentalities* (Cambridge).
  (1991a) *Methods and Problems in Greek Science* (Cambridge).
  (1991b) 'The definition, status, and methods of the medical τέχνη in the fifth and fourth centuries', in *Science and Philosophy in Classical Greece*, ed. A. C. Bowen (London) pp. 249–60.
  (1990/1992) 'The theories and practices of demonstration in Aristotle', in *The Boston Area Colloquium in Ancient Philosophy* VI (1990), ed. J. J. Cleary and D. C. Shartin (Lanham) (1992) pp. 371–401.
  (1992a) 'Democracy, philosophy, and science in ancient Greece', in *Democracy. The Unfinished Journey*, ed. J. Dunn (Oxford) pp. 41–56.
  (1992b) 'The Agora perspective', *Extrême-Orient Extrême-Occident* 14: 185–98.
  (1992c) 'Introduzione all'edizione italiana di *Polarity and Analogy*', *Polarità ed Analogia* (Naples) pp. 20–4.
  (1994) 'Methodological issues in the comparison between East and West', in *Is it Possible to Compare East and West?*, ed. H. Numata and S. Kawada (Tokyo) pp. 23–36.
  (forthcoming) 'Theories and practices of demonstration in Galen', in *Festschrift G. Patzig*, ed. M. Frede and G. Striker (Oxford).
Lloyd, G. E. R. and Sivin, N. (1993) 'Tao and Logos: comparing ancient Chinese and Greek science', *Newsletter for the History of Chinese Science* 5: 165–6.
  (forthcoming) *Tao and Logos*.
Loewe, M. (ed.) (1993) *Early Chinese Texts: a Bibliographical Guide* (Early China Special Monograph Series 2, Berkeley).
Long, A. A. (1982) 'Astrology: arguments pro and contra', in *Science and Speculation*, ed. J. Barnes, J. Brunschwig, M. Burnyeat, M. Schofield (Cambridge) pp. 165–92.
Long, A. A. and Sedley, D. N. (1987) *The Hellenistic Philosophers*, 2 vols (Cambridge).
Lonie, I. M. (1978) 'Cos versus Cnidus and the historians', *History of Science* 16: 42–75 and 77–92.
  (1981) *The Hippocratic Treatises 'On Generation', 'On the Nature of the Child', 'Diseases IV'*, Ars Medica Abt. 2, Bd. 7 (Berlin).
Loraux, N. (1987) 'Le lien de la division', *Le Cahier du Collège international de la philosophie* 4: 101–24.

Lovejoy, A. O. (1936) *The Great Chain of Being* (Cambridge, MA).

Machle, E. J. (1993) *Nature and Heaven in the Xunzi* (Albany).

McKirahan, R. D. (1992) *Principles and Proofs: Aristotle's Theory of Demonstrative Science* (Princeton).

Mahoney, M. S. (1968–9) 'Another look at Greek geometrical analysis', *Archive for History of Exact Sciences* 5: 318–48.

Major, J. S. (1993) *Heaven and Earth in Early Han Thought* (Albany).

Manuli, P. (1983) 'Lo stile del commento', in *Formes de pensée dans la collection hippocratique*, ed. F. Lasserre and P. Mudry (Geneva) pp. 471–82.

  (1992) 'Galien et le Stoïcisme', *Revue de Métaphysique et de Morale* 97: 365–75.

Manuli, P. and Vegetti, M. (1977) *Cuore, Sangue e Cervello* (Milan).

Marsden, E. W. (1971) *Greek and Roman Artillery: Technical Treatises* (Oxford).

Matthen, M. (1988) 'Empiricism and ontology in ancient medicine', in *Method, Medicine and Metaphysics*, ed. R. J. Hankinson, *Apeiron Supp.* XXI, 2 (Edmonton) pp. 99–121.

Maula, E. (1974) *Studies in Eudoxus' Homocentric Spheres* (Helsinki).

Meakin, K. (1990) *Pre-Platonic Ontology of Mathematics*, Ph.D. dissertation (Cambridge).

Meritt, B. D. (1961) *The Athenian Year* (Berkeley).

Millar, F. (1977) *The Emperor in the Roman World* (London).

Millett, P. C. (1989) 'Patronage and its avoidance in Classical Athens', in *Patronage in Ancient Society*, ed. A. Wallace-Hadrill (London) pp. 15–47.

Miyasita, S. (1967) 'A link in the westward transmission of Chinese anatomy in the later Middle Ages', *Isis* 58: 486–90.

Mondolfo, R. (1956) *L'Infinito nel pensiero dell'antichità classica*, 2nd ed. (Florence).

Moraux, P. (1968) 'La Joute dialectique d'après le huitième livre des *Topiques*', in *Aristotle on Dialectic*, ed. G. E. L. Owen (Oxford) pp. 277–311.

  (1973) *Der Aristotelismus bei den Griechen*, vol. I (Berlin).

  (1984) *Der Aristotelismus bei den Griechen*, vol. II (Berlin).

Moravcsik, J. M. E. (1974) 'Aristotle on adequate explanations', *Synthese* 28: 3–17.

Mueller, I. (1981) *Philosophy of Mathematics and Deductive Structure in Euclid's Elements* (Cambridge, MA).

  (1982) 'Aristotle and the quadrature of the circle', in *Infinity and Continuity in Ancient and Medieval Thought*, ed. N. Kretzmann (Ithaca, NY) pp. 146–64.

Nagashima, N. (1973) 'A reversed world: or is it?', in *Modes of Thought*, ed. R. Horton and R. Finnegan (London) pp. 92–111.

Nakamura, H. (1960) *The Ways of Thinking of Eastern Peoples* (Tokyo).

Nakayama, S. (1966) 'Characteristics of Chinese astrology', *Isis* 57: 442–54.

(1969) *A History of Japanese Astronomy* (Cambridge, MA).

(1984) *Academic and Scientific Traditions in China, Japan and the West* (trans. J. Dusenberry) (Tokyo).

Needham, J. (1956) *Science and Civilization in China*, vol. II: *History of Scientific Thought* (Cambridge).

(1959) *Science and Civilization in China*. vol. III: *Mathematics and the Sciences of the Heavens and the Earth* (Cambridge).

Needham, R. (1987) *Counterpoints* (Berkeley).

Needham, R. (ed.) (1973) *Right and Left: Essays on Dual Symbolic Classification* (Chicago).

Neugebauer, O. (1975) *A History of Ancient Mathematical Astronomy*, 3 vols (Berlin).

Ngo Van Xuyet (1976) *Divination, magie et politique dans la Chine ancienne* (Paris).

Nivison, D. S. and Pang, K. D. (1990) 'Astronomical evidence for the *Bamboo Annals'* chronicle of Early Xia', *Early China* 15: 87–95.

Nylan, M. and Sivin, N. (1987) 'The first Neo-Confucianism: an introduction to Yang Hsiung's "Canon of Supreme Mystery" (T'ai hsuan ching, c. 4 B.C.)', in *Chinese Ideas about Nature and Society*, ed. C. LeBlanc and S. Blader (Hong Kong) pp. 41–99.

Osborne, R. (1994) 'Athenian democracy: something to celebrate?', *Dialogos* 1: 44–58.

Owen, G. E. L. (1957–8/1986) 'Zeno and the mathematicians' (originally *Proceedings of the Aristotelian Society* LVIII, 1957–8, 199–222) in *Logic, Science and Dialectic* (London), pp. 45–61.

Pankenier, D. W. (1981–2) 'Astronomical dates in Shang and Western Zhou', *Early China* 7: 2–37.

Peerenboom, R. P. (1990) 'Natural law in the *Huang-Lao Boshu*', *Philosophy East and West* 40: 309–29.

(1993) *Law and Morality in Ancient China* (Albany).

Peterson, W. J. (1989) 'Some connective concepts in China in the fourth to second centuries B.C.E.', in *Gleichklang oder Gleichzeitigkeit* (*Eranos Jahrbuch* 57, 1988) ed. R. Ritsema (Frankfurt) pp. 201–34.

Porter, J. (1980) 'Bureaucracy and science in early modern China: the imperial astronomical bureau in the Ch'ing period', *Journal of Oriental Studies* 18: 61–76.

Pritchett W. K. and Neugebauer O. (1947) *The Calendars of Athens* (Cambridge, MA).

Qian Baocong (1963) *Suanjing Shishu* (Beijing).

Rawlings, H. R. (1975) *A Semantic Study of PROPHASIS to 400 B.C.* (Hermes Einzelschriften 33, Wiesbaden).

Reding, J.-P. (1985) *Les Fondements philosophiques de la rhétorique chez les sophistes grecs et chez les sophistes chinois* (Bern).

(1986a) 'Greek and Chinese categories: a re-examination of the problem of linguistic relativism', *Philosophy East and West* 36: 349–74.

(1986b) 'Analogical reasoning in early Chinese philosophy', *Asiatische Studien* 40: 40–56.

(1993) 'La Pensée rationnelle en Chine antique', in *Contemporary Philosophy: a New Survey*, vol. VII, Asian Philosophy, ed. G. Floistad (Dordrecht) pp. 165–93.

Rehder, W. (1982) 'Die Analysis und Synthese bei Pappus', *Philosophia Naturalis* 19: 350–70.

Renfrew, C. (1987) *Archaeology and Language: the Puzzle of Indo-European Origins* (London).

Robinson, R. (1936/1969) 'Analysis in Greek geometry' (*Mind* NS 45, 1936, 464–73) in *Essays in Greek Philosophy* (Oxford) pp. 1–15.

Roux, S. (1992) 'Le premier livre des *Equilibres plans*. Réflexions sur la mécanique archimédienne', in *Mathématiques dans l'antiquité*, ed. J.-Y. Guillaumin, Université de Saint-Etienne, Centre Jean-Palerne Mémoires XI, pp. 95–160.

Sandbach, F. H. (1985) *Aristotle and the Stoics* (Cambridge Philological Society, Suppl. vol. x Cambridge).

Sato, T. (1986) 'A reconstruction of *The Method* Proposition 17, and the development of Archimedes' thought on quadrature, Part I', *Historia Scientiarum* 31: 61–86.

(1987) 'A reconstruction of *The Method* Proposition 17, and the development of Archimedes' thought on quadrature, Part II', *Historia Scientiarum* 32: 75–142.

Schofield, M. (1991) *The Stoic Idea of the City* (Cambridge).

Schofield, M., Burnyeat, M. and Barnes, J. (eds.) (1980) *Doubt and Dogmatism* (Oxford).

Schwartz, B. (1959) 'Some polarities in Confucian thought', in *Confucianism in Action*, ed. D. S. Nivison and A. F. Wright (Stanford) pp. 50–62.

(1985) *The World of Thought in Ancient China* (Cambridge, MA).

Scolnicov, S. (1975) 'Hypothetical method and rationality in Plato', *Kant-Studien* 66: 157–62.

Sedley, D. N. (1982) 'On signs', in *Science and Speculation*, ed. J. Barnes, J. Brunschwig, M. Burnyeat, M. Schofield (Cambridge) pp. 239–72.

(1989) 'Philosophical allegiance in the Greco-Roman world', in *Philosophia Togata*, ed. M. Griffin and J. Barnes (Oxford) pp. 97–119.

Sharples, R. W. (1990) 'The school of Alexander?', in *Aristotle Transformed*, ed. R. Sorabji (London) pp. 83–111.

Shaugnessy, E. L. (1983) *The Composition of the Zhouyi*, Ph.D. dissertation, University of Stanford.

Sivin, N. (1969) 'Cosmos and computation in early Chinese mathematical astronomy', *T'oung Pao* 55: 1–73.

(1978) 'On the word "Taoist" as a source of perplexity. With special reference to the relations of science and religion in traditional China', *History of Religions* 17: pp. 303–30.

(1986) 'On the limits of empirical knowledge in the traditional Chinese sciences', in *Time, Science, and Society in China and the West*, ed. J. T. Fraser, N. Lawrence and F. C. Haber (Amherst) pp. 151–69.

(1987) *Traditional Medicine in Contemporary China* (Ann Arbor).

(1992) 'Ruminations on the Tao and its disputers', Review of Graham (1989), *Philosophy East and West* 42: 21–9.

(1995a) 'Text and experience in classical Chinese medicine', in Bates, ed. (1995), pp. 177–204.

(1995b) 'Comparing Greek and Chinese science', in Sivin (1995e), ch. 1.

(1995c) 'The myth of the naturalists', in Sivin (1995e), ch. 4.

(1995d) *Science in Ancient China: Researches and Reflections*, vol. I (Aldershot).

(1995e) *Medicine, Philosophy, and Religion in Ancient China: Researches and Reflections*, vol. II (Aldershot).

Smith, W. D. (1973) 'Galen on Coans versus Cnidians', *Bulletin of the History of Medicine* 47: 569–85.

(1979) *The Hippocratic Tradition* (Ithaca, NY).

Solmsen, F. (1929) *Die Entwicklung der aristotelischen Logik und Rhetorik* (Neue Philologische Untersuchungen 4) (Berlin).

Sorabji, R. (1980) *Necessity, Cause and Blame* (Oxford).

(1983) *Time, Creation and the Continuum* (London).

(1988) *Matter, Space and Motion* (London).

Sperber, D., Premack, D., and Premack, A. J. (ed.) (1995) *Causal Cognition: a Multidisciplinary Debate* (Oxford).

Staden, H. von (1982) 'Hairesis and heresy: the case of the *haireseis iatrikai*', in *Jewish and Christian Self-Definition*, vol. III, ed. B. F. Meyer and E. P. Sanders (London) pp. 76–100, 199–206.

(1989) *Herophilus: the Art of Medicine in Early Alexandria* (Cambridge).

(1995) 'Anatomy as rhetoric: Galen on dissection and persuasion', *Journal of the History of Medicine and Allied Sciences* 50: 47–66.

Stephenson, F. R. and Clark, D. C. (1978) *Applications of Early Astronomical Records* (Bristol).

Suppes, P. (1981) 'Limitations of the axiomatic method in ancient Greek mathematical sciences', in *Theory Change, Ancient Axiomatics and Galileo's Methodology*, ed. J. Hintikka, D. Gruender, E. Agazzi, vol. I (Dordrecht) pp. 197–213.

Szabó, Á. (1974–5) 'Analysis und Synthesis (Pappus II, p. 634ff. Hultsch)', *Acta Classica Universitatis Scientiarum Debreceniensis* 10–11: 155–64.

Tannery, P. (1930) *Pour l'histoire de la science hellène* (Paris).

Taylor, A. E. (1928) *A Commentary on Plato's Timaeus* (Oxford).

Tóth, I. (1966–7) 'Das Parallelenproblem im Corpus Aristotelicum', *Archive for History of Exact Sciences* 3: 249–422.

Unschuld, P. U. (1985) *Medicine in China* (Berkeley).

Vegetti, M. (1979) *Il Coltello e lo Stilo* (Milan).

(1983) *Tra Edipo e Euclide* (Milano).

Vitrac, B. (1992) 'A propos de la chronologie des oeuvres d'Archimède', in *Mathématiques dans l'antiquité*, ed. J.-Y. Guillaumin, Université de Saint-Etienne, Centre Jean-Palerne, Mémoires XI, pp. 59–93.

Volkov, A. (1994) 'Nombres et nombres', *Extrême-Orient Extrême-Occident* 16: 5–11.

(forthcoming) 'Calculation of π in ancient China: from Liu Hui to Zu Chongzhi', *Historia Scientiarum*.

Volkov, A. (ed.) (1994) *Sous les nombres le monde* (*Extrême-Orient Extrême-Occident* 16) (Paris).

van der Waerden, B. L. (1960) 'Greek astronomical calendars and their relation to the Athenian civil calendar', *Journal of Hellenic Studies* 80: 168–80.

Wagner, D. B. (1978a) 'Liu Hui and Tsu Keng-chih on the volume of a sphere', *Chinese Science* 3: 59–79.

(1978b) 'Doubts concerning the attribution of Liu Hui's commentary on the *Chiu-Chang Suan-Shu*', *Acta Orientalia* 39: 199–212.

(1979) 'An early Chinese derivation of the volume of a pyramid: Liu Hui, third century A.D.', *Historia Mathematica* 6: 164–88.

Wardy, R. B. B. (1992) 'Chinese whispers', *Proceedings of the Cambridge Philological Society* NS 38: 149–70.

(forthcoming a) *Chinese Whispers*.

(forthcoming b) 'Rhetoric', in *Le Savoir grec*, ed. J. Brunschwig, G. E. R. Lloyd, P. Pellegrin (Paris).

Waterlow, S. (1982) *Nature, Change, and Agency in Aristotle's Physics* (Oxford).

Watson, B. (1964) *Han Fei Tzu, Basic Writings* (New York).

West, M. L. (1971) *Early Greek Philosophy and the Orient* (Oxford).

Xi Zezong (1981) 'Chinese studies in the history of astronomy 1949–1979', *Isis* 72: 456–70.

Xi Zezong and Po Shujen (1966) 'Ancient oriental records of novae and supernovae', *Science* 154: 597–603.

Yabuuti, K. (1973) 'Chinese astronomy: development and limiting factors', in *Chinese Science: Explorations of an Ancient Tradition*, ed. S. Nakayama and N. Sivin (Cambridge, MA) pp. 91–103.

Yamada, K. (1979) 'The Formation of the *Huang-ti nei-ching*', *Acta Asiatica* 36: 67–89.

(1991) 'Anatometrics in ancient China', *Chinese Science* 10: 39–52.

Yosida, M. (1973) 'The Chinese concept of nature', in *Chinese Science: Explorations of an Ancient Tradition*, ed. S. Nakayama and N. Sivin (Cambridge, MA) pp. 71–89.

Index

Ideas in Context

Edited by Quentin Skinner (General Editor), Lorraine Daston, Wolf
Lepenies, Richard Rorty and J. B. Schneewind

Titles marked with an asterisk are also available in paperback